INVISIBLE FORCES

INVISIBLE FORCES

Modern Strategy Principles from the Aerie of IBM

JOEL CAWLEY

Joel Cawley Publications:
  Invisible Forces—Modern Strategy Principles from the Aerie of IBM
  The Fifth Paradigm—A 21st Century Strategy for America

Produced by Dan Levine

ISBN-13: 978-1-7332754-1-5 (paperback)
ISBN-13: 978-1-7332754-0-8 (eBook)
Library of Congress Control Number: 2019911083

CONTENTS

INTRODUCTION

THE YEAR WAS 1997. I had been at IBM just over 16 years. I had been a developer, systems engineer, sales rep, marketing manager, offering manager, and strategist. I had led sales teams and had been in charge of several software and hardware offerings. I was now just under a year into my first assignment in Corporate.

It was late on a Friday evening. My colleague and I were sitting in the office of Larry Ricciardi, officially the head of legal, but in reality, the consigliere for the recently arrived CEO, Lou Gerstner. We were in IBM's Corporate headquarters. The office was unlike any other in that mid-century modern building. The furniture was old-world European, probably Italian. There were no overhead lights, nothing even vaguely fluorescent, just a desk lamp and a pair of floor lamps that cast the kind of subtle golden light that proclaimed this was not a regular corporate office. Almost a year earlier we had been charged by Gerstner to write a strategy for IBM that would be "hard hitting, fact based and an in-your-face declaration of what the company needed to do." We had submitted our first draft that past Monday. The summons to Mr. Ricciardi's office had been curt and abrupt.

When we arrived in his office Friday evening he was equally succinct. He said, "This is too controversial to be useful. You are dangerously close to the fatal flaw of any strategist—the destruction of your own credibility." And then, "I'll give you until Monday to come up with a plan, and ten days to get it done. If that doesn't work, feel free to find a job elsewhere." He turned his back. We were dismissed.

So began what would eventually lead to over 20 years of work on strategies at the top of IBM. In the course of those years I investigated, customized, developed, and attempted to apply strategy concepts, methods, and doctrines from the most traditional to the highly avant-garde. While there were lots of theoretical discussions in that process, at the end of the day every concept had to undergo the acid test of practical usability. It had to survive skeptical colleagues. It had to work in the real world. It had to be supportable and understandable to clients, partners, and investors. And, it had to be repeatable. One-time flukes were of little interest. The IBM portfolio ranges from capital- and IP-intensive semiconductors to labor- and skill-intensive services and operates in geographies ranging from North America to China, India, and beyond. It also encompasses the management of both maturing businesses and the introduction of whole new business areas and models. This real-world laboratory provided a unique crucible to examine and test the best strategic thinking from all over the world. Through those decades I learned a lot about what works and what doesn't. This book embodies those lessons.

In addition to exploring the best strategic concepts of the last half century I had the opportunity to watch the world evolve through a series of remarkable changes. I worked alongside technologists charting the future of semiconductors. I helped clients explore what seemed at the time like risky excursions onto the web. I worked with flamboyant and radical true believers from the open-source community. I rubbed shoulders with "white hat" security experts as they outmaneuvered the frauds and swindlers of the world. I led the early business incubation work on Watson. I traveled the world working with clients and negotiating deals in Europe, India, and China. None of these experiences, nor the countless others, were in a passive or academic role. In every instance, there was some urgently pressing business issue or opportunity. It was a remarkable perch from which to observe an incredible period in business history.

I learned a great many things, one of which is how little most of us really know about how the world works. I'm not referring here to political maneuvering, graft, or any other cynical behavior—though I've certainly witnessed my share. I'm referring to the world of global business. The basic concepts of what a business is and what it does are often rooted in an economic model that dates from the industrial era of the 19th century. Adam Smith used the metaphor

of an "invisible hand" to describe how market forces guide resource alloca-
tions in unplanned and unexpected ways. In our modern world, that invisible
hand is joined by other invisible forces like global standards and the necessity
of collaboration across firms and around the world. It is these forces that cause
trucks sold in Texas to be shaped by policies in Beijing, and that cause the largest patent holders to license those patents to all.

The original invisible hand is still an important force in the world.
However, the economic value that guides that hand is increasingly embedded
in services, and those are increasingly rooted in the digital domain. Digital
assets are non-rivalrous, have zero marginal costs, and enjoy near instanta-
neous global reach. As a result, Smith's invisible hand has also been joined by
the invisible forces around network effects, viral adoption, and the vitality of
the digital commons. The most valuable raw materials in the modern economy
do not come out of the ground, they come from cell phones, sensors, and the
digital exhaust of businesses. And, they come from people.

In fact, probably the greatest collection of invisible forces are those that
are rooted in people—what they know, what they believe, what they invent,
and, most of all, what they value. Those factors are eternal. What's new is that
the people that matter—and therefore the knowledge, beliefs, inventions, and
values that matter—come from every corner of the globe. The 19th-century
model was at least partially real and does still exist, but it's a very poor conceptual foundation for modern businesses and economies.

I had the good fortune to work with three successive CEOs—Lou Gerstner,
Sam Palmisano, and Ginni Rometty. Each brought to IBM their own particular
skills, beliefs, and styles. Each had their signature impact on IBM's business
and culture. Each also presided over a particular combination of challenges
and opportunities for IBM. Gerstner famously took over an extremely troubled
company on the verge of being broken up and dismembered. He reversed those
plans, righted the ship, and set it on a course for success. Palmisano brought an
intense focus on profitability and led IBM's aggressive embrace of China, India,
and other emerging geographies. Rometty faced a portfolio where everything
of any size was eroding and everything that was growing was too small to lift
the company. Each era brought new issues and opportunities and new lessons.

I have organized this book into those three eras. Each section begins with the actual history of what happened in IBM. These are the real-world decisions we confronted, what we did, why we chose that path, and how well it worked (or didn't). Those stories aren't organized in any sort of academic theory or structure. They reflect all the messiness and wrong-footed thinking that always happens in the real world. From the outside it may have appeared as though we were making systematic progress toward a clear goal. In reality, we were far more often groping our way forward in darkness that ranged from dim outlines to total blindness. While not well formed in the academic sense, there are still countless strategic lessons in those stories. I will spell those out as they arise.

Each section then proceeds to a set of chapters on strategic principles, concepts, and methods. Many of these were informed by some of the leading strategic thinkers of the last 20–30 years. Those concepts were tested and adapted to the specific issues at hand in IBM. Some concepts fared well, and their influence can be readily seen in IBM. Others did not hold up. These chapters will spell out those learnings. Most of my focus is on the things we found that worked. With a few exceptions, I have spared the reader the details of the many dead ends we explored in our journeys. The strategy chapters in the Gerstner section focus on basic fundamentals and introduce IBM's Business Leadership Model. The chapters in the Palmisano section build from those fundamentals by reviewing the three most common causes of strategic derailment and how to avoid or manage them. The final collection of strategy chapters focus on the modern frontiers of business strategy. Most of these final topics also raise complex implications for public policies. This book does not attempt to resolve those policy issues. My objective is simply to highlight them and to frame them in the context of what contemporary businesses need.

I obviously survived my early encounter with Larry Ricciardi. The remainder of that story, along with dozens of others, are spelled out in the pages that follow.

NOTE: The scope of the term "business strategy" warrants a short sidebar. One of my early mentors in strategy, Bruce Harreld, used to say, "the difference between military strategy and business strategy is the existence of the customer." It's never good business strategy for your customers to be caught in the crossfire between rivals. Despite our best intentions, this did happen to us on at least one occasion, as you'll see later in this book. Nonetheless, the central aspect of customers and what they value is an important principle for business. In fact, as this book unfolds it will become clear that I see this as the vital heart of business strategy.

Business strategies also exist across multiple levels. There are strategies for individual businesses, strategies for portfolios, and strategies for investing. Individual businesses come in many different flavors and stages of evolution. Portfolios can be optimized for financial results, risk mitigation, or operational dimensions like common go-to-market or delivery infrastructures. Investing strategies can focus on solid revenue, cost, and expense fundamentals; on stock market measures, where P/E ratios dominate; or on "exit strategies" for start-ups, which may focus on suitability for strategic acquisitions. We will touch on many of these dimensions in the course of this book.

Over the course of my career in strategy I have benefited from the thinking and ideas of numerous contributors to the library of business strategy. Many of these individuals worked with myself and my team at various points in our journey. All of them faced a challenging, testing audience looking for immediate and practical advice on specific issues. I would particularly like to acknowledge Adrian Slywotzky, Michael Tushman, Charles O'Reilly, Thomas Friedman, Rita McGrath, Clayton Christensen, Geoffrey Moore, Gary Hamel, Michael Treacy, Stephen Coley, Michael Porter, Lawrence Lessig, Brian Arthur, Hal Varian, Charles Ferguson, and Joseph Pine. The specifics of what each of those thinkers brought us will become apparent.

IBM: The Gerstner Years

My name is Ozymandias, King of Kings;
Look on my Works, ye Mighty, and Despair!
Nothing beside remains, Round the Decay
Of that colossal Wreck, boundless and bare
The lone and level sands stretch far away

—Percy Bysshe Shelley, "Ozymandias"

INTRODUCTION

OUR STORY BEGINS with Gerstner's arrival at IBM. Like the mythical Ozymandias the once proud, arrogant and haughty IBM leaders had fallen. IBM had just experienced what at the time was the worst loss in the history of US business. John Akers, Gerstner's predecessor, along with the board of directors, were in the midst of a grand strategy to break up the company and sell off all the pieces. The proceeds would be returned to the shareholders. Nothing of substance would remain. That was the plan and actually had been for well over a year. Many of us were actively engaged in the process. Disentangling all the different connections, chargeback schemes, and internal accounting was a nontrivial task. Many of the top executives were ecstatic. They felt certain that once freed from corporate restrictions and overhead they would thrive. It was incredibly naïve.

The crisis we faced is usually attributed to the market shifting to a paradigm of computing known as "client/server." This paradigm entailed the usage of PCs as "clients" connected to "servers" which were usually either based on Unix/RISC systems or were PCs themselves. This was in contrast to the preceding paradigm in which "terminals" connected to "host" systems. It may seem bizarre that the subtle technical differences between these two paradigms would cause such an impact.

Indeed, for most of IBM's leaders it was unfathomable. After decades of intense competition, IBM had emerged as the unquestioned leader of the older paradigm. Our executives were proud and arrogant, our relationships with our customers were as strong as ever. It was IBM that had embraced the nascent, hobbyist movement of the original PCs and brought them into the business world. We were the trigger for its early growth. We still regarded PCs as an entertaining side show. In fact, it seemed like a part of the computing industry that was mainly driven by gaudy, splashy events like the annual Comdex shows in Las Vegas. Those shows were scheduled every year to coincide with a highly racy event held by the adult film industry. It wasn't something to be taken seriously. How little we knew at the time.

However, it was a paradigm shift. The shorthand name of "client/server" was an accurate description of one aspect of the technology associated with the paradigm, but it did nothing to convey the deeper transformations that were under way. The host systems IBM had been so successful selling were deployed in special rooms with raised floors that allowed cooling ducts, vents, and cabling to be spread all over the room. The cables were as thick as my wrist. The ventilation systems carefully filtered out any speck of dust that might cause problems for spinning disks holding the precious data of the company. The high priests of these environments were incredibly protective and restrictive about what they would allow to be deployed in these pristine environments. These restrictions were not limited to hardware. Software and applications were even more complex and fragile, and the frequent source of problems. In no small measure, IBM's success was based on our command of these environments and the people and tools we deployed to help those high priests. When things were running smoothly they might give us a hard time, but when things went wrong they would be prostrate at our feet desperately looking for the help only we could provide. And, we all knew it.

That's the paradigm that was really changing. The buyers were shifting. CIOs still mattered and dominated our time, but the new systems were being bought by individuals and department heads. Those systems were not being deployed in the "glass houses" we knew so well. They were being set up in closets and under desks. The individuals who managed them often did so as an adjunct to their primary job. The PC phenomenon had exploded the number of people with knowledge and skills to run systems. As these deployments grew in size and complexity, small businesses began springing up all over the world that would help departments address their growing management needs. The department heads who were responsible often wanted as little as possible to do with their internal IT organizations.

In addition to these small service companies, a number of larger companies were emerging to compete with IBM. They did not rely on sales to the high priests in the IT organization. They built their businesses understanding the new paradigm and directly targeting the new buyers. The IT organizations themselves were changing. They knew all too well that the organizational resistance they faced from within their own business was an indication they needed to adapt. They couldn't leave behind the glass-house infrastructures that were still absolutely critical to their businesses, but they began shifting more and more resources toward supporting what had become an irresistible wave.

That was the paradigm shift that was endangering IBM. Even though it was happening right under our noses we had trouble recognizing it for what it was. Most senior IBM executives were incredibly ignorant about what was happening. Even when warned by customers, analysts, or front-line employees their arrogance made it impossible for them to grasp. We were beset with the disease of arrogant ignorance. That disease is almost always fatal. We were also incredibly complex, with matrixed measurements all over the company. Internal debates about who could take credit for a successful sale were more important than a candid discussion about the many others we were losing. The eventual result was a dramatic collapse, leading to the ouster of Akers and the hiring of Gerstner.

CORPORATE TRANSFORMATION

Among the many early changes Gerstner implemented was an overhaul of the key functional/staff leadership positions. He brought in new leaders from outside IBM for marketing, communications, finance, legal, IT, and strategy. Each of these outside leaders set about making major changes both at a corporate level and, over time, throughout the organization.

The focus, discipline, and skill improvements led by the new CFO, Richard Thoman, had an immediate impact. They were the spearhead for dramatically driving down costs, most of which came in the form of headcount reductions, both voluntary and through layoffs. One of the recurrent themes throughout this book will be the impact leaders have on culture. Under Gerstner's new leadership team those cultural changes came fast and furious. There was a *Wall Street Journal* article published at the time telling a detailed story about Thoman personally reviewing an organization's expenses. This article was noted by many long-term IBM executives that I knew personally at the time. I recall one particular comment from a division president in which he said, "OMG this guy is actually counting envelopes!"

Leaders sometimes wonder how to affect culture. It's actually both easy and unavoidable. Culture emerges from the stories people tell about their leaders. Those stories will be told. Yes, measurements and rewards are important, but human culture is rooted in stories and businesses are built on humans, on people. Leaders need to know that and consciously manage the stories that will define them and shape their organizations.

Thoman and Gerstner began tackling an internal measurement practice known as "drag." IBM had always been a company focused on hardware, in particular the host or server systems that ran mission-critical functions for businesses. Those were still big businesses, but they were increasingly surrounded by spending on other items like terminals, printers, and software. The groups in IBM who were building and selling the big systems wanted to be able to take credit for all these add-ons as well. They built arguments and complex models that they used to assert how much "drag" they should be credited with. At one point the CFO added up all the "drag" being credited across the company and concluded we would have to be three times our size for all of that to be correct. The internal squabbles and debates were endless and, from a market standpoint, fruitless. This had to go. It would take many years before it was expunged completely, but Gerstner made it clear from the beginning that all he wanted to hear about from his leaders was their results, not the results of others that they wanted credit for.

The cost and expense targets set by Gerstner and the collective leadership team were deliberately aggressive, intended to provide operational improvements and financial flexibility for future changes. It was painful but relatively swift. Without those prompt actions, none of the rest of this story would have been possible.

Gerstner's new leader for Strategy and IT was Bruce Harreld. Mr. Harreld had been a partner in BCG and an IT leader for Boston Market. He, like Gerstner, had a customer's perspective on technology. This was invaluable but needed to be supplemented with the perspectives of those who had experience conceiving, developing, building, selling, shipping, and maintaining technology. Mr. Harreld brought in to his team a handful of IBMers to bring those skills, along with organizational familiarity and relationships with key leaders. I was one of those individuals.

I had been in IBM for about 15 years. I had worked in many roles and across many parts of the business. I had seen a lot and been party to the plans at the time to break up IBM. I had definite points of view about what was right and wrong with the company. I had no idea how little I actually knew.

Shortly before I took this new role in IBM, Charles Morris and Charles Ferguson had published a seminal article in *Harvard Business Review* titled "How Architecture Wins Technology Wars." This article spelled out a set of strategic principles specific to the IT industry. They asserted that having direct control of key technology "architectures" was the most powerful means of ensuring long-term success and profitability in the technology industry. This article captured the essence of what I and many others believed. We had a simple strategic diagnosis of IBM's problems. It was captured by the phrases "Architecture wins technology wars" and "IBM doesn't control any meaningful architectures." I came to the corporate strategy team with the fervent belief that to help IBM I needed to get agreement on that diagnosis and then on a path to fix that problem. It's worth noting how little this has to do with the important aspects of the paradigm shift described in the introduction to this section. A hint at the learnings to come.

Over the past several decades these beliefs in the keys to strategic success in technology have been developed on a vast scale. Countless articles and books have been written aimed at dissecting the details of exactly how this formula works. Those learnings were and still are widespread and so embedded as to be "unquestionable" for many extremely knowledgeable and successful individuals. Even today the belief in this collection of insights drives the current valuations of companies like Apple, Facebook, and even Tesla. One of the most important themes of this book is the exploration and discovery of both what is correct as well as the deep flaws and errors in this set of principles. At this stage of the story, it was simply one of the many things I had wrong.

TOWARD A SHARED VISION

The corporate strategy team had several functions including working with finance on the long-term budget and resource allocation processes and plans. My task, along with a few colleagues, was different. We were asked to write a "comprehensive, hard hitting, fact-based document" that would "tell IBM what to do and why." We felt we already knew many of the answers but that we lacked details, particularly around the "facts" and the "why." We set out on an effort to gather all of that data.

We read and interviewed the authors of countless industry and financial analyst reports. We met clients and distilled their feedback. We spoke with business partners and captured their hopes and fears. We visited labs and research groups across IBM. We spoke with futurists on trends and scenario planners of possible forks in the road. We filled the walls of our "war room," as we called it, with documentation, quotes, and insights from all these sources. Then we sat down to write our conclusions.

The first draft had a long, up-front section on the trends in the market, what we had heard from clients, what competitors were doing, and what we saw coming on the technology front. At the time, the Internet was exploding in everyone's consciousness. This combination of technologies and standards had been around for a long time but was suddenly working in ways very few had foreseen, and few really understood. It was obviously a game changer, but the specific actions needed to capture value from the trend were still unclear. We felt the key was in software, specifically the software that would embody the "architectures" of the internet. As a result, the first sections we drafted focused on actions for IBM's Software Group.

We sent our draft in to Gerstner, his key lieutenants, and the executive who ran the Software Group at the time, John M. Thompson. Mr. Thompson was a longtime IBM executive, highly regarded not only for his background in the industry, but also as an extremely thoughtful and respected leader. He was tough, but fair, thoughtful, and deeply passionate about getting IBM back to the stature we all felt was our destiny. His response to our draft, handwritten in the margin, was "If I believed half this stuff, I'd fire myself." That was when we were summoned to our fateful Friday evening meeting with Larry Ricciardi.

After our abrupt dismissal from Ricciardi's office, we huddled in a conference room down the hall. We knew we couldn't abandon all the work and insights we had gathered. We had very little time. We ended up rewriting our work to maintain the hard-hitting market facts and realities we had found but changed our recommendations. Instead of "telling IBM what to do" we wrote the recommendations as a set of questions. The market facts framed those questions. This was much more palatable for IBM's senior leaders at the time.

We called this document "IBM Global Market Trends" and it was then used to organize an all-day strategy conference with Gerstner and his direct reports. Each topic followed the same pattern. We would lay out our market findings, sources, and suggested questions. Gerstner would then personally lead a discussion with his team. He began each section by asking "do you all agree with what these guys just said" and from there went into "what are we doing about it and what should change." At the end of this conference John M. Thompson thanked us and told us it was the best strategy session he'd been to in years.

With that success under our belts we did the same the following year. The year after that we did it again. The year after that, Gerstner arrived at the conference and stated, "I hope there was nothing important in the last three chapters because I never got there." Others in the room asked, "what are all these smarmy questions at the end of each chapter? If you guys have a point of view, why don't you just say what it is?" The year after that, they killed the whole process.

Why do I tell this story and what was going on here? One of the most cited topics in senior leadership is the power of a shared vision. When Gerstner arrived at IBM, not only was there no shared vision, there was very little shared understanding of the market. It was common for different groups to hire outside consultants with the purpose of developing their own view of the world. These views were not limited to the areas of the business relevant to their group. They included the whole market. Including how different outside consultants viewed other parts of IBM. We didn't use the phrase at the time, but what was happening was each group was developing and documenting their own "alternative facts." There could be no hope of a shared vision when there was no foundation of a shared understanding of the facts—of reality.

Those early strategy conferences were one of the many tools Gerstner used to rebuild the basic foundations of an effective leadership team. A related initiative was put in place at the time by the marketing organization. While our work focused on client, competitive, and technology dynamics, they set out to get management control of the basic metrics of the market. How big was each segment and how fast were they growing? The only way to agree on what share of a market IBM had was if you could agree on the size of that market. Many market based metrics were being plumbed by Human Resources into the executive compensation structures and therefore needed management independence and auditable integrity. The market sizing numbers were essential but only made sense when combined with the rest of the story we were assembling in the strategy organization. It was this combination of shared insights on trends and agreement on basic facts about the market that were necessary foundations to agree on strategies.

Ironically, this was also the period when Gerstner made his famous quote about "the last thing IBM needs is a vision." Most management textbooks and consultants mean something quite bland when they talk about "vision." They're usually referring to some sort of tripe nonsense. We had zero time for anything like that. We did, however, need a shared understanding of *reality* and where we intended to focus our energies and resources. We needed depth, breadth, and details. It was embodied in 50–100 page documents, not 3x5 cards. By the time we shut down the Global Market Trends work, every senior executive was capable of presenting that material to any audience. There were no longer any "alternative realities." It was a remarkable change and had a powerful impact on the leadership culture.

REVITALIZING THE CULTURE

While this essential plumbing was being developed, Gerstner was busily driving another subtle but profound cultural evolution. IBM has a long history of being a customer-focused organization. For many years, almost all of IBM's top executives came to their roles through time spent in the sales organization. When I was a young systems engineer and then sales representative, my team leads imbued in me a bone-deep commitment to our customers. In those days, my desk was located at the customer location. That's where I went to work every day. They were my closest friends. I had drinks and played softball with them after work. My first day at the customer location included a 30-minute meeting with the customer's director of IT operations where he lectured me on how he and his team worked … and how I needed to work now that I was a part of *his* team.

Commitment to customer value was a part of our history. However, it had weakened and lost focus as we went through our internal trials and tribulations. Gerstner brought all that back with a vengeance. He started at the most primal and basic level. He decided we needed to remain an integrated firm, because that's the value he kept hearing customers wanted from us. It was our unique raison d'être. What he also observed is that those customers were rooting for us. They could be harsh and challenging critics, but they dearly wanted us to succeed. That reservoir of value is something most established brands have and that most pundits and analysts severely underestimate.

There was a customer conference in Chantilly, Virginia, that became a deep and enduring part of the legend of Gerstner in IBM. This event had thousands of people and hundreds of CIOs in attendance. Toward the end of the conference there was a discussion panel where all of Gerstner's direct line executives were on stage taking questions from customers. A question came up from the audience, the specifics of which are lost in time. What happened next will not be forgotten by those in IBM. The IBM executive on stage gave an evasive, politically correct answer. It wasn't anything egregious. Similar things happen at customer conferences all over the world by lots of companies and by countless executives. However, in this instance Gerstner stood up and challenged the IBM executive. He rejected his evasive answer categorically and demanded the customer be given a straight answer. He sided so completely with the customer that every IBMer in attendance realized the customer mattered more than literally any IBM executive of any level. Word spread like wildfire. Few IBMers used texting back in those days, but by the end of the next 48 hours I doubt there was a single IBM executive anywhere in the world who hadn't heard the story. Stories spread and with them so does culture.

One of the downsides of sourcing so many general managers from the ranks of sales is that many of IBM's general managers at the time had pretty shallow business skills. They had great relationship skills and knew how to close deals but didn't know how to run a business. As a whole they tended to rely on functional staff organizations for many key business details. The strong, top-down controls put in place by finance, that were so essential to survival, tended to exacerbate this disconnect from operational fundamentals. Gerstner knew this had to change—he wanted full ownership and business accountability from all his line general managers.

He set about driving this cultural shift in his first division- and group-level strategy reviews. IBM general managers in the past would bring bulleted presentations with few details and lots of ambiguity. They would rely on attendant staff members to answer any probing questions and would hide amidst the ambiguity whenever the questioning got tough. Few really knew how they stacked up versus their competition beyond the basics and even those were generally little more than sales platitudes.

Gerstner rejected all of those traditional behaviors. Strategies now needed to be written in prose with full sentences. They needed to state clear and unambiguous conclusions, implications, and plans. They needed to be defended, not through reference to a staff-written document, but by the direct understanding, belief, and passion of the general manager. And then the results needed to be delivered. It was a dramatic change in expectations and one that many executives at the time would struggle to meet. Which then served to open doors for a new generation of senior leaders—another element in Gerstner's comprehensive transformation agenda.

EMERGENCE OF SERVICES AS A BUSINESS

One of the most important achievements under Gerstner was the successful building of IBM's services business. It was Sam Palmisano who led that effort, directly resulting in his elevation to CEO when Gerstner retired. As a business, it started from very little. IBM had always enjoyed a fantastic reputation for the services it provided customers. Some of those services, like maintenance, were explicitly paid for under contract. However, many other services were "free," meaning they were implicitly embedded in the prices paid for IBM's hardware and software offerings. These "free" services were a substantial element of IBM's value to clients and were often a major reason for the customer's decision to buy from IBM.

The market shifts described earlier were ripping this model apart. Services businesses were growing rapidly in the market, but they were independent from any specific technology provider. The growth of the PC industry meant that more and more people were becoming familiar with computers. Basic services were often of little to no value. The open standard of the PC business had also triggered an explosion of suppliers in every imaginable category. These trends were not limited to PCs and consumers. They spread across the whole IT industry. As a result, corporate IT organizations were now dealing with literally hundreds of suppliers. There was no longer any such thing as an "all IBM shop." Services that were bundled with IBM hardware sales and focused only on IBM offerings were simply out of step with what customers actually needed and wanted.

This complexity was also what Gerstner had heard in spades. Customers were building their internal skills rapidly, but the range and depth needed to stay abreast of the industry was growing even faster. This meant that while almost every customer had definite needs for services the specifics varied enormously. What was precious for one could be considered utterly useless for another. Very few saw significant value in skills or services that were limited to a single vendor, including IBM. The need for services was exploding, and IBM had a strong reputation for excellence, but the business model we had used throughout our history would no longer work. In fact, in a perverse way, what had once been a source of differentiation for IBM's offerings was becoming a problem. Embedding relatively standard services that were narrowly vendor specific was driving up costs, not value, and value is what matters.

The solution was to break out the embedded services and drive them as specific business areas in their own right. These services now needed to be managed as distinct revenue and profit sources. They needed the attention of dedicated management teams, with associated investments, innovations, and operations.

We had resources and skills all over the world, deployed to our largest customers. Those customers had never been asked to pay for those resources, they were "just there." That needed to change. Some of those customers saw enough value from the IBM team that they were willing to begin paying for them. Some of the IBMers involved found this an easy transition. These folks had embraced the new innovations, brands, and modes of computing. They had made friends and relationships with individuals outside the IT organizations in their customers. They were proud of their own skills and the distinct value they brought. In some cases, it was an easy transition.

But for many situations, it was nearly impossible. Clients had taken these resources for granted for so long that being asked to pay for them was a non-starter. Many of the IBMers were equally uncomfortable. Part of the challenge was that these individuals were all members of IBM sales teams. The best field personnel, particularly systems engineers, had always seen themselves as advocates of the client first. This was an integral part of the pride and excellence of the IBM organization. Despite these beliefs, it was nearly impossible for both they and the customer to see them as independent from IBM sales.

The emerging IBM services organization felt it was essential to establish this kind of independence. Without it, they were certain we could not be competitive as a "real" services company. Whether customers ever truly believed or valued this vaunted independence is debatable. What was unquestionable was the need to establish a distinct organizational culture around services as a business. The IBMers who had been providing services as an extension of our sales resources needed to be converted to true service personnel in a separate organization. Some would make it. Many, maybe most, would not.

New management practices needed to be implemented. One of the early learnings was that a single badly structured, scoped, written, or delivered contract could wipe out the profitability of dozens of good deals. As a result, we knew we needed new quality control processes. The term "delivery" now meant something quite different from the hardware business. Whole organizations, processes, and nomenclatures were built around "delivery." The IBM culture celebrated winning deals, but the true value for the client was either achieved or failed through delivery. We needed to begin celebrating delivery excellence as much as closing sales. This would prove to be a consistent leadership challenge.

New service offerings needed to be conceived, tested, and deployed. In the world of services these processes didn't happen in some laboratory. They happened in the field, in the client's shop. The "development" process was hyperfragmented, tuned to each geography and client. The resulting organizational structure was completely foreign to IBM. There was literally no single person you could talk to about offering plans and results. Everything happened on the ground, in the geographies and in the client. This led to fantastic flexibility, but made it extremely difficult to identify, capture, and invest in specific services assets. Unfortunately, this would be another chronic leadership issue.

These unfamiliar organization, process, and management dimensions couldn't be readily measured and managed in the same way as the rest of the portfolio. Services contracts were won in one year and then delivered and monetized over many years. This meant we needed to track and report on signings and backlog "waterfalls." It meant changes in resources and results often took several years to unfold, for good or ill. It's like the difference between steering a small speedboat versus a giant cruise ship. You adjust the helm, and then wait.

There was only one organization in IBM with any experience at this. That was the Federal Systems Division that had worked on large-scale contracts for the US government. They had robust processes capable of putting men on the moon. They were skilled at managing federal procurement with all the attendant time scales, agencies, and documentation. They didn't really know how to run a commercial business, but they gave us a nucleus to build from.

And, build we did. One of the unplanned events that helped accelerate our growth was the Year 2000, or Y2K, scare. This derived from the historical practice of software developers to hard code date fields with only two digits. The date "1982" would be coded as "82." It was sloppy, but nearly universal at the time. The question everyone had was what would happen to this software when the date reached 2000? "00" would be interpreted incorrectly as being before "82" not after. There were widespread fears of massive disfunction that could unintentionally propagate all over the globe. Even though these fears were greatly exaggerated, the reality was inescapable. A lot of software was going to begin making a lot of mistakes.

While the coding involved was simple, the overall task was not. Essentially every piece of software had to be inspected and altered to avoid these errors. For many companies that could easily number in the thousands of packages. In some cases, the actual source code was either lost or not up to date itself. It was a global mess and literally every single company was going to have to deal with it in some fashion.

I recall an event that happened to me at the time. I was on vacation driving across the country exploring back roads and out-of-the-way places. I happened to stop at a diner in a small town somewhere in the middle of Ohio. As I was eating I overheard a conversation between three farmers sitting at a nearby table. They were talking about Y2K. One of them had done his research on the subject and was explaining to the others what they needed to do to ensure they didn't have any problems. A small, local company was going around to all the farms helping them inspect, upgrade, or replace any software on any of their systems. It made me realize just how incredibly widespread this issue was.

The issue was also a gold mine for the services business. Fixing these problems was inescapable. But, it was also a one-time bubble. Once complete, the resources to do the work would no longer be needed. It made no sense to hire permanent employees to handle this. It was a perfect fit for a services value proposition. While it was laborious, at a technical level it was also relatively easy. Everyone knew what to look for and how to fix it. It made it easy for us to get a footprint established across the market.

Completely unbeknownst to us at the time, it was also the entry point for a handful of small Indian services companies to establish their own footprints in the west. We will return to this in great detail later in our story.

The kinds of services I've been describing so far are referred to as "professional services." They involve hiring skilled professionals to tackle specific tasks with specific deliverables in specific time frames. At the same time that we were getting this business off the ground, we were also building a very different service business, the outsourcing business.

The basic idea of IT outsourcing is for the service provider to take over all of the capital and labor associated with a company's IT operations and to then manage those resources on behalf of the client. These are large, complex deals. They involve substantial capital and are written for long terms. Electronic Data Systems had been one of the early pioneers in this category of service and we were intent on catching and surpassing them.

Our established position as longtime trusted partners with major customers gave us a great foundation. After all, we were taking over the technology "hearts and lungs" of these clients. The sheer size and strength of the IBM balance sheet meant the capital was readily manageable. We leveraged this further by linking the IT capital to our leasing business. It was a great fit for IBM and one that Gerstner would later describe as the most incredible business opportunity he had ever seen, not just in IBM, but anywhere.

This was Sam Palmisano's baby and it was growing like gangbusters. At one point, when the growth seemed to stall, Sam addressed his direct reports in a staff meeting. He looked at his top three lieutenants and told them that from now on there would be a new management system. He turned to the first and said, "you find them." He turned to the second and said, "you kill them." He turned to the third and said, "you skin them." In less colorful language what he was referring to was qualifying sales opportunities, closing deals, and managing delivery. It wasn't the most sophisticated organizational diagnosis and intervention, but it worked. Double-digit growth returned.

This "big game hunter" mind-set is deeply rooted in IBM. The colorful language was unique to Sam, but the cultural fixation on winning large deals is everywhere. When the market opportunity matches that culture it's a fantastic asset. Unfortunately for IBM, as we will see several times in this book, there are many opportunities in the market where this culture is anathema.

The services business had become huge. It was over $10 billion in annual revenues and was still growing in double digits. However, it wasn't very profitable. In part, this was due to the nature of the outsourcing deals which were usually constructed in a fashion where the profits were primarily in the later stages of the contract. In part, it was due to our relative immaturity in constructing and delivering professional services contracts. We had learned that a single bad deal could easily wipe out the profits of ten great deals, but we still hadn't learned how to consistently avoid that one bad deal.

We needed a business that would fuel profits, not just revenues.

The Middleware Strategy

What everyone in the IT industry knows quite well is that software is highly profitable. Software is also at the heart of the IT architectures described earlier as the keys to winning in technology. While the growth of services was explosive, software was a major focus from the very earliest days of Gerstner's tenure.

When Lou arrived, IBM had software assets and capabilities scattered all through the business. Every hardware business had extensive, and unique, software offerings. For the most part, those investments had historically been made to drive demand for hardware. In addition to spanning all of IBM's platforms, the portfolio covered everything from operating systems to applications and tools. It also encompassed something that would come to be known as "middleware," which included things like database management systems and transaction processing systems.

IT software systems can be thought of as buildings with multiple floors. Operating systems are like the basement that sets the footprint and foundations of the building. The upper floors house applications and tools and are where people come to get work done or to live. In between are the systems that provide plumbing, heating, and electricity that make the upper floors livable. It is this latter category that became known as "middleware" and that has driven IBM and much of the technology industry to this day.

In the early nineties IBM had well-established and mature operating systems that were closely tied to their respective underlying hardware businesses. The middleware portfolio of the time was scattered across the business, primarily aligned with different hardware groups, though not nearly to the extent of the operating systems. IBM had pulled together its diverse application portfolio into an organization known as the "Application Solutions Line of Business" or ASLOB. This organization also housed IBM's portfolio of personal computer software including IBM's alternative to Windows known as OS/2.

Just as we noted earlier in the services discussion, building and managing a software business is quite different from a hardware business. When you build a piece of hardware you need to pay for all the underlying componentry. Every nut, bolt, microprocessor, or wiring harness has to be paid for. This is true for every single thing you build. These directly associated costs can amount to a substantial portion of the revenue you get from the sale of hardware. It would not be uncommon for this cost percentage to be 60%–70%. In the case of personal computers, it could be as high as 80% or even more. The rest of the businesses expenses including development, sales, marketing, and profits all have to come from the remaining 20%–40% which reflects the "gross margin" of the business.

In software, this is all turned upside down. Once you've built a piece of software it costs almost nothing to make essentially unlimited copies. There are direct costs associated with the distribution of those copies, but that's tiny. There are more substantial costs associated with supporting all those copies, but even that is tiny in comparison to the component costs of building a piece of hardware. Software is inherently a high "gross margin" business. While those margins are impressive, the development, sales, and marketing expenses can also be quite high, particularly at the stage of industry maturity in the early to mid-90s. At that time, the "net margin" after all costs and expenses were included might not be all that different between a hardware business and a software business.

The details of how the business results were delivered could not have been more different. Very successful, longtime IBM executives whose experiences were almost entirely in the hardware business found themselves making horrendous mistakes running software businesses. As a collective team, we didn't know how to price, promote, sell, support, develop, deliver, or manage software as a business. While this was true to some degree across the board, it was particularly true in the areas of application software and in software for the PC market. In the overall market those areas were booming. In IBM, they were floundering and losing literally billions of dollars. This had to change.

There were two key approaches used to tackle the issue. First, we pulled all the software assets other than operating systems into a single organization that became IBM Software Group. While this organization did not have direct ownership of the operating systems, it did provide functional guidance to those teams and, depending on the context, included those in its reported business results. The mission of this team was to lead IBM not just through the delivery of those different software offerings, but also on the larger agenda of transforming IBM into a software powerhouse with people, skills, and processes optimized for the current and emerging software industry.

To accelerate this process, IBM also embarked on two major software company acquisitions. Lotus in 1995 and Tivoli in 1996 not only brought major offerings to IBM's portfolio, they also brought people and processes rooted in precisely the areas IBM lacked. The Lotus portfolio overlapped with a substantial chunk of IBM's existing, and failing, PC and office automation software. It was relatively easy to shift both internally and externally to the much more prominent Lotus packages. A much greater challenge was with OS/2.

I'll describe the strategic flaws of OS/2 later. For now, it's enough to note that this rival to Microsoft's Windows was losing in the market every day. It was a hard reality to face. We had made uncountable commitments to clients all over the world that we would stick by them if they embraced OS/2. This included our best customers in the banking industry. At the time, the majority of ATM machines around the world had OS/2 behind the scenes. Inside

IBM, the executives who had made those commitments felt a deeply personal imperative to "fight to the death." It was also clear, however, that this very fight was crippling our ability to move on, to shift our focus to fights that were winnable and that would make a difference in the market. John M. Thompson led the work to look at our options and embark on a strategy that would not "surrender" but would let us move on. We set out to "stabilize" the package, ensuring that no customer would be abandoned, but also de-escalate this particular competitive fight with Microsoft. It was an emotional set of decisions, described at the time by many in IBM as our "Vietnam moment."

With that decision behind us, we set out on a strategy to first consolidate our existing portfolio of middleware and then strive to lead the emerging category of middleware for the internet. The internet middleware market was inherently "cross platform." Every system in the world would eventually be connected to the internet which implied that anyone developing for this market needed capabilities that could be delivered on any platform. As a result of IBM's diverse hardware portfolio, we had been wrestling with various aspects of this technical challenge for over a decade.

Our principle competitor was once again Microsoft, but this time the cross-platform reality of the market gave us an advantage. We had an unexpected ally in Sun whose Java platform offered an important part of the cross-platform formula. They were unfortunately also fierce competitors in the hardware arena which was the beginning of IBM learning how to simultaneously cooperate and compete with others. Our clients all wanted to leverage their existing systems and assets in their internet plans. By now, we had pretty solid teams of development, marketing, and sales who knew how to run software businesses and who were passionately committed to winning, specifically against Microsoft. We had consolidated every potentially relevant software asset under an umbrella brand named Websphere. The actual technical integration of those components was proceeding. Not as rapidly as some wanted, but compared to others in the market we were doing fine. However, it was not enough.

We weren't "losing," but we also weren't making much progress. Our market share remained abysmal and while the overall internet middleware market had not yet really exploded we were not positioned for success when it did. With little to lose the general manager, Tom Rosamilia, decided to reach out to an organization called "The Apache Group." This was a loose collection of individuals who were part of the open-source movement and who had created a crucial element of internet middleware known as an "HTTP server." If there was any single element of internet middleware that *had* exploded it was the Apache HTTP server. Tom sought to strike a deal for IBM to embed Apache software inside our Websphere offering. This might seem like a simple idea, but for the technology industry it was revolutionary. It was also done with no small amount of trepidation. How would this group react? Would we be able to build an ongoing relationship that was healthy for our customers? Would we be able to work with this loose collection of outsiders? Would it actually help?

One of IBM's traditions dating back to the original Watson Sr. was to nurture its "wild ducks." This tradition has waxed and waned over the years. In the mid to late nineties, IBM's wild ducks were going wild about the internet and were often themselves members of numerous open-source initiatives. The wild ducks were unanimous and emphatic—embracing open source was not only possible but essential. There were many different "flavors" of open source each of which took different approaches to the management of the intellectual property associated with their offerings. The license model used by the Apache Group was probably the easiest and most accommodating to the strategy IBM was seeking. As long as we respected the IP of the Apache contributors, they would respect and make no claims to the IP that IBM was adding all around them. We also acknowledged that if we were going to "exploit" their IP as we intended, we needed to be full-fledged members of their community, actively making contributions to the core IP of Apache. From our perspective, we needed to do this anyway since we knew we needed to be in a position to provide full technical support to our clients. The only realistic way to do that with open source was as a full member of the community. Everybody had a different definition of what they wanted in a "win," but the various demands were sensible, reasonable, and eminently workable. We could do this. We could do it as a win-win-win for the open-source community, for IBM and, most of all, for our customers.

The model that emerged was revolutionary and the results extraordinary. Websphere rapidly grew share in every category. The existing installed base of Apache users suddenly had a wide range of upgrade options available to them from the Websphere portfolio. Small skunk works teams in companies all over the world that had been doing exploratory work with Apache could now go to their corporate IT organizations and tell them a commercially supported version was available from IBM. We had found the beginnings of a new formula. The next phase of this evolution, our highly public embrace of Linux, will be described in the Palmisano era. A great deal of strategic work needed to be done before we reached that stage, but the crucial first step happened here, with Apache and Websphere.

It's worth noting the pragmatic mind-set behind this whole set of events. At the time, open source was regarded by many as a set of political manifestos. Most of our competitors, particularly Microsoft, adopted an ideological stance with open hostility toward the movement. We were certainly aware of all those currents in the market but chose to open a dialogue and see what was possible. Instead of hostility, we brought respect and a direct acknowledgment that these folks had created something of real value. To their credit, the Apache Group took the same stance toward us. None of us at the time had any idea how powerful this combination of commercial and social interests would become. We had unknowingly thrown a line around an invisible force that would propel IBM for decades and that powers much of the technology industry to this day.

Another groundbreaking development that stemmed from our experiences with Websphere was the creation of a technical framework to enable rapid integration of software assets into a coherent overall package. Reusing components had been a holy grail of software developers for decades. There had been progress to some degree, but failure was far more the norm. Some of this is technical and relates to inconsistencies between architectures, designs, and coding styles. Some of it is cultural. In addition to the usual NIH problems there are countless ways that managers and measurements can work against the best plans for reuse. As noted above, Websphere started as a bit of a branding exercise, throwing a lasso around a bunch of different components.

Once customers started buying into that branding promise, we really needed these pieces to begin actually working as an integrated whole. There were many different techniques used to achieve this, but two in particular stand out.

First was the appointment of a group of senior technical leaders to an IBM-wide Architecture Committee. The mission of this committee was to do design reviews of existing and planned software assets specifically to ensure the maximum possible reuse of existing assets. They focused on both the design architectures as well as the components themselves. If reworking an existing component would enable it to be used much more broadly they would call that out and work to get it done. They were given substantial veto powers if they saw designs that failed to live up to their plans. They could get a bit imperious in the process. In fact, some of them were deeply disliked by many top developers, but it was effective.

The second element was a management intervention by Steve Mills. Steve had been one of the key leaders who had driven the evolution of the Software Group. By this point he was in charge of the whole organization and would remain so for decades. At the time, there was a practice in IBM, that was prevalent across the industry, for the users of a particular component to pay a "transfer price" to the organization that "owned" that component. As far as Steve was concerned all those assets were "owned" by IBM and there was literally zero cost being incurred by the originator of the asset. It made no sense to burden usage decisions with some sort of artificial measurement, so he unilaterally abolished the practice. It was a simple, but profoundly liberating move.

Once we figured out how to readily reuse IBM's assets we realized many of the same techniques would also work with external assets. These could come from open-source communities as described above, or they could come from acquisitions. This ability to rapidly and effectively integrate newly acquired assets into the existing portfolio was crucial. We were all familiar with what had happened to Computer Associates, CA. Under their CEO, Charles Wang, CA had embarked on an aggressive growth strategy fueled almost entirely by acquisitions. For a while, this strategy yielded great results. However, the lack of true integration of the acquired companies and their assets began to drive up costs and complexities. Eventually, CA's meteoric growth came to a crashing halt. We were not going to make that mistake.

§

Based on what we had done internally with Websphere we felt confident we could avoid the problem. We began to ramp up our acquisition activities specifically of small software companies with assets that could be embedded into Websphere and other major IBM software brands. A standing "deal committee" was established to speed the flow of decisions, and a crucial new business capability was born in IBM. Over time we developed the processes, measurements, management systems, skills, and culture that enabled IBM to be extremely effective in identifying, qualifying, acquiring, and integrating software companies. From these small beginnings, acquisitions grew to become one of the primary means of adding to the IBM Software portfolio.

Overall the software portfolio was reasonably healthy. But, there were some crucial exceptions. One of the foundational elements of the middleware category are database management systems, or DBMS. At a macro level, IBM appeared fairly strong in this category. Under the covers there was a different story. IBM's strength was deeply rooted in the IBM mainframe and proprietary midrange systems. Outside that stronghold, specifically in the rapidly growing Unix and PC markets, IBM struggled. Oracle was and remains deeply embedded in the Unix market and Microsoft was steadily gobbling up share across PC server installations.

REALITY OF "CO-OPETITION"

This reality created a significant problem for IBM's Unix hardware business. They simply could not be competitive unless they worked closely with Oracle. Doing so created huge issues for the IBM teams who saw Oracle as one of IBM's top competitors. The tensions between the organizations grew steadily. The teamwork Gerstner had worked so hard to establish and the ability for IBM to deliver a completely integrated and optimized technology stack to clients was in jeopardy.

These tensions eventually boiled over in a meeting of IBM's top executives with wild accusations being made around the room. Senior executives were openly calling each other "traitors" or "communists." Gerstner stepped in and asked the corporate strategy team to come up with a resolution. Most of those top executives believed there simply was no solution. They thought we would have to deliver some sort of "edict" that would force one side or the other to accept a compromise that would inevitably cause them to lose competitiveness in the market. At this stage, Oracle was far and away the most problematic situation; however, the same issue lurked everywhere. In an open market with many possible options for clients, an integrated portfolio like IBM's could easily be driven to a lowest common denominator where IBM's share was driven by the weakest element, not the strongest. The stakes were actually quite high.

Within the corporate strategy organization, we had recently begun using a methodology known as "Decision and Risk Analysis" or DRA. We had folded that method into a decision process we called the Strategic Decision Process. This process and the associated methods will be described in more detail later. One aspect of the process was for the project team to interview the major stakeholders and gather from them all the issues and decisions they felt were essential to be evaluated. These issues were then assembled into an overall analytic model that allowed us to examine the outcomes arising from the various strategic options under consideration against a range of market uncertainties. The initial model for the Oracle project had over two thousand variables, every single one of which at least one major stakeholder felt was crucial.

This illustrates why the organization found the problem so intractable. Nobody could hold in their head the possible trade-offs and outcomes of two thousand variables. No two individuals shared the same beliefs about which of those were important and which irrelevant. The DRA method we were using is particularly powerful at dealing with exactly this type of complexity. What emerged was a realization that almost all of the two thousand variables did have the potential to change, for better or worse, the results for IBM. However, very few of them were "decision relevant." In other words, most of them had essentially the same impact regardless of what we did.

In actuality, we found there were only three variables that really mattered to the "decision." Once we could show everyone that that was the case all the energy could be focused on just those three areas. It took less than ten days from that point to understand how we could have our cake and eat it to. It was another month before we had written down the specific operational and behavioral rules and guidelines that reflected that approach. In the eighteen years since then we revisited the rules only once to make minor revisions. It became another key part of the IBM arsenal of organizational capabilities and competencies.

The other weakness in the software portfolio was in application software. IBM had lost literally billions of dollars in the application software business. Application software is the heart of what makes computers valuable. There had been a stage in the evolution of the market where clients wrote most of their applications themselves. That had changed and now clients wanted to source most of their application needs from outside vendors. The huge range of applications along with the enormous diversity of clients meant that the overall application software category was highly fragmented. There were thousands and thousands of different companies, most of whom were quite small and specialized. Attempting to match that enormous volume of specialized capability was a major contributor to IBM's losses in the application software. It was structurally ill-suited to a company like IBM and far better delivered through an open market. Many of these companies were also partners with IBM and played an essential role in delivering value to our clients. The partner network was both huge in number and huge in importance. We did not want to endanger those relationships by competing with them.

There were two major application categories that had not fragmented. In fact, they were consolidating down to a small handful. One of those was what used to be called office automation. This included email, calendaring, spreadsheets, word processing, etc. This was the heart of what Lotus delivered in competition with Microsoft. Nobody in IBM ever questioned our desire to win against Microsoft, but many had doubts about whether the Lotus portfolio was up to the task. In addition to being well established in all the relevant channels—training, installation, and support organizations—Microsoft was highly adept at creating "suites," or bundles of packages. Lotus had been a clear leader in many areas but found themselves in a steadily deteriorating market position. I will devote a full chapter to all the strategic issues and lessons that come from this particular set of battles.

The other major consolidating category was in Enterprise Resource Planning, or ERP. In the ERP space the clearly emerging leader was SAP. IBM needed to decide whether to try and compete with SAP or partner. SAP needed to make the same decision with respect to IBM. While both companies decided the partner path was preferred, the reality was always strained. When SAP began venturing into areas of the middleware stack that IBM viewed as strategic, those stresses threatened to bring the partnership activities to a halt. The principles and methods we had developed for managing the co-opetition with Oracle in DBMS now needed to be applied to SAP as well.

That left the question about what to do with all the other IBM application software assets and associated clients we had from our history. We had a large portfolio with well over three thousand different offerings. Most of those had a handful of clients at best. IBM wasn't going to continue investing in those assets but didn't want to leave those clients stranded. There were a lot of clients that could be impacted. In some cases, just stabilizing the software so it wouldn't fail was enough. In other cases, we found ways to divest or spin out the assets. In all cases, we extracted ourselves as gracefully as we could from any future obligations. By the end of this process we had converted our strategy to one that, with a few exceptions, relied almost completely on partners for application software.

Cleaning Up the Hardware Portfolio

This divestiture process was also happening on a much larger and more emotionally charged scale in the hardware business. IBM's history was rooted in hardware. Many of the most fundamental hardware technologies in the industry were invented by IBM. IBM had faced countless competitors in the hardware business including companies like Sperry, Burroughs, and DEC. Many of those no longer existed or had exited the hardware business completely. There were always competitors, but in hardware IBM felt it reigned supreme.

One of the first hardware organizations to come into scrutiny under Gerstner was the Technology Group or TG. TG had been formed when Akers was planning on splitting up the company. As the name implies it housed the development and manufacturing of the key underlying technologies of IBM's hardware business. Specifically, this included LCD displays used in laptop PCs, Hard Disk Drives or HDDs used in storage devices of all kinds, and semiconductor logic chips used in systems. Under Akers this group had been given both the direction and free reign to establish themselves as independent businesses no longer captive to IBM and to explicitly become suppliers to other hardware companies.

This strategy had worked to some degree. TG had succeeded in developing supplier relationships outside their captive IBM users. While almost nobody at the time knew it, Sun was actually one of IBM's largest customers. That had brought additional revenues and, importantly, manufacturing volumes that enabled the technology production processes to operate on a competitive cost basis. In the context of an open market it was no longer possible to maintain competitive economics strictly as a captive supplier. Even at IBM's scale the overall market was just too large. The TG structure and mission enabled IBM to stay abreast of these economics, but the model was under great stress.

The first major shift in strategy was around the display business unit. IBM's research team has an annual process in which they bring forward the outlooks around key technology trends for the next ten years. In one of those reviews they showed graphs on the increasing resolution of display technology. There was a line running through the middle of the chart. The line was labeled "limits of human visual acuity." We would be crossing that line in the next few years. There were still many areas open for valuable innovation in displays. Things like form factors, dynamic color balance, and power consumption are all areas that are still delivering differentiation for LCD producers. However, the PC use cases IBM cared about were mainly rooted in screen resolution and we could literally see the writing on the chart designating the end of that source of differentiation. It didn't take long to decide this was no longer a business IBM needed to own and we sold it to Toshiba.

The next piece of the technology business on the block was the Hard Disk Drive or HDD business. This hit much deeper, right into the heart of IBM. IBM had invented the HDD and had led every aspect of the technology for several generations. Much of that period had been about cramming more and more bits onto larger and larger platters. There had been a slip in IBM's leadership when the industry began shifting to smaller platters organized in redundant arrays called RAID drives. IBM was slow in making this shift and, once it did, found it hard to catch up with others who had made the moves earlier.

HDD revenues were down. In order to maintain the targeted expense-to-revenue ratios set by the TG financial model they had been steadily dropping investments in development. We had made our financial targets but had fallen behind competitors. The team still had the business of supplying HDDs to IBM's storage business but that group was beginning to complain and the outside customers were leaving for other suppliers. By the time this all became evident to the Corporate team, we had reached a point where a major reinvestment would be needed to bring the organization back to full competitiveness. There was no guarantee that that investment would actually yield sufficient results. The IBM storage business using the HDDs was divided over whether they needed internally developed HDDs or whether they'd be just as well-off sourcing from one of the various outside suppliers. In fact, there were a lot of voices who believed we'd be *much* better off sourcing from the market. For those who had lived IBM's history of innovation in HDDs it was a horribly painful decision, but we divested the business to Hitachi.

IBM's storage business was struggling too in its competition with EMC. Those struggles came from many sources. The many missteps by the HDD division were part of the story. The storage industry, and EMC in particular, had also shifted the basis of competition. It was no longer enough to simply deliver improved capacity or access speeds. EMC was now introducing all kinds of functionality through software embedded in the storage subsystem itself. This was still a hardware device, but the competitive dynamic was shifting to the functionality made possible through embedded software and IBM was struggling to keep pace. Those struggles continue to this day.

Another troubled part of the hardware portfolio were IBM's proprietary midrange systems. These systems were unique in the market and had been designed from the beginning to appeal to small and midsize businesses as well as small departments. Part of their appeal was how much embedded capability they included. These systems came with both operating systems as well as most of the middleware all included. In addition, they were sold through channels that would preload all the application software and handle installation and training. They were "closed," but if you could live within that enclosure everything worked smoothly and reliably. It was a model that Apple would successfully apply to the PC market many years down the road.

The departmental users of these systems were rapidly moving to PCs, but the small and midsize businesses had a harder path. Some of these companies had grown into pretty large enterprises and were demanding ever larger systems to support their growth. They were also struggling to find enough flexibility of software sourcing within the relatively smaller pool of companies focused on these systems. IBM began including Intel chips under the covers allowing companies to run PC software while still retaining the benefits of the integrated systems management inherent in these systems. These actions helped, but the writing was on the wall. When companies were confronted with the need to inspect, upgrade, or replace every piece of software to avoid Y2K issues many took that opportunity to migrate to either the rapidly growing capabilities of PC servers or to the well-established ecosystems based on Unix. The era of the proprietary midrange systems was rapidly coming to a close.

RESURRECTING THE MAINFRAME

This brings us to the IBM mainframe business. Gerstner is given credit for a great many things, but possibly the most important was what we did under his leadership with the mainframe. Like the midrange systems just discussed, the IBM mainframe was at odds with every trend in the market. Essentially, every analyst had concluded that the mainframe was a relic and would be totally absent from the market within 10 years if not 5. I had numerous discussions with these analysts. One of them guaranteed me the last mainframe would be unplugged by 2001 at the latest. They were all wrong.

In addition to the adverse market perceptions there was a less well understood technology problem as well. The IBM mainframes depended on semiconductors made with a process known as bi-polar. Most of the semiconductor industry used a process known as CMOS. Once again, the ten-year outlook from Research showed a dangerous reality. The steady gain in performance from each generation of chip technology was continuing at an incredible pace in CMOS. Bi-polar was ahead, but its pace of improvement was slower and there were indications it could slow even further in the future. If we didn't shift to CMOS, the mainframe would soon be overtaken by CMOS-based Unix systems. For IBM to shift to CMOS would require literally billions of dollars of investment. An entirely new semiconductor fabrication plant would need to be built. That alone could cost in excess of $3–5 billion.

The problem was further compounded by a timing issue. If we made the shift when we needed to stay on a ramp that would keep us ahead of the CMOS based Unix competitors, we would have at least one generation where we would fall behind the bi-polar based plug-compatible mainframe competitors from Japan. We would face 12–18 months during which these fierce competitors would be able to offer their own bi-polar mainframes at better price/performance and with completely seamless migration from IBM.

If you think about this situation from the perspective of the classic beliefs about business strategy you would come to only one conclusion: leave it behind. After all, it's a textbook example of a cash cow—profitable, but no growth and no prospects. Investing would take many billions of dollars and several years. The investments are filled with technical and operational risks. The whole process exposes the business to enormous competitive risks. Any MBA student would conclude to leave it alone—milk it for what you can and move on.

Instead we doubled down on our commitment. We built the fab. We migrated the systems to CMOS. The Japanese competitors stayed on bi-polar and gained exactly the advantages we had forecast. We sold our socks off for the 12 months when we were competitively exposed. Then we went further. Now that we were CMOS based, it was possible for us to offer smaller systems. We could offer systems that could operate in the environments where you found Unix servers with less environmental coddling. We started positioning this as a "reinvented" mainframe that was now a "server" just like the Unix systems. We did suffer some setbacks and losses. But, then we came roaring back.

After a single generation, the Japanese plug compatibles found they were no longer competitive and had no hope of recovering. We were able to aggressively target all their clients. The Unix competitors no longer had a competitive technology story with any substance. They could and did position themselves as "open" versus "proprietary" and that did carry weight. However, the IBM mainframe was unmatched by anything at the time in reliability and seamless scalability.

The Unix systems would continue to grow both in scale and capability. There was a slow steady erosion as clients made shifts to those alternatives. Every analyst knew about this and continued their drum beat about the end of the mainframe. There were not a lot of new mainframe clients, but there were more than most analysts realized. Mainframes have always been most valued by clients who needed very large-scale, 24/7/365 availability, in particular supporting high-volume transaction processing. These were banks, governments, the back-office operations of telecommunications companies, etc. As these kinds of companies in China, Russia, and other emerging geographies began to get large they all gave a hard look at using mainframes from IBM, and many chose to do just that.

We will come back to the mainframe story in later chapters. These days, the mainframe market is relatively stable with a simple cyclicality based on when each new generation is introduced. Throughout the last several decades these systems have delivered truly mission critical capabilities to our clients. They've also provided IBM with the profitability and cash flow undergirding much of the company. None of that would have been possible had we not made the hard decision under Gerstner that we did. This decision, that violated so many established precepts of strategy as well as the strident advice from analysts, was one of the most important and truly strategic decisions we ever made.

GERSTNER SUMMARY

Gerstner had saved the company. He had shed several perennial money losers and reinforced the core hardware legacy of the business. Through acquisitions, management moves, and sheer persistence he had built a truly competitive software business. That organization had developed business innovations that were having substantive impacts on the whole market. The internet wave was in full swing and IBM was right in the middle of it, helping our traditional clients embrace all the possibilities. The services business had exploded. It was already in double-digit billions in annual revenues and was still growing at double-digit rates. No other traditional technology company could boast anything like it. The market was evolving, and IBM was back in a leadership role participating in and driving that evolution.

We had not abandoned our core and we had significantly expanded it. What had once been a set of hardware product businesses surrounded by a thin veneer of software and services was becoming a business whose future value would be almost completely embodied in those extensions. Each of those business categories had required the assembly and construction of entirely new models of business with unique investment principles, value propositions, profit sources, partnerships, skills, and culture.

And, it all began with a series of cultural transformations rooted in shared insights, shared values, and a shared vision of what was happening in the market and IBM's future role.

Leadership really does make a difference.

STRATEGY: THE BASICS

WHILE IT MIGHT seem obvious, one of Gerstner's fundamental transformations was to expect his senior executives and, specifically, his general managers, to be wholly responsible for their business results. Finger pointing, blame shifting, or taking credit for an organization on cruise control became intolerable. A crucial part of that accountability was the development, articulation, and execution of their business strategies. Both he and I believe that strategy should not be some arcane discipline housed in an ivory tower. It's a core part of what general managers do and something any general manager must understand and be able to articulate.

First, let's look at what constitutes a "Strategy." Many executives will happily state that their "Strategy" is to be the "market leader." Or, they will declare their strategy is to "beat XYZ competitor." They might assert they've decided to be the "lowest cost producer" or the "highest value provider." Those all sound like "strategies," but in reality, they're closer to statements of what we will call "strategic intent" than actual "strategies."

"Strategies" are choices we make about things under our control. We make those decisions based on "outcomes" we hope to achieve. Whether we achieve those outcomes or not is a function of the various "uncertainties" that are not under our control. We can decide on a "strategy" to grow by dropping our prices 25%. That's under our control. We may or may not achieve the desired "outcome" of growth. Whether we do or not depends on "uncertainties" about customer price elasticities and competitive responses. This is a crucial concept to get right. Desired "outcomes" are not "strategies" because they are not under our control.

If outcomes are not strategies then what would be considered a strategy, specifically a strategy for a business? This topic has been studied for generations. There are lots of variations on the subject, but at its core a business strategy includes a coordinated set of choices along the following key dimensions:

- **Target Market(s)**
- **Offering(s) that embody a Value Proposition for that Market**
- **Value Capture mechanism**
- **Ability to sustain the creation and capture of value**
- **Scope of activities directly owned by the business**

There are numerous classic sources that have contributed important insights for all five of these topics that will be referenced throughout this book. Michael Porter's Five Forces framework is one of those classics, particularly on the mechanisms used to sustain the business. The Four Ps of marketing described by Philip Kotler and others is another basic and very useful tool for ensuring all aspects of a value proposition are addressed. Geoffrey Moore offers similar insights along with his observations about the stages of market evolution as a function of buyer segments. This has been both accurate and practical in my experience. Similarly, Clayton Christensen's deconstruction of the factors leading to an "Innovator's Dilemma" is right on the money, though I disagree with his conclusion that innovation is nearly impossible for incumbents. Less well known is Michael Treacy's work on value propositions. He asserts that the value creation of any business can be decomposed into three basic building blocks of "operational efficiency," "customer intimacy," and "innovation." In my experience, trying to apply this with too much rigor quickly gets far too academic. It is, however, a useful tool for thought experiments and one used frequently in this book. I've found that the classic growth-versus-share structure from BCG is a tool that needs caution in the real world. We will cover the dangers of the "cash cow" concept in several sections. Finally, over the last couple decades there have been substantial additions to these classics by people like Hal Varian, Carl Shapiro, and others. They have emphasized the new strategies rooted in unique aspects of the digital revolution. These more recent concepts are vitally important to understand, but also fraught with overly simplistic interpretations.

WHAT COMES FIRST–CONTROL VERSUS VALUE

One of the most crucial and elusive elements of business strategy is how to design a business that will be able to sustain its value in the market on an enduring basis. In Porter's classic Five Forces paradigm the answer is to create and use barriers to entry for competitors and to switching by customers. Scale economies and scope economies are probably the most familiar entry barriers along with things like patent protection and gaining control of the supply of a crucial resource. Most of his concepts aim toward creating some sort of monopoly or near monopoly position somewhere in the process. As the digital revolution has grown, this logic of market power has increasingly focused on the notion of "control." What were thought of as competitive "barriers" are now thought about with a language around gaining "control" of some segment of the market.

For many strategists and business analysts this has become such a paramount focus that all other aspects of business strategy have been deemed secondary. They will explicitly and emphatically assert that with the right "control" strategy in place, customers and value propositions don't actually matter. In fact, even to suggest they do is proof that you don't "get it." In the technology industry, this belief is so pervasive and so deeply embedded it amounts to a near religion. It manifests itself every time you see a company take actions to exert control even when those actions are hostile to customers. Well, I do "get it" and nonetheless have become an apostate. The reasoning behind this rejection and my assertion of the primacy of value will become apparent over the course of this chapter.

To begin, we need to understand why so many highly intelligent and well-informed business strategists believe in the "control paradigm." There have been decades of work done to develop this set of beliefs. Boiled down to its essence the core logic can be embodied in the following statement: "Architectural control points" enable the creation of "de facto standards" that lead to "network effects" that create "lock-in" and allow one to "control" the market. These are powerful new "invisible forces" that have enormous effects on markets and competitive dynamics. Let's look at each of these terms one at a time.

Let's start by returning to the analogy of a building for understanding software architectures. Once a building's architect has decided on the placement of things like air ducts and elevator shafts the owner of a specific floor can't change any of those things and must work with them as they've been defined. If you were hoping for a big open-air atrium right where a bunch of mechanical shafts have been placed, you need to revisit your plans. If I as the architect suddenly decided I wanted to compete directly with the company providing air handlers I could unilaterally change the shape, size, and placement of the air ducts to ensure the competing suppliers equipment didn't work at the same moment I offered something that fit the new specifications perfectly. In this way architectural decisions or changes can make competitive offerings obsolete.

In the technology industry, this observation led to a whole class of competitive strategies. Providers of foundational software like operating systems or middleware can introduce technical changes that make a competitor's offering that runs on top of those foundations inoperative, inefficient, or irrelevant.

This tactic has been used repeatedly throughout the technology industry. There's a famous phrase supposedly prevalent in Microsoft in the late 1980s and mid 1990s which was "Windows isn't done until Lotus doesn't run." I can't vouch for the truth in that, but I can say that in that period each new release of Windows did indeed create headaches for Lotus around changes that negatively impacted their offerings. In many, probably most, cases it was less about malicious acts and more about Microsoft's steady evolution of their operating system (OS.) Knowledge about those plans was well known to their colleagues on the application side of the business so they were able to ensure when new OS features emerged their application software immediately reflected the changes. When you control the evolution of the technologies that define an architecture, you can coordinate that evolution to the advantage of anything you have running within or on top of that architecture.

There is no question architectural control is a real invisible force that has been leveraged hundreds if not thousands of times over the years. This part of the control paradigm is accurate.

Standards are the next key element in the paradigm. Standards can be de facto or de jure and they can be open or proprietary. Standards make markets. In particular, standards enable markets to become very large. One of the most famous historical examples was the video format war between VHS and Betamax. It was the establishment of the VHS standard that enabled the rapid growth of the video industry. Device makers knew what capabilities they needed to include and there were ample sources of components they could draw from that matched that standard. Producers knew what format they needed to ensure the widest audience. Video stores knew what they needed to stock, and consumers knew that whatever video they got from whatever store they went to would work on whatever device they had at home. Standards do create boundaries to innovation in some areas but, at the same time they reduce uncertainty for both customers and suppliers and greatly expand the market.

VHS was the "open de facto" standard while Betamax was more "proprietary" and required licensing from Sony. The de facto nature of the standard was crucial in enabling VHS to win, creating a template for how to establish market making standards. Open standards that require de jure approval from some sort of standards body are hamstrung by the slow consensus process those bodies require. As a result, the standards are frequently based on a least common denominator and almost always slow to evolve. In contrast, a de facto standard can evolve as quickly as its provider can deliver. A de facto standard that is truly proprietary will always have limits to the scale it can achieve. De facto standards that are "open" in the sense that they are well documented and that anyone can implement them without prior licensing or fees can grow to unlimited scale. There are those who would argue that an "open de facto standard" is an oxymoron, but within the industry, particularly during this period, it was a perfectly acceptable notion. The crucial point here is that standards enable markets to grow to vast scale with a richness and dynamic no single vendor can match.

There is no question this is another incredibly potent invisible force that shapes markets in the technology industry and many others as well. As the global marketplace has developed, this invisible "market shaping" power is slowly but steadily shifting to China. This element of the paradigm is also valid.

Network effects expand on the notion of a standard for a given device and focus on the standards that enable devices to interoperate. If the world only has one fax machine that has no value. When there are thousands of fax machines suddenly they become useful. If those thousands don't all work together then we're back to zero value. It doesn't matter how cool you think your new fax machine is, if it doesn't work with everything that already exists it's useless. Most important, network effects can apply to people just as much as technology interfaces. The fact that there are lots of people using Windows or on Facebook means there are lots of places to go for help, there are common understandings about "how things work," and there's a common language in the market around systems and how one interacts with them.

Once again, there is no question network effects are an important invisible force and a valid piece of the paradigm.

The phrase "lock-in" has a pejorative flavor, but it accurately captures the result technology companies believe they are pursuing under this pervasive paradigm. Once enough volume has been achieved around a de facto standard, and once there are widely dispersed and active networks of users, it becomes essentially impossible to move to an alternative. While the switching cost for any individual user might be manageable, the collective switching cost for the entire network is both astronomical and requires a coordination that is impossible to achieve. As the examples have illustrated, the standards and network effects are not artifacts, they are essential to the realization of the core value in the first place. Precisely the features that create value also create lock-in.

And, again, these switching barrier dynamics are quite real.

There is no single point in the rationale behind this paradigm that is wrong. All are valid, and the conceptual work done around these different invisible forces that continue to shape the technology industry have definitely added to our understanding of strategy. These are all concepts that strategists should understand and use where appropriate. When I first joined the corporate strategy team I agreed with all of this and brought those beliefs to the work I was doing. But, something wasn't quite right.

The first inkling I had that something wasn't adding up came as a result of a project we did looking at strategies for how IBM could team up with Netscape. The phenomena described above all depend on large volumes. Individual PCs used as "clients" to access "servers" had that sort of volume. IBM had very limited presence on those devices, certainly nothing with the volume to challenge Microsoft. Netscape, however, had grown rapidly to establish itself as the de facto standard web browser and was reaching volumes that allowed them to make a challenge to Microsoft. The browser technology was also evolving as a "container" that would begin to create an actual foundational architectural alternative on Windows devices. The whole industry was watching this unfold and IBM had an opportunity to create an alliance with Netscape that might disrupt many existing trends.

We launched a project to look at a range of alternative strategies. The team we assembled defined four different options. Two of them were based on the control point paradigm outlined above with two different targets for possible architectural control. The third option basically amounted to "leave all this tech stuff to others let's just focus on services." The fourth strategy, added late in the process at the suggestion of a top sales executive, was for IBM to be the "agent of the customer," whatever that meant.

The analysis was quite complex. We had to model the different architectural intercept points. We had to look at what would be needed to achieve sufficient volumes and how that would manifest as competitive advantages. We had to look at variations of the market and competitive responses to our various actions. We even modeled what would happen if Netscape suddenly turned on us at different inopportune moments. Despite all the complexity, everybody assumed the winner would be one of the control point strategies. We had debates about which one, but no doubts those were the invisible forces we needed to harness.

Eventually we began getting analytical insights from all our hard work. It was stunning. The "services only" strategy wasn't great, but the "agent of the customer" strategy was winning by miles. It wasn't even close. In every variation, every simulated market or competitive twist it came out on top. The architectural control strategies did okay in some scenarios, but never came close to what our agent of the customer modeling was showing. Most IBM senior executives hearing about the results just assumed we'd made some sort of mistake. Maybe we set up the models wrong. Maybe they weren't properly calibrated. Maybe we just fed them bad data or had brought in a bunch of team biases.

The result created real doubts for me personally. I went back through all the details of how the model was constructed. I boiled out all the extraneous complexities and got down to the core elements driving the results. I decided that while the model could have been done differently, it was not logically wrong and wasn't missing anything that would change the outcome. I then started playing with all the key inputs and assumptions to see if I could get a different result. Nothing I felt had any credibility changed anything. Then I reverse engineered the model to figure out what inputs *would* change the result. Those inputs were not credible, nor did they fit any existing market data.

The final stage of acceptance was to step back and create a completely abstracted representation of the underlying mathematics. What I found surprised me enormously. Essentially what we were modeling was a set of flows through an interconnected, but "leaky" network. Putting aside all the technology, you could think of this as a set of water sources connected to pipes with junctions and valves controlling the flow to downstream reservoirs. At each junction, some of the water flowed to each connected pipe with the distribution probabilities ranging from 0% to 100% at any given point. We were attempting to divert the flows by intercepting them at their earliest point. What the simple math showed me is that this type of cascading logic attenuates extremely quickly. Far more so than my intuition presumed. Any strategic logic that says, "if I can capture point A then I'll have an advantage getting point B which will set up point C and allow me to win at point D" doesn't work. The math doesn't work. At least not if all the junctions are interconnected. If what you really want is at point D, then go there directly. I began to have doubts about the whole paradigm. All the forces were real, but did they actually work in combination the way everyone assumed?

During this period Gerstner had asked us to do a presentation to the IBM board of directors simply to educate everyone on this whole collection of strategy concepts. We did so, and it was so well received several board members asked us to come give the same presentation to their boards. It also began a more in-depth dialogue with Gerstner himself. This led to a major debate between Gerstner and Bruce Harreld on a company plane en route to a conference in Florida. Harreld's account of this discussion culminated with Lou cornering him against a bulkhead of the plane and saying, "let me get this straight, you're telling me your strategy is to lock-in our customers and then screw them on price. Well, let me tell you that is NOT what the IBM company is about!"

Months later, in a similar encounter, I was having a discussion about a particular strategy with Nick Donofrio, IBM's Executive Vice President of Technology. Nick is a legend in both IBM and the industry and a man of towering personal integrity. He turned to me at one point in our discussion and said: "stop using the word control. Nobody wants to be controlled. Do you want to be controlled? Our mission is to support our clients not control them."

Both of these leaders were giving unmistakable messages and guidance on values. Not in some abstract, academic way but viscerally from their guts. Many of the top IBM strategy executives at the time felt Lou and Nick were just wrong, that they were underestimating the power of these invisible forces, they were just too "old school." But with the doubts that had been rising in my head about the whole paradigm I felt we needed to challenge ourselves. I didn't really know where my work would lead and I had numerous questions, but I also strongly agreed with the values Lou and Nick were espousing.

It was time for us to tackle the subject directly and decide for ourselves what we were going to believe. We were all familiar with the examples used by every single pundit to construct their control paradigm logic. What about counterexamples? Confirmation bias is a powerful and seductive source of systemic errors for even the best of us. Every pundit was relying on essentially a single set of market data around the success of Microsoft and Intel in the PC market. The few other examples trotted out were almost always fragments that illustrated one or another of the underlying factors described above. Our debate wasn't with any one of those. We knew each one of them was valid. The debate was whether they actually worked in tandem the way the theory of the paradigm predicted.

The competition between Lotus 123 and Microsoft Excel provided an interesting case study. This example was frequently cited by those articulating the architectural control paradigm, but those references almost never really looked at what actually happened. Prior to Microsoft's entry in the spreadsheet category, Lotus was the clear, undisputed leader. It had every single element on the architectural control paradigm in place and in its favor. Spreadsheets, and specifically Lotus 123 spreadsheets, were everywhere and served as the foundation of countless business processes and systems. The inventors of the spreadsheet could never have dreamed how fundamental this simple tool would become to not only the analytics and modeling activities that were its intended target, but also as the foundation for countless business processes themselves. In that role, Lotus 123 was the architectural foundation of a whole generation of applications.

Lotus 123 also had all the characteristics of an open de facto standard including powerful network effects. Adoption was incredibly widespread. It was the tool used by everyone in any sort of finance or modeling role. It defined the standard for the exchange of data between departments, organizations, and companies. Training could be found literally anywhere in the world in any modest-sized community. Users traded spreadsheets that could be embedded in other models and traded data in the format used by Lotus. These standards were so ubiquitous and powerful that even today when Lotus 123 itself is as rare as a dodo bird, the 123-file interface is still the most commonly found format in the market. Lotus had every element of the control paradigm in its favor, so why did they lose?

The argument from the architectural control crowd is simple. They assert that the operating system was and is a more powerful architectural force and that Microsoft used that to overcome the less powerful control possessed by Lotus. To see if that's true let's look at what actually happened.

This was the era when PC applications were evolving from a command line interface to a full graphical user interface, or GUI. Microsoft was at the forefront of driving this transition. They did in fact use their control of the GUI embodied in the operating system to establish the standards for the GUI used by applications. The actual "form" this "control" took was that they used the exact same GUI elements in their applications that they did in their operating system. This meant that a user only had to learn one set of "standards" for things like how to open, close, or resize a window. We all know those little red, yellow and green dots. We all know how to grab a corner with a mouse and drag it to change a window size. We all learned those "standards" by working with Windows, and then Microsoft made the same standards available in their applications. Because their application developers knew what new "GUI widgets" would be coming in the operating system interface before anybody else, they could implement those standards in their applications faster than anybody else, specifically Lotus. This is a concrete illustration of the major elements of the architectural control paradigm at work and Microsoft explicitly and aggressively used every piece of the formula.

So how did it work? As you'd expect from the model, Microsoft introduced a full GUI capability for Excel before Lotus. Lotus announced they would have their own version "soon." "Soon" stretched out for months with customers waiting to hear when Lotus would have its own GUI version of 123. Eventually Lotus announced a firm date, which happened to be over a year after Microsoft. That's a very long delay. It was particularly perplexing to the market because the actual process of implementing the Microsoft GUI was simple. Microsoft wanted the whole market to embrace their GUI, so they had made available programming libraries that any developer could use simply and freely to give their application a full GUI. Many developers were suspicious that Microsoft had kept secret versions available only to their own internal developers. Regardless of whether that was true, it was indisputable that Microsoft had deliberately made it very easy for anyone to implement their GUI.

None of this was why Lotus was late. The problem Lotus was dealing with was a complete rewrite of the code for 123. The original version had been written in assembler and was tightly tied to both the older generation of Intel chips and the DOS operating system. This was making it impossible to evolve the offering as the underlying platforms evolved. Lotus was rewriting the code into C to fix this problem. But, that was a huge undertaking.

The fact that Lotus would be a year late disappointed customers, but for the most part they stuck with Lotus. Microsoft made share gains, particularly among first time users, but overall Lotus maintained its dominant lead. Which is clear evidence of the power of this combination of forces. Network related switching barriers are quite real.

Then a year passed, and the promised date arrived, only to have Lotus announce it would be delayed again. After a short while, it became apparent they would be delayed another year. They were now two years later than Microsoft and a year behind their own committed schedule. Customers were very frustrated by this. The GUI paradigm was demonstrably better for most users, in particular novice users, and its absence was becoming a major weakness. Furthermore, the missed delivery promise was a breach of faith for their largest and most important clients.

Customers began shifting to Microsoft, though it was still more a slow, steady erosion than any sort of mass exodus. During this period Microsoft stepped up their game with two key moves, one of which was aimed at the overall market and one of which was specifically targeted at Lotus. From the beginning, Excel had offered a "key stroke compatibility" mode that allowed power users to bypass the GUI commands and use simple keyboard shortcuts. Excel had its own version of these keystrokes but had also set out to ensure that anybody coming from Lotus 123 could use the commands they were already familiar with. This "123 emulation" had evolved to the point where it was good enough for almost anybody other than the most devoted power user to readily shift to Excel. They had directly addressed one of the individual user switching barriers though it did nothing to really address the network effects.

They also began bundling several major office application tools including spreadsheets, word processing, presentation graphics, and email. This bundle would become what we now know as Office. The relatively seamless integration that put all the tools one needed into a single package was very popular with customers. It also provided a concrete value to customers when all these tools worked together, had common interface and file standards, and could be bought and supported from a single supplier. It met a number of key user needs of the time.

By the end of this period Lotus finally shipped its updated version of 123. It was almost three years late and, by the time it finally shipped, had missed two different committed dates. It was competitive as a standalone offering, but by this point Microsoft had shifted the competitive bar to the fully integrated suite of professional tools. The slow customer erosion became a full mass exodus.

As the example illustrates, there are certainly many places in this story where the forces of the architectural paradigm were in play. However, are those the real reasons Microsoft won? Or, is it because Lotus was three years late with a crucial capability, missed major client commitments, and eventually fell so far behind they couldn't catch up? For the true believers of the control paradigm, that's an easy question to answer. I wasn't so sure.

This example also highlights how the real and observable presence of different aspects of the paradigm leaves open the question about whether those forces are in fact determinative. Which opens the question about whether the original source of the whole paradigm is as definitive as its supporters believe. In large measure the paradigm was developed to answer the question "why did Windows win"? Specifically, how did it win versus OS/2? Here was this tiny company, formed by a Harvard dropout, who was a supplier to the dominant computing vendor of the time, and who began competing with the very company, IBM, they were supplying. From the perspective of simple market power, IBM was in a vastly stronger position than Microsoft. The hobbyist and consumer markets were growing, but this was still a market that had been made by IBM with its access to large customers and their wallets. Furthermore, any computer science professor at the time could cite numerous underlying technical aspects of OS/2 that were more advanced and sophisticated than what at the time was still fairly rudimentary technology from Microsoft. Things like task switching, interrupt handling, and file management system were all indisputably technically superior in OS/2 than they were in Windows. Yet, Windows won. Why?

This question led to the development of the entire paradigm, and countless volumes have been written to elucidate the answer through different aspects of the theory. As we saw earlier, I don't dispute those points, but I do want to ask whether there were other factors involved. If we understood those better, would those factors lead one to question whether the real explanation was the architectural control forces or those other factors?

When trying to diagnose business strategy questions I like to start with the basics. Let's start with the product itself. How did OS/2 actually stack up versus Windows? The technical advantages mentioned above were real and widely understood at the time. However, they had essentially no relevance to the actual buyers of PCs. PCs were used by individuals who were typically executing one task at any given instant. The basic task switching in Windows was more than adequate for almost all users. Similarly, interrupt handling and file system advantages which were technically real were hard to illustrate with any credible real-world examples of people using PCs. In fact, it was so hard to come up with usage scenarios that exploited the underlying technical advantages that even after years in the market IBM was unable to cite any major examples that were relevant for individual users of PCs.

These technical capabilities might have been relevant for the high end of the file-and-print server market, which was dominated by Novell at the time. However, IBM made no serious effort at positioning its offerings in that space. The positioning strategy adopted by IBM was a "better Windows than Windows." In that positioning, the only places where IBM was actually "better" were places few users cared about. In the areas users did care about, OS/2 was definitively *not* better. For most applications it also required usage of a Windows emulation mode under OS/2 that was clunky to access and created incompatibility issues between the applications and data in Windows and those under OS/2.

Adding to the positioning problem, when IBM introduced OS/2 we also introduced a new line of PCs called PS/2. While OS/2 was available and would run just fine on Compaq or any other PC, IBM deliberately muddied the water with its branding. Many buyers were confused by this. Would PS/2 only run OS/2? Would OS/2 only run on PS/2s? The intended strategy was to use the "superiority of OS/2" to help drive sales of PS/2 branded PCs, but what it actually did was confuse the market.

The next issue had to do with price/performance. It was true that an OS/2 PC was capable of running just as fast as a Windows PC. However, to do so, it needed a great deal more memory. IBM liked to say that memory was a commodity so that didn't matter. However, like diamonds or gold, it was a commodity that happened to be very expensive. Users could choose between a low memory OS/2 configuration that would be comparable in price to a Windows PC, but measurably slower, or one that was the same (not better) performance but cost a great deal more.

On three of the classic four Ps of marketing OS/2 was a loser. For the actual buyers of PCs, the product was inferior, the positioning strategy exacerbated these weaknesses, and the price was substantially higher. What about the fourth P, "place?" This relates directly to the assessment of IBM's marekt-making power with business buyers. At first glance this would seem to be a key source of strength for IBM and it was one of the major factors analysts sought to understand.

The reality was quite a bit different from the superficial appearance. IBM has always sourced a disproportionate amount of its market strength from its relationships with businesses. This strength is skewed to larger enterprises and is centered on the IT organizations of those large enterprises. As mentioned in the opening chapters, it was normal for IBM to deploy its resources right alongside the people in those organizations. We played softball with them, hung out together, and worked side by side when things went either right or wrong. But, PCs were being bought by individuals and departments scattered across the organization. Those distributed buyers wanted as little meddling as possible from their IT brethren. They would tolerate a certain amount of procurement-linked volume negotiations, but after that they wanted full independence. Not only did IBM not have relationships with most of those buyers, its deep association with the IT organization was often at least as much a detriment as a positive.

Furthermore, the actual "place" where most of the buying was happening was not part of IBM. These systems were being bought from dealers and business partners who were in turn buying from distributors. IBM was far removed from the actual buying process and had little visibility into the details of what was being bought, by whom, and for what purposes. This arms-length reality was equally true for our friends in the IT organizations. They also had limited visibility, often relying on monthly or quarterly reports from a variety of dealers and partners who were scattered around the country or the world and who each handled reporting in different ways. They knew as little as we did.

Internally, outside of the original organization that created the IBM PC, most of IBM's leadership simply didn't understand this market. They didn't use PCs themselves. They relied on secretaries and analysts for most tasks and actually used a mainframe-based package for email and calendaring. They didn't understand the bottom-up, organic adoption from departments. They couldn't understand why our CIO buddies wouldn't simply edict the use of IBM PCs and OS/2. Many still believed these were just novelties on the distant perimeter of what mattered. There were many IBMers, in fact thousands, who knew better and who argued accordingly. However, IBM's market power was weaker than many realized and we were hopelessly mired in internal debates often dominated by those with no real understanding of the market.

On all the basics—product, price, positioning, and place—OS/2 was a loser. In some ways, the miracle is that IBM had as much success as it did, not that Windows ended up winning. The observations about the invisible forces arising from architectural control and network effects are all quite real, and they certainly contribute to our understanding of what was happening, but I would be hard put to claim they mattered more than our poor performance on the fundamentals.

Let's now return to the story of Netscape. As noted earlier, Netscape was becoming a dominant presence on the desktop. In the accepted paradigm of architectural control this was an intolerable threat for Microsoft. They set out with a vengeance to eliminate that threat and used every trick they could come up with to do so. The early releases of Microsoft's alternative, Explorer, were not very competitive. The key factor in the market was ensuring that any website would render properly on the screen and Explorer trailed Netscape in this regard. Following the principles of competing through architectural control, Microsoft set out to leverage their presence both in the operating system on the client device as well as on the servers that ran many websites. They introduced a variety of low level embedded networking protocols that they felt would allow them to exploit performance advantages. They introduced variations on HTML protocols than embraced the standards set by Netscape and then "extended" those standards in ways that would only render properly on an Explorer browser. This became known in the industry as an "embrace and extend" strategy. None of those tricks worked all that effectively.

Then they tried bundling the browser with the operating system and giving it away for free. This raised a number of antitrust reactions, particularly in Europe, but they managed to pull it off anyway. However, at least initially, it also produced no meaningful results. Netscape's dominant position remained. Despite all of the technical and market tricks, Explorer just wasn't as good a browser as Netscape and that good old fundamental competitive principle meant they weren't effective in dislodging them.

Microsoft was catching up, however. One of the things they are justly famous for is not giving up. They continued working on getting the basic offering to be more competitive. When they reached the point where the offerings were truly comparable then, and only then, did all their other initiatives begin to really work. Once the offerings were comparable, the fact that Explorer was free and came bundled with Windows really did mean there was no room for Netscape to compete. There are those who believe this is a further illustration of the architectural control paradigm. To my thinking this is just a very traditional example of how monopolies are able to exclude competitors through bundling and pricing. If architectural control had really worked as its believers claim, then Microsoft would have been able to achieve *sales* in this new category of software. They would have created an entire new revenue and profit source for their company. Instead, they were forced to add features and development costs to an existing offering with no incremental revenues and possibly some modest profit erosion.

Let's return to the IBM strategy for Netscape. We described earlier how the "agent of the customer" strategy was the clear winner. What did that mean? Under its grandiose name what it really amounted to was helping customers avoid lock-in and ensure they had options, specifically the option to leverage the existing assets they had in place. Many of those assets were IBM technologies so "agent of the customer" in many ways really meant ensuring that those clients that wanted to leverage existing IBM assets could do so without undue sacrifice. IBM's revenue and profit were centered on the servers used to power websites, not on the client devices used to access those servers, which is where Microsoft's presence was centered.

The theory of architectural control held that Microsoft's ability to "control" those client devices would enable them to "force" customers to choose their server technologies as well. Their control of point "A," the browser on the client, would influence intermediate points "B" and "C," leading to "control" of point "D," the world of server technologies that IBM was worried about. The architectural control strategies IBM had considered were aimed at fighting Microsoft at points "A" or "B," on the client, with the belief that that would flow through to point "D" the server technologies. In contrast, the "agent of the customer" strategy focused on weakening the linkages between points "A," "B," "C," and "D"—reducing "lock-in"—and on maximizing the value of the IBM offerings at point "D," the server. In every scenario, with even the wildest assumptions, this was far and away the most effective strategy.

As our examples have shown, even when the competitive dynamics are kept strictly within the world of client technologies, the actual effectiveness of extending one dominant position to another strictly by leveraging architectural control is very weak. When that same trick is tried across multiple platforms, each of which has its own set of market and technical dynamics, the actual power to "control" customer behavior is limited. What our analysis also showed was that both we and our customers were much better served when we focused directly on the offerings and technologies that mattered to both of us rather than fighting distant competitive battles in hopes that somehow those results would flow through. Once again, back to basics.

At the time, we felt that it was important for us to ensure we did in fact reduce the linkages between technology elements, reducing the spread of lock-in and providing a more open, level playing field. This was a core part of the strategic fight with Microsoft over the programming model for the web. IBM was aiming for well-defined interfaces, open standards, cross platform interoperability, and other fundamental approaches to maximize customer choices. For some of us, the value to the customer was the central feature of the strategy. Others tended to view the situation as more about reducing Microsoft's market leverage. In either case, we felt an urgent need to drive and lead these efforts. In hindsight, I don't think I'd change any of the specific things we did as part of that effort. However, I do believe we underestimated how pervasive and powerful the overall market was in driving to these same goals. As Nick Donofrio so forcefully told me, customers don't like to be "controlled."

Basically, we reached the conclusion that the best way to ensure our success in the server technologies we cared about, was to build the best offerings for our clients. Duh. Those offerings needed to deliver differentiated capabilities and needed the flexibility of working across the disparate technologies in the market. We didn't need to obsess about loss of control to some outside lock-in. The "value" we delivered our clients WAS the invisible force that mattered both to them and to us.

IBM's strategy for Websphere, our collection of web server software technologies, emerged from all of these learnings. We focused on an open programming model with the flexibility of supporting whatever client or networking technologies existed in the market. We leveraged open source as much as possible, since none of those technologies were differentiating and the open-source footprint allowed us to maximize our unique value. We focused our resources on building and delivering differentiating capabilities on top of that foundation. Many of those features were focused on enabling our clients to get the maximum value out of their existing data and application assets, and many of those were based on existing IBM technologies. We didn't need to waste time and resources fighting pyrrhic battles over client technologies and we didn't need to worry about open-source architectures being leveraged to undermine our success. This strategy was spectacularly successful, delivering literally billions of dollars of results to IBM for well over a decade. It flew in the face of all the industry wisdom and beliefs, yet still it worked.

One of the more interesting examples of the importance of "value based" strategies over "control based" strategies is probably Apple and the mobile phone market. This is more than a bit ironic given how internally control oriented the Apple culture is. For most of its history, Apple was the poster child for the downside of closed, proprietary systems. In comparison to Windows and Intel based systems, their market presence was minimal. They were used as the proof point for how immovable the PC market had become because of the network-based lock in effects around Windows.

The early Macs used Apple's internally developed operating system and ran on PowerPC chips from IBM. When they moved to Intel, many pundits predicted they would collapse. The belief was that the Intel migration would reduce the strength of Apple's network effect and cause them to be further swamped by Wintel systems. Nothing of the sort happened at all. They worked hard to ensure the migration would be relatively painless for both customers and partners and the market proceeded with barely a hiccup.

When they introduced the iPhone, they made no attempt to link those phones to their existing PC architectures. They used a different set of chips and wrote a new operating system for the device. They focused on making the device incredibly appealing to consumers, not on arcane architecture debates. They focused on what was valuable. The explosion of the iPhone has lifted their PC business immeasurably, but none of that was based on some sort of control point logic. Consumers liked the experience provided by their phones and decided maybe the same delight could be found in Apple's PCs. The brand was associated with a specific value proposition and it was that value that drove consumer behavior.

The contrast with Microsoft could not be greater. Microsoft's primary strategy for the phone market was to try and leverage their PC install base. They sought to duplicate the PC experience, even though that wasn't particularly suited to what people wanted from their phones. Nobody wanted a Windows phone. Even when they acquired Nokia, a company with a strong track record in phones, they remained focused on leveraging Windows instead of focusing on providing real value to phone buyers.

There's a widely held belief in the technology community that the eventual winner in the phone market will be Google and Android. This belief is based on the comparison to the early days of the PC market. Android is viewed as the "open" alternative to Apple and is presumed to be on the same market dominating path as Windows. It is certainly the case that Android devices outnumber Apple devices. The people who choose Android usually do so because they prefer the experience provided by the more open environment. They don't like the hand holding inherent in the Apple experience. To date, that hasn't meant all that much downside for Apple. In any case, the actual competitive realities are being driven by the good old basics of relative value, price, and availability, not some technical fight about architecture.

I want to close this chapter with a more philosophical observation about this topic. The notion of "control" has been a part of business strategy thinking for a very long time. There's this notion that if only we can achieve XYZ then all will be well. We can sit back, put our feet up, and take it easy. The language around "entry barriers" or "exit barriers" provided a polite way of talking about this, but underneath the real desire was a hunt for "control." This is a vision or a dream for a future state where things are static, where passive behavior is sufficient for success.

I believe this is an illusion. In today's globally competitive market I don't believe any company can "put its feet up and take it easy." I believe the only real source of "control" is the sustained delivery of value. It is only because clients choose you again and again that you sustain your success and that choice has to be earned again and again. I do strongly believe that different business designs can either help or hinder that process. Good business design includes the explicit recognition of how a firm creates value and how that can best be sustained. If your organization is dependent on client insights to drive value, you need skills, culture, and measurements aimed at ensuring a sustained flow of those insights. If you drive value through operational efficiencies, you need the ability to recognize and implement those opportunities. If you rely on innovation you need programs, skills, and a culture that generate repeated discoveries and inventions.

To summarize: the core of good strategy is a business designed from the ground up for the sustained delivery of unique value to clients. It is important for companies to maintain control of their ability to deliver that value, not to try to control their customers.

In essence, value *is* control. ... Control is *not* value.

UNDERSTANDING MARKETS

A solid understanding of customers is the key to a good business strategy. This is one of those simple eternal truths that is taken for granted far too often. Many companies rely far too heavily on the anecdotal understandings they glean from direct interaction with existing clients. There's no question this is a crucial, in fact, probably foundational, source of understanding. As we will discuss, IBM, particularly under Ginni Rometty, has just such an unhealthy reliance. Every executive I've ever worked with is aware of the dangers when this becomes your sole source of insights. Yet, they still do so. Why?

Part of the problem is that the formal data gathering methods are far too often focused exclusively on tactical insights. The results are then packaged in a way that causes senior executives to wonder just what they're supposed to do with the materials. Probably the majority of the general manager–level executives I have worked with through the years will, in moments of candor, admit they rarely find anything actionable or useful. They spend thousands of dollars, get the results, and then have no idea what to make of it nor what to do with it.

This is true despite the explosion of available data and insights. Companies are spending ever increasing sums to better understand, target, and serve customers even as their most senior executives become ever more removed from understanding what all those insights mean for their business. I will cover the explosion of new data sources later in this book. In this chapter, I'm going to focus on the traditional, classic means of gathering and using data along with the problems companies have getting anything actionable from that work.

Our primary focus here is on insights that have strategic relevance. This starts with the most basic market sizing data such as revenue size, growth rates, etc. Most executives and companies have no problems understanding and using this data. It's a standard ingredient in quarterly earnings reports, discussions with analysts, and almost every market strategy project. This is usually available in a standard form and most companies will just buy this from some consultant that specializes in market sizing for their industry.

For IBM, the market sizing process involved the synthesis of literally hundreds of external data sources. These were organized by offering category, geography, client size, industry, and time period. One of the underlying inputs to this market analysis was itself a collection of multiple sources that provided detailed macro-economic forecasts. The management of this process was centralized in Corporate Marketing who then outsourced much of the underlying mechanics to specialized outside analyst firms. Those firms followed IBM developed guidelines and methods to create economic forecasts to our unique specifications. Over the decades a great deal of work has been done to identify leading indicators of various events. These tools proved their worth in the 2008 downturn. For most in the market the shift itself wasn't apparent until September or October of that year. IBM spotted it in July, giving us time to adjust resource levels downward all over the globe. All that overhead was worth it for IBM, but not something most companies will bother with.

Moving on from basic market sizing is the shift to insights around what drives customer behaviors. This is where the problems begin to crop up. There's a whole host of work done by organizations every day to test offering concepts, validate design studies, explore feature trade-offs, and the like. Any competent offering manager will draw from this repertoire on a regular basis, and every study will be loaded with direct and obvious offering implications. Very little of that rises to the level of strategic insight which is part of the reason that senior executives can find it tedious. They want to know that their offering managers made their decisions on the basis of good data, but don't really need or want all that underlying detail. It's important, but not strategic. At least, not usually so.

This kind of data is rarely available in an "off the shelf" form and usually requires commissioning some form of market study. This is one of the places where unavoidable issues arise. The insights needed by offering managers can often be achieved through the use of focus groups and simple surveys. Those methods are relatively inexpensive, quick, and perfectly fine for what they need. If companies have developed the right sort of strategic framework these studies can usually be connected to that framework. However, these simple studies usually cannot be used to create that strategic framework in the first place.

There's a big difference between the insights gleaned from simple surveys that ask prompted, multiple choice questions about preferences versus MaxDiff, discrete choice, or conjoint studies. Basic questions will always be biased by the respondent's assumptions about what is expected from them. They will also consciously steer their answers toward what they want you to believe about them, which may or may not have any bearing on their actual desires. Almost nobody ever answers a question in a way that would imply a willingness to pay a higher price. Yet, every day that's exactly what people do all over the world. It's these kinds of deeper insights that become valuable contributors to strategy development.

The more complex methods mentioned, along with an ever-growing list of others, all offer these deeper insights. The challenge with all of them is that they're more lengthy and expensive to administer. This forces trade-offs on the range of topics you choose to explore, how deep you go on any one of them, and the scope of the potential market you include. You really don't want your offering managers spending all that money and/or limiting the scope of what they need to learn as a result of using these tools. However, when you need to understand things like price elasticities you have to use the more expensive methods. A simple survey on price will be next to useless.

Studying business customers introduces a range of additional issues and opportunities. Almost all studies attempt to apply established consumer techniques in a business context. Even though this is the universally used approach, it has a couple deep flaws. The biggest issue is that business decision making is almost always a collaborative process. It may range from simply getting feedback from a CFO to a full committee process, but whatever the range it's almost never a solitary decision.

The consumer techniques businesses rely on all have an unstated assumption that the respondent is the sole decision maker. Since this is never the case, business surveys rely on their own tacit assumptions about who the "actual" decision maker is, versus who is an "influencer." They then assume that understanding that decision maker's criteria will be meaningful. It may be useful, but it's almost never determinative. The collaborative process and impact of various influencers is far too important. Having led countless major and minor corporate decision processes I can attest that none of those assumptions or techniques would have been predictive of our final conclusions.

This is a nontrivial problem. It may be that some future technique might create a breakthrough, but for now this remains a real hole in the repertoire of "business-to-business" strategists. An interesting example of a counterintuitive finding on the role of influencers in corporate decision processes comes from a piece of work we did analyzing the PC server market. We were doing a conjoint study where each question offered respondents two different servers to choose from. The different features associated with each test case were varied systematically and then analyzed statistically to discern which features actually drive selection. We had done lots of studies like this in the past, so we had a baseline on many of the key attributes. What we did uniquely in this study was we asked each respondent to identify whoever in the organization they thought was most important to their decision. In each choice set we then placed a statement saying whether that person was either in favor of a given choice or opposed. We were measuring the importance of the influencer not by asking the respondent that question directly but rather through our observation of how the influencer's opinions impacted their choices in our study.

The results were fascinating and also quite revealing about the market for PC servers. All kinds of potential influencers were identified by respondents, from the CEO, CFO, and CIO down to the individual technicians who provided deskside support. When we measured the impact those individuals had on purchase decisions none of them had any "favorable" impact at all. Far and away the largest sources of influence were the low level technical support team. They also had no "favorable" impact, but they did have substantial "negative" impact. If they did not want to work on a specific offering or brand, then nobody up the line was going to try and force that on them. We discovered it was a waste of time trying to get a CIO to want IBM. The key was ensuring the tech support team simply wasn't against IBM. The invisible decision force that mattered most was hidden in the lowest level of the organization.

While this example was interesting and gave us a useful insight it was not a formula that could be replicated in most situations. As noted in the opening of this chapter, probably the single most used method for market insights was through client advisory councils. IBM has hundreds of these structures. They exist at all levels. The highest level advisory council meetings are attended by the CEO and all his or her direct reports. A typical agenda might start with follow up from prior meetings and then have a series of discussions in which an IBM general manager would present a set of planned offerings, events, or changes and then get feedback directly from the clients in attendance.

There are obviously lots of problems when relying heavily on these sources. They are by definition all anecdotal and qualitative. They're also skewed by the selection of clients to participate. We get input from our "friends," not those who are outside our inner circle. It's a dangerous source. This reality was something both Lou and Sam recognized. They would always insist on balancing or testing the insights from these sessions with other sources. Ginni understands the risks, but her orientation to direct client feedback was and is very strong. She too would sometimes seek confirmation from other sources, but in her case the balance usually skewed to the direct comments. The result is those qualitative inputs from a limited and biased set of sources had, and still have, a substantially disproportionate impact on IBM's perceptions of the market. This common strategic flaw for incumbents was identified by Clayton Christensen and is one that has caused numerous problems for IBM, particularly in the Rometty era.

In the context of strategy development, probably the most useful analysis centers on segmentation. Segment understanding and selection sits right at the foundation of good strategies. In the consumer context, the segments are often based on various socioeconomic and demographic factors. In the business context, industry and enterprise size are common starting points. There are lots of sources for this kind of standardized data. Like the basic market sizing data, it's important to include this in the overall data gathering plans. However, like the simple surveys done by offering managers this data is almost always inadequate for good strategy development. In both the consumer and business markets, this foundational data needs to be augmented with other "needs based" or "value based" insights, like our price elasticity example.

Segmentation is as much of an art as it is a science. There are important trade-offs that drive the process. The publicly available data can be readily gathered and used. However, when the association with actual customer value is low—which is the norm—it may offer zero value to strategy development. Conversely a pure "needs based" analysis may be fascinating to strategists but utterly useless in practice for marketing and sales. Similarly, strategy development involves working with a small number of large segments from which to select, while sales and marketing will be hunting for a large number of small segments to provide better targeting and a more personalized experience. The phrase "segment of one" is both a dream for sales and online marketing and a nightmare for strategy. Picking a single customer, no matter how good, is a guaranteed recipe for eventual strategic failure.

In addition to the higher costs and operational disconnects, there are other problems with the various methods used to derive strategic insights. In the normal approach, one of the methods mentioned above is performed on a large, demographically diverse population. This data is then analyzed statistically to identify clusters of common patterns. Typically, the research firm will then examine those clusters and come up with some sort of memorable name to give it. As an example, they might label one cluster as "disappointed novelty seekers" while another might be "happy millennials." Unfortunately, the names themselves have a strong tendency to become the primary drivers of subsequent work. The underlying details tend to be left behind. The names will almost never capture the full characterization of the cluster. This makes these kinds of statistically derived structures tricky in practice.

The other challenge for these tools is developing a segmentation that can be used effectively over extended periods, multiple data sources and multiple studies. A fancy clustering analysis that can't be connected with any other source and that requires adding substantial overhead to future studies will not be useful for most firms. The clusters are far too often mathematical constructs that exist only in the context of the original study.

An example of a segmentation study that did produce important strategic insights comes from IBM's Unix Server business. At one point in the evolution of that line we introduced an extremely complex and sophisticated dynamic clustering capability. This feature had gotten great feedback from our advisory councils, had tested well in early ship programs, and was being positioned as a major differentiator for our high-end offerings. At launch, this critical differentiator was included in all of our high-end models and was a key selling point. The only problem was it didn't seem to be lifting our results.

After much debate, we did a piece of market research to find out the problem. As part of that work, we tested the price elasticity of this specific feature along with every other aspect of the offering. The initial findings were puzzling. Despite all the rave anecdotal feedback we'd gotten from clients, the actual research showed no value from the feature at all. The overall market wouldn't pay anything for the feature. Zero. The good news is that finding matched what we were seeing in the real world. The bad news was we still didn't know why.

What we learned by analyzing the data was that under the covers there were (and still are) two very different segments of buyers of high end Unix servers. One segment strongly valued leadership technologies and features. In fact, that's what led them to Unix based solutions in the first place. They believed the Unix market was where the cutting edge of technology could be found. The other segment felt all that new technology just made their environments more complex and difficult to manage. They really just wanted consistent price/performance improvements with no underlying feature or operational changes.

The first segment was the group that had been telling us how cool our new technology was and they were quite happy to pay a meaningful premium over the base to get it. The other segment not only wouldn't pay more for the feature, but actually would pay *less* because of the perceived added complexity. The two segments were roughly equal in size so on a quantitative basis when added together netted to zero.

The tactical solution was simple. By making this technology an optional upgrade and charging only those clients who chose to buy it, we could serve both markets. The strategic implication was there was almost half the market being poorly served by both IBM and all our competitors. We were all maniacally focused on the leading technology buyers and nobody was really focused on the part of the market that wanted leading price/performance in an operationally simple package.

Unfortunately, this kind of strategically useful insight is not the norm. All of the factors we've described contribute to the problem. The simple "off the shelf" data is necessary, but not sufficient. The projects that gather data needed and used for basic offering management don't provide strategic insights and should not be burdened with the added costs and complexities of the tools that would. The tools that do generate good strategic insights are often incompatible with the operational deployment of those insights. They are also frequently difficult to replicate across studies and time periods.

There's no magic wand that solves all this. In large measure, it comes down to recognizing where problems arise and working to avoid or minimize them. It also makes clear that strategists cannot simply rely on studies done in support of other activities. Strategy development needs its own market analysis and those studies must be carefully constructed to provide both replicability and operational relevance. There are emerging techniques, particularly in the consumer market, that I have found useful to create the needed operationally relevant strategic frameworks. These are designed around predefined clusters that can be readily identified and have proven strategic value. We will discuss one particularly intriguing version of this approach in a later chapter.

The final, and in some ways most important part of the insight process is finding and sharing the "stories" hidden in the data. I have seen great analytical work ending up going no further than a binder on an analyst's bookshelf. The insights have to be extracted from all the complexity of the study and its methods and translated into clear business implications. It needs to be "actionable" and the communication of the insights needs to be structured around the actions at least as much as around the insights themselves. Carefully picking a few anecdotes that are representative of the study findings is also quite useful. When done well, it can connect the discussions that arise in an advisory council with the more wide-reaching formal research process. People will remember the stories surrounding those anecdotes long after they've forgotten any actual data they see. That's the natural human process and as along as the stories reflect the actual data there's no reason not to take advantage of it.

STRATEGIC BUSINESS DESIGN: STRATEGY
Business Leadership Model

Strategy Framework	Strategic Intent	Market Insights	Technology Insights	Business Design
Execution Framework	Major Processes and Activities	Measurement & Management Systems	Skills	Culture

We used several strategic frameworks over the years to diagnose various problems. Eventually we developed an overall framework we used as our consistent model for both developing new strategies and evaluating strategic issues.

This model, which we called IBM's Business Leadership Model, has both a Strategic framework and an Execution framework. In this chapter, we'll discuss the Strategic topics and cover the Execution topics in the next chapter.

There are four interconnected pieces of the Strategic framework in our model. These are: Strategic Intent, Market Insights, Technology Insights, and Business Design. The first three can be thought of as inputs to Business Design. The Business Design elements will feed directly into the Execution framework. This entire framework is built around the business philosophy discussed in our opening, with the central focus on the sustained delivery of value to clients.

Defining a strategic intent is the starting point for the development of a strategy. It's not the strategy. It's a statement of intent which could be translated into a set of measurable objectives. It might be something like "be the low-cost leader in ABC" or "be recognized for the best customer service." This will flow through many later stages of the strategy process. It gives business leaders an opportunity to begin shaping how the business will function by defining the unique raison d'etre for the organization. As noted earlier, one of the most common mistakes is to act as if this "intent" is actually the strategy itself. It's not. The actual strategy will define how this intent will be achieved—what we will actually "do."

Market insights are obviously critical to good strategies. These include many different dimensions including clients, their needs, how they use our offerings, what partners participate and what drives their economics, who the primary competitors are, either directly or through substitutes, etc. In the prior chapter, we covered some of the issues associated with gathering good strategic customer insights. One of the challenges across all market insight activities is being able to detect emerging trends, or weak signals amidst all the rest of the material. I will discuss some of the specific methods used for this including our VC relations process in the chapter on innovation programs.

One process we put in place under Gerstner was the creation of dedicated competitive intelligence teams. For each company on a specific list of approximately a dozen competitors we had dedicated teams whose sole responsibility was to maintain detailed understanding of everything those competitors were doing. The teams assigned to this task immersed themselves in everything about those competitors. They attended their customer conferences, called in to their quarterly earnings calls, attended meetings with analysts and stockholders and built profiles of every one of their executives. We also built financial models to reflect their underlying business results analyzing both revenue results and profit contributions. Each competitor on that list also had a senior executive defined as the "competitive champion" who, in addition to their primary line job, was responsible for leading his or her competitive insights team. The direction to those senior executives was that at literally any time Gerstner wanted to be able to call them and get an immediate and up to date briefing on what the competitor was doing. Over the years those teams proved to be invaluable sources of incredibly rich insights.

Technology insights include both internal roadmaps as well as the activities in the broader market. It should also include any adjacent technologies with potential for relevance. In IBM, while there is active business unit participation throughout, the overall process is primarily led by Research. IBM Research is not only one of the crown jewels of the company, it's also one of the crown jewels of the country, if not the world. There are roughly a dozen labs across six continents, including major labs in both India and China. Those labs have a remarkable degree of independence and work every bit as extensively with universities and outside organizations as they do with IBM line groups.

In the Gerstner era, the technology outlook was called the Ten-Year Outlook and mainly focused on forecasting the next steps in highly quantifiable things like semiconductor price/performance or storage density. This tended to be hardware focused although there were definite discussions on things like database or transaction processing technology trends. These were important inputs and, as described above, provided the trigger for several of the most important strategies IBM developed. Specifically, the strategies for the Display Business Unit, the Hard Disk Drive Unit, the Unix Server business and the Mainframe business were all initiated after technology reviews indicated important shifts on the horizon.

The strategic intent, market insights, and technology insights are all inputs for the creation of a business design. In IBM's Business Leadership Model, the business design is the heart of the strategy. It involves a coordinated set of decisions across the five dimensions of Target Market(s), Value Proposition, Value Capture, Scope of Activities, and Sustainability of the strategy. This methodology and much of its terminology is derived from Adrian Slywotzky—both from his book, *The Profit Zone*, as well as his direct interactions with IBM in the development of various strategies.

The business design begins with the identification of the target market and a distinct value proposition for the business. These are highly interdependent dimensions of the business design and almost always are worked in tandem. Sometimes the process starts with the client segment and sometimes it goes the other direction. The key is to end up with well aligned and understood value propositions and clients who want that value. One common problem is using overly generic definitions that provide little guidance or focus for the business. When done well, a clear and distinct market segment and value proposition can motivate a great deal of strategic insight and action.

Even more important is avoiding definitions that are little more than a tautology. I've seen many situations where a business will assert its value proposition and then declare that its target market is whoever wants that value. That's not useful. Its okay to start with the value proposition, but then the onus is on the strategist to determine who actually *does* want that value with some set of actionable identification factors.

As noted earlier, one of the useful conceptual tools we used over the years to think about value propositions is from the work of Michael Treacy. His work classifies value propositions as being rooted in one of three primary sources—client intimacy, operational efficiency, or offering innovation. A firm with a value proposition centered on client intimacy has processes, skills, and resources tuned to understanding exactly what a client needs and customizing or tuning offerings to those client specifics. A firm based on operational efficiencies is maniacal about driving out costs and delays in every operational process, both their own as well as their suppliers' and even their clients. Innovation value focuses on the repeated, sustained delivery of new and valuable innovations.

Obviously, every company has some element of all of these. Treacy's argument, however, is that each of these focus areas requires trade-offs in the others. For example, the tuning and customization of a client-intimacy firm is anathema to those seeking the ultimate in operational efficiency. Innovation firms almost always start with the innovation itself and then look to find which clients might want it and how best to get it to them. And, an operational efficiency company is happy to provide every customer with whatever color they want as long as it's black. We never spent too much time on the issues in these trade-offs, but we did regularly ask ourselves which of these classes of value would be the best strategy for a given space.

Two examples can illustrate the variety of value propositions that arise from these fundamental primitives. The mainframe business has always needed to be close to or ahead of any other server on price/performance. However, its unique value proposition was its reliability, availability, and scalability. Every part, component, and subsystem are aimed for the highest reliability in the industry and the overall design philosophy ensures that even when a part fails the system remains available. These high availability systems were also designed for seamless scalability with zero intervention. All these technical innovations were geared toward ensuring these "mission class" systems could be trusted and operated efficiently. The systems themselves were expensive, but the intent was to minimize the *total* cost of ownership for those client workloads that needed true 24/7/365 operations. It might not be readily apparent, and, given the high prices, might seem counterintuitive, but the core value proposition was actually focused on client operational efficiencies.

The IT Outsourcing business was also geared toward an operational efficiency value proposition but did so in a very different fashion. The phrase we used was "your mess for less." We would take on all your assets, operations, people and resources, and then manage them through systemic best practices to reduce costs. The level of actual client intimacy was off the charts, but the real value we were selling was efficiency. An interesting observation that suggests the accuracy of Treacy's theory is that we tried several times to shift our value to be a bit more based on how well we knew the client. We developed several strategies over the years to try to make that pivot but none of them really worked. The people and processes we had in place were so deeply wired for a focus on efficiency that we never got traction on using these relationships to drive a different type of value.

One of the critical dimensions of value proposition work is a focus on the competitive context. Marketers will often use the phrase "unique value proposition." There's no question competitive uniqueness is important, but the details of what makes it unique can be complex. The prior two examples were both focused on operational efficiencies, but each achieved that value through radically different methods. How the value is achieved can be as important as what the value is. In almost all situations, businesses with an operational efficiency value will need a cost basis that is at least equal if not superior to competition. That cost basis might not be what marketers usually mean by competitive uniqueness, but I guarantee it will drive competitive strategies. Innovation value strategies might seem to have inherent competitive uniqueness. After all, the whole idea behind the strategy is delivering new innovations. However, the relative value of substitutes and the meaningfulness of the innovations in a competitive context will determine the real power of the strategy. Similarly, customer intimacy strategies will derive their competitive uniqueness from a combination of the depth and accuracy of the insight with the ability of the firm to deliver something relevant to the insight. In actual practice, many of the truly unique competitive aspects of the business will be temporary and tactical. The key is to design the business to constantly reinvent and deliver these competitive advantages on a consistent basis.

The next key element of a business design is around value capture. Essentially this means what does the client actually pay for and how do they pay for it. This may seem trivial, but again there are a wide range of options both in how the business is designed and how things actually work in practice. In the PC business, sales and procurement is almost always focused on the PC itself, but most of the actual value capture came from various add-ons like mouse pads. Few, if any, companies designed themselves to operate this way. These realities only emerged as the industry began realizing where the profits were found in actual practice.

The mainframe business is another one where a great deal of the value captured by IBM is not in the sale of the server itself. These machines were the foundations for the sale of a large portfolio of software and services. We counted those business results in other units, but we were acutely aware they were tied to the underlying mainframe installation. The combination of the mainframe and all its associated software and services also provided the critical mass of business that made it affordable to have extensive sales resources deployed with that client. Those resources could then be effective selling the rest of the IBM portfolio. This formula became less important over time as IBM expanded in so many different dimensions, but in the early days the simple presence of an IBM mainframe was a central factor in our ability to capture value.

"Scope of activities" refers to the selection of which elements of the business to own directly, versus which to get from suppliers, from partners, and from the general market. At first glance this element may seem less "strategic" than the others. However, it's important that this set of decisions align with the rest of the strategic business design choices. If your strategy is based on a value proposition rooted in sustained innovation, you need to ensure you have the resources to deliver that stream of innovations. There may be others involved in the process as well, but if you don't have direct control of the core aspects of your value proposition, the business design will fail. Similarly, if your strategy is based on client intimacy, it's critical not to be disintermediated from your customers.

Scope can also have important impacts on costs, asset intensity, flexibility, and speed. Sometimes greater control leads to improved flexibility and speed, but sometimes it's exactly the opposite. You may be better off sourcing from a wide set of suppliers than getting saddled with the sunk costs of an under-utilized asset. These choices often involve critical trade-offs and getting the formula right can substantially affect long-term competitiveness.

In our earlier example, I described the decision to build a new semiconductor fab in conjunction with the mainframe migration to CMOS. There were many trade-offs involved with that decision. While CMOS is relatively standard in the industry, the specific formula used for IBM's mainframe chips is quite different. Had we wanted to source from an outside supplier we would either need to further complicate our migration or we would have had to find a supplier willing to create a modified process to support our needs. Either of those would introduce additional technical risk. Being dependent on an outside supplier for such a critical component would also increase our supply and quality risks. The specific details of IBM's semiconductors embody an enormous body of intellectual property including patents, copyrights, and trade secrets. Sharing all of that with an outside supplier could introduce substantial IP risks. On the other hand, building, maintaining, and operating a fab is incredibly expensive. Adding to that, the production volumes needed to fully utilize the fab far exceeded IBM's own needs, meaning we would have to sell that extra capacity to others. This example illustrates the importance and complexity of these kinds of "scope" choices. In the end, we built the fab. We also eventually created a whole new business model centered on that investment and its associated IP which is a story for a later chapter. The strategy needed to encompass all these decisions and resources.

We've already devoted considerable material on the final element of business design which is sustainability. That obviously has nothing to do with the environmental context of that word. Rather, it refers to how the business design will enable the firm to sustain its ability to deliver on its unique value proposition to its clients. Any successful business will attract competitors and, in today's global marketplace, these will arise quickly and can come from anywhere. As we've seen, this aspect of strategic business design has its origins in the classic "Five Forces" Porter model which has been substantially expanded in recent decades through the development of the control paradigm. While none of these are as important as a solid value proposition, they are critical to a good strategy and should not be neglected.

Each value proposition category brings its own distinct strategic vulnerabilities. As noted above, the Achilles heel of client-intimacy strategies is disintermediation. In today's global market, the weak spot for many operational efficiency strategies is sourcing from low cost geographies. Innovation strategies are often rooted in technical excellence and can be vulnerable to those with access to superior customer insights. It's "innovations that matter" that are important, not just innovation in its own right. Good business design anticipates competitive challenges aimed at these kinds of weak spots and includes mechanisms to deal with them when they arise.

The overall business design sets the context for the offering plans, roadmaps, marketing strategies, partnerships, pricing, and all the other specific actions aimed at achieving the desired results. Most of these will be covered in the section on aligning execution. In practice, at least some basic version of all of these decisions will have contributed to the thinking on the business design itself. While this has been presented as a linear path, it's almost always highly iterative.

Having established this framework and nomenclature we can now use it to discuss some of the key strategies we dealt with. In the early days of the web it was often the case that inside large organizations the groups building web applications were distinct from the main IT organizations. They were also often viewed as somewhat renegade, using technologies most IT organizations were still unsure of, including Apache open-source software. The Apache open-source strategy with Websphere enabled us to bring those two groups together. We were using the technology the web experts preferred and we were assuring the IT organization it was safe and supported. That gave us a value proposition important to both groups that we could then enhance with all the various capabilities we were assembling in Websphere. The target market was the union of those two groups and the value proposition was a stream of innovation on top of a secure, fully supported, open-source foundation. IBM's value capture was in all those software extensions, as well as through services contracts rooted in providing secure integration between the web applications and the existing IT infrastructure. This strategy required us to expand our scope of software activities to include providing resources that became regular contributors to the open-source elements we were using. In the early stages, most of that came from the personal free time of IBM's programmers rather than true dedicated resources, but as our involvement in open source grew we eventually created a dedicated organization to fill those roles. The big worry raised by technology analysts was on how sustainable this model would be. They feared our innovations would be hollowed out by the open-source "cancer" at our foundation eventually leaving us with nothing of value. They were applying the logic of the control paradigm that we had decided was far less dangerous than they assumed. We certainly did debate and understood the concern. However, we also saw an enormous mountain of software that was extremely valuable to our clients and we were gaining confidence that gave us enough market power to prevail. Some pieces might become irrelevant or might be replaced with open source options in the future, but the vast majority we were confident would continue to be valuable. We also saw literally no end to the number of innovations companies were going to need. The strategy is still going strong almost 20 years later. Value really does matter.

That success is in stark contrast to the original PC business. The prevailing wisdom asserts we failed because the microprocessor and operating system were "architectural control points" that enabled Intel and Microsoft to capture the vast bulk of the value. As we've discussed, there's a degree of truth in that line of thinking, however, it's incomplete. After all, Dell has made a great deal of money in PCs for a very long time despite not having any of those assets.

The business design template helps reveal a more complete picture of how deeply the IBM design was flawed. The original target market could be characterized as bringing a set of cool technologies from the world of hobbyists into the mainstream world of business. That part was sound. However, IBM's real roots were in the IT organizations of those businesses and these systems were going to be bought by individuals and departments that IBM had never done very well with. The value proposition and scope designs were even more deeply flawed. The main sources of valuable innovation were in the microprocessor, the operating systems, and the application software, none of which IBM was providing. By turning all sales and fulfillment operations over to partners, IBM had almost no visibility into how clients were actually using these systems. The actual production processes were heavily outsourced both upstream and downstream making an operational efficiency value proposition impossible. As a result, none of the fundamental sources of a value were accessible to IBM. In contrast, Dell, with its direct model had a design that enabled them to readily tap into these last two sources of value.

With IBM's heritage in selling hardware systems we just assumed we would capture value in the sale of the PCs themselves. However, once competition arrived, the prices on the PCs completely collapsed making the systems themselves profit-free and forcing the profits to come from elsewhere. The scope decisions made it very difficult to tap into any of these means of value capture. Finally, from a sustainability standpoint there were essentially no barriers to entry and minimal switching costs. IBM got by for a few years on brand loyalty but that waned as companies like Compaq and Dell who were solely focused on PCs began proving themselves and building their own brand followings. It was a fatally flawed business design. All the possible sources of value creation and value capture had been turned over to others and there was no way to make even the modest early success sustainable.

STRATEGIC BUSINESS DESIGN: EXECUTION

A well thought out business design creates the strategic architecture of the business. In this section, we'll talk about aligning the strategic execution framework with that business design. It's all well and good to develop a business design, but without effective execution its academic at best. There's a phrase we frequently used in IBM that goes, "vision without execution is hallucination."

Everyone understands this so why do so many strategic post-mortems include the phrase "we had a great strategy, but the execution was flawed." Part of the issue is that execution is complex, highly variable, situationally dependent, and spread throughout the organization. Despite this reality, there are a number of specific focus areas that leaders can use with significant impact on the organizations ability to execute a given strategy.

In IBM, we selected four of these: critical processes and tasks, management and measurement systems, skills, and culture. The first two we usually referred to as the "hard axis" while the second two we thought of as the "soft axis." The "hard" elements are ones that can be easily reduced to detailed specifics. Strong operational managers and executives love working on these. The "soft" elements can have a "touchy feely" aspect that makes some executives uncomfortable. In many ways those are actually the most powerful leadership tools, particularly when driving change. All four are essential to building a strong execution capability aligned with the strategy.

Let's walk through each strategic execution element in a bit more detail. Throughout this discussion I'll continue the example of the strategy IBM used to accelerate the success of Websphere by embedding Apache.

We begin by looking at the critical tasks and processes associated with the strategy. In a business as complex as Websphere there are literally hundreds if not thousands of tasks and processes, some of which are pretty generic. Our focus will be on those processes that need to be rethought based on the specifics of the new strategy. In this case, we are sourcing a number of absolutely critical components of the offering from an open-source organization. There are obvious tasks like negotiating and executing a license agreement with that organization. Once in place, the contract itself will have terms we need to manage. These could relate to proper documentation and sourcing references. They could also relate to agreements on sharing changes to the open-source code. We also need processes to ensure proper isolation of that set of code from the core IP in Websphere so as not to inadvertently give away things that are important to IBM. In the description of the strategy we talked about how we knew we would need to become ongoing contributors to the Apache open-source assets. Therefore, we need processes to ensure we are doing that on an ongoing basis. We also need to revisit our different support organization processes. What process will we use to handle problems when they come up? How will we determine whether a bug is in IBM code or in an open-source component either coded by IBM or a potentially unknown open-source contributor. What process will be used to resolve the problem in the latter case.

The reader can easily imagine how this logic unfolds. Almost every process needs to be examined to see whether there are changes and, if so, what those are. The management and measurement systems flow directly from these task and process decisions. Every process needs to fit into a management system and any critical elements need some sort of measurement. An obvious interesting example in this case is around quality controls, release processes, and change management. All of those processes already exist and have measurements that are used for decisions, corrections and incentives. What defect measurements will be used for release decisions? How will defects in the open-source elements be tracked and what management system will be used to ensure timely resolution. In the world of enterprise IT when a client's system is "down" and not functioning its referred to as a "severity one" problem. IBM's fame with enterprise clients is the urgency and effectiveness with which we handle these situations. How will we ensure the presence of open-source components does not detract from these measurements and how will we prove that both internally and externally? The entire strategy is based on a belief that embedding Apache will enable dramatic market share gains. What measurements will capture this? How will we track and measure placements of Apache and clients who subsequently choose Websphere? What goals should we set for these critical measurements?

Executing the resulting strategy will also require new sets of skills as well as a rebalancing of existing skills. We obviously now need developers with in-depth knowledge of Apache. We also need people skilled at working collaboratively with outsiders who are incredibly diverse in backgrounds, cultures, and motivations. Those are interpersonal and management skills that can be hard to find among hard-core developers. Not only must they be found, but they're now quite important and probably need increased compensation or some form of appropriate recognition for their contributions. The essence of the strategy also requires that we understand the features and capabilities clients want on top of the basic Apache. Those are skills we needed before, but they're actually a bit more important and may need to cover a wider gamut of needs than we addressed in the past.

Finally, we need to address the cultural aspects of the strategy. Some people may regard this as an abandonment, or hollowing out, of IBM's software. Some may harbor views that are hostile to the contribution of others, particularly when they view open source as vaguely socialist. The open source movement does have highly vocal members many of whom are critical of corporate interests in general. We need to handle all these worries, neutralizing some and taking actions to explicitly address concerns in others. We need to demonstrate that success will be defined by growth in the market and will be rewarded in ways appropriate to contributions.

It is only by thinking through and explicitly addressing all these questions that it becomes possible to execute the new strategy. There's another phrase we often used which was "if you change the strategy, but not the execution environment you will NOT get the new strategy. You'll get the old strategy, poorly executed." This is a crucial point. Whenever the strategy changes, its essential to revisit all the key dimensions of its execution. If there are no changes to processes, management systems, measurements, skills or culture there will not be a new strategy in the real world.

It's also important to notice how measurements fit into this picture. They flow directly from the assessment of critical tasks and processes and those flow straight from the business design of the strategy. Measurements are not strategy, even when they reflect the heart of the allocation of resources and the reporting of business results. In the context of an operational business this observation also applies to the entire domain of finance. It's very common in large organizations to either give undue credit or blame to finance. This is a classic case of the tail wagging the dog. It can also be a specific example of how critical it is to change execution when the strategy changes. If the resources needed for the strategy are not allocated appropriately we will once again get the old strategy executed poorly, not the new strategy.

The final point, which we will explore a bit more in the discussion of innovation programs, is just how extensively one needs to examine the different aspects of the execution environment. The example above gives a small taste of the range of things that may need to change in order to execute a new strategy. When a strategy allows most of the processes, management systems, measurements, skill and culture to remain intact or undergo small tweaks in special situations it may seem easy to execute. The challenge in those situations is ensuring the differences are sufficiently prominent that they actually get changed and to avoid falling back to the familiar. In contrast, when every aspect needs radical change it may be nearly impossible to execute with existing teams and resources. Good strategies are tailored to and specific to a given organization every bit as much as they are to the opportunity in the market.

STRATEGIC DECISIONS

One of the processes we formalized fairly early in the Gerstner era was our approach to complex strategic decisions. This may seem like a fairly "wonky" topic and, indeed there's more than a little corporate bureaucratic process in this chapter. However, it's one of those things that really does make a difference over the long haul. We often think of corporate decisions as being made by someone like the CEO or board of directors. However, in the real world important decisions almost always involve teams of stakeholders of various sorts. All of those participants have strong personalities and strong opinions. Having them actually function as a team and collectively execute the resulting conclusion is far more challenging than one might think.

Throughout the tenures of both Gerstner and Palmisano many strategic projects were aimed at dealing with chronic business performance problems. In the early years, the selection of which problems to tackle was usually driven by Gerstner himself and often took the form of "what's really going on here, can it be fixed, or should we just divest it?" Business performance issues always have lots of people willing to point a finger at someone else. In an organization as complex as IBM, with interdependencies and matrixed responsibilities everywhere you turn, finding out "what's really going on" was never easy and the blame game had a tendency to run rampant.

At the start of a project it's important to identify the key stakeholders that need to be included. Basically, any executive who will own responsibility for the execution of any of the "controllables" under consideration should be included from the very beginning. The formation of this "Steering Committee" can be tricky and requires judgement on both the issues at hand as well as the personalities and relationships of the various executives. We often spent a great deal of effort tweaking the project scope to get a Steering Committee we felt would be both effective in reaching a good decision and able to execute the result.

Decisions are always made in the context of other decisions. One of the tools we used in IBM is something called a "decision hierarchy." In most situations, a specific set of decisions is bounded by some number of prior decisions that will be treated as "givens." Furthermore, there are lots of downstream decisions that will be made in subsequent work, often by other teams, that will be framed by the decisions we are making at this moment. In our example on the mainframe, the strategic decision to invest needed to include assumptions about all major cost elements, including estimates on how much it would cost to build a new fab. Once that decision was made there were still thousands of subsequent decisions about the size of the fab, its location, the tooling and layout, etc.

This process of "Framing" which "controllables" are in consideration for a specific decision is the first step in what we referred to as our Strategic Decision Process. In defining the controllables that are in scope it's important to agree on what prior decisions will be treated as "givens" and which are on the table for reconsideration. One also needs to decide which controllables can and will be deferred for later consideration.

The other key element in the "Framing" step is agreeing on what outcome(s) are to be used in evaluating the decisions as well as the "uncertainties" that must be factored into that evaluation. Those "uncertainties" need to include the risks around our actual ability to execute the things we've defined as "controllable." In our mainframe example, there were lots of uncertainties and execution risks around our ability to build the fab and deliver the needed semiconductors with the performance, quality and schedule assumed in our plan.

Once a decision is "framed" we can then define different "alternatives." Good decision making always requires serious consideration of real alternatives. If you haven't looked at real alternatives, then you haven't really made a "choice." You've just followed a path. These alternatives might be different ways of achieving an agreed "outcome." They might also be based on asserting that a different "outcome" altogether is a better option. In our earlier example of a price-based share strategy, we might consider dropping prices only 10% or we might assert that price-based share gains are counter-productive and instead we want to invest to deliver a new set of capabilities that we think will be a better approach to that objective. One of the keys to good decisions is ensuring these alternatives really do reflect the range of options available and credible to the firm.

When dealing with persistent business performance problems it can be tempting to assume the root causes are deep and strategic. This can lead to the construction of quite elaborate hypotheses and alternatives. In fact, one of the major learnings from my decades of strategic problem-solving is to focus on the basics first. Classic issues around undifferentiated products, cost or pricing problems, poor enablement, insufficient sales resource, or even basic quality problems were far more often the real source of persistent problems. The classic "four Ps" of marketing around product, price, positioning, and placement are classic for a reason.

As we will discuss in a later chapter, it's also important to recognize when those basics are not the problem. When the root cause is an actual shift in the underlying markets and value propositions, the full strategic business design paraphernalia needs to be employed.

The next step in the decision process is the analysis of the different alternatives in the context of the major uncertainties against the outcome(s) we're seeking. It's tempting to ask in this process "which alternative is the winner" and sometimes things are that simple. More frequently, however, the actual winner is either a hybrid of the good ideas from different alternatives or one alternative that's been modified considerably to improve its robustness to the various uncertainties. That examination process yields the actual decision.

This four-step process—Framing, Alternatives, Analytics, and Decision—can range from a simple one-hour discussion to a three-to-four-month project. The simple version may skim over the more formal complexities, but will still benefit from the key disciplines, in particular the distinctions between controllables and uncertainties and the consideration of real alternatives. The longer versions almost always benefit from formalized checkpoints and reviews around each stage. The amount of time and effort spent on each stage varies enormously across projects. In some cases, the big debates are around clarifying alternatives. In other cases, it's around understanding all the risks and their impacts. In my experience, it's always best to frame the project to ensure completion in under three or four months. Projects that go longer than that tend to run adrift and get lost in their own complexities.

Over the course of a typical project the Steering Committee would meet a minimum of twice, but more often four to six times. If the project was reasonably well understood by the key stakeholders, we might meet first to review the framing and alternatives and then a second time to review the results of the analysis and to make the decisions. Much more frequently there would be a couple of meetings needed to get the framing and alternatives finalized and then several to review various stages of the analysis before leading to a final decision meeting.

When we first introduced this process to the company it met with a lot of cultural resistance. Project teams felt very insecure going to senior executives with interim work products that did not include final recommendations. They felt awkward asking executives if we had included the right elements in the framing and if the alternatives really reflected the range of debate in the organization. Senior executives who were accustomed to being the final arbiter of any decision found they had to interact with their peers during the process. The formalisms around controllables and uncertainties often didn't suit their free-wheeling style or their homilies around "just win, baby."

It is interesting to observe how much this has changed over the past couple decades. These days the formation of a steering committee, the scheduling of a series of checkpoints in advance, the identification of the final decision forum and many of the disciplines around framing and alternatives are automatic for most IBM senior executives. Many senior leaders still have trouble with the formalisms I've been describing. It's still common for an executive to provide input that mixes controllables, uncertainties and outcomes into a giant hairball. We learned over the years not to try and force the formalism onto folks like that. We would take their "hairball," go off and unpack it, put it into a coherent structure and come back and show it to the executive. Some would react by saying "however you want to form it is fine with me." Others would be fascinated to see how their intuitive beliefs could be structured in a methodical way. Leaders like that would often start using the structure to clarify and sharpen the point they were after. What was once foreign and uncomfortable has slowly become just "how we do things around here." Getting to that point required a great deal of leadership for the projects, the process and the results.

More than anything it was the good results that made this process stick. In the early days, we essentially only embarked on one of these projects at the direct request of Gerstner. We were very careful to stay focused on the integrity of the process and the analytics. We had no axe to grind and brought no preconceptions to the project. We were only being asked to engage when there were strong differences of opinion about what IBM should do or when the options and possible outcomes were highly complex. In that environment, we knew that just adding another point of view wasn't helpful to anybody. We needed to help the senior executive team involved to get to a decision they could trust and execute. Over time, as we developed a reputation for getting good results, we began getting requests from places other than just the Chairman's office. The first time a general manager called me up and said, "why don't you come by and let's see if we can figure this out before Lou sends you after me" I knew we had turned the corner.

We also observed a number of failure modes to good decisions. There are studies that claim 70%–80% of project failures stem from poor framing. I can attest that sounds credible particularly in the absence of a formal process and when the decision involves multiple organizations. It is quite common for a member of a steering committee to assert "XYZ is a decision I've already made, so as far as I'm concerned that's a given." Or to say, "we don't need to look at ABC in this project, that's mine to figure out once we're done here." Depending on the project, those positions could be either perfectly workable or a complete derailment. It's crucial to find that out early and to resolve it if there's a problem.

The other common problem we had with framing, particularly in the early years, was getting alignment on scope and decision schedule. Everyone wants fast decisions. Sometimes the things done to get a fast decision actually make it take much longer. I can remember one project where I did my usual introductory remarks at the project kick-off. When I was done I looked around the room and everybody was looking at their shoes or out the window. I started asking questions. It turns out this was the sixth time this exact same team had been asked the exact same question. In all five prior efforts, they had been told they only had 30 days to reach a decision. After five projects, they were no closer than when they began. I had to insist with their Senior Vice President that my version of the project was going to take 90 days, but I guaranteed we'd get to a solid conclusion. He wasn't happy with that but consented and we finally got his issue resolved—in 90 days.

The failure to consider real alternatives is another major source of bad decisions. It's very common for people who have already made up their minds to create a ridiculously under resourced option along with a completely unaffordable option and then claim they chose the "one in the middle." It can also be challenging for teams to develop enough depth of thinking around all the alternatives for them to be effectively evaluated. Sometimes you'll have leaders who really don't want to consider anything other than what they've already concluded. All of these can be managed, but it does require a level of strength and rigor from the project leaders.

The failure modes in the analytic phase are numerous. Most common is to underestimate the level of uncertainty in both the market and our own execution. Execution risks are particularly sensitive to assess. No senior executive wants to admit they may only deliver a fraction of what they commit. This topic is also fraught with political agendas. In the context of addressing businesses that are underperforming, this can get particularly tense with certain observers and participants eager to get into a "blame game." In the course of these discussions you also need to watch out for what we would now call "alternative facts." False assumptions about what has happened in the past or in other organizations can take on a life of their own and badly distort the decision process.

One of the most common failure modes I've encountered is what I call the "drunk under the street light" problem. This is a reference to the old joke where a passerby sees a drunk scanning the ground carefully under a streetlight. The passerby asks if he can help and the drunk says, "I dropped my keys." After carefully looking over the ground and finding nothing the passerby finally asks, "exactly where were you when you dropped your keys?" The drunk then points to his car on the far side of the parking lot. To which the passerby exclaims, "then why are you looking over here?" To which the drunk responds "because the light is better over here." People will often focus on the data they have rather than the data they actually need. Decisions can be hopelessly twisted around in the process.

The final step of actually making the strategic decision is also a source of many failures. Probably the most common failure in IBM was a disconnect between the decision, the operational changes embodied in that decision and the financial implications flowing from the decision. After all the work on distinguishing the true controllables and deciding which we would do, many teams then failed to actually put those changes in action or did so in very incomplete ways. The decision process was almost always done separately from the annual budgeting process. As a result, when it came time to do the actual budgets there were often huge discrepancies. The tendency to rely on financial targets as a surrogate for strategy would rear its head and the action-able decisions that everyone believed had been made would be left in tatters. One colleague used the expression "the decision isn't made until the resources are actually allocated." I would add that the decision isn't made until the opera-tional execution changes are actually deployed. Both failure modes happened with more frequency than any of us would like to admit.

One final observation about the failure modes of strategic decisions has to do with how some individuals approach these kinds of situations. I've laid out a logical path from framing to alternatives to analysis and finally to decision. Some people just don't operate that way. For some people, until they know what the decision is, they are unable to discuss any alternative or analysis. If any of those might lead to a decision they don't like, then they just won't engage in any way at all. They fear being trapped by logic or data and having to accept something they don't want. This is a kind of "backward decision process." Until they know the answer is one they like they won't agree or even discuss the question. I found this mode of operation to be far more common than one might think. In some cases, we could use the formalized alternatives to allay their concerns. If their specific desired conclusion is clearly spelled out as one of the alternatives they might be able to engage. Far more frequently, we simply needed to wait until nearing completion before we tried to bring them into the thinking.

IBM: The Palmisano years

No Company is an Island.
Value creation is achieved through value add...
by building on the work of others.

Introduction

Sam Palmisano brought a management style that was distinctly different from Lou Gerstner. Lou was elite, patrician, intimidating and highly formal. On at least one occasion I can recall him leaving a meeting saying he was on his way to an opera performance at Lincoln Center. Sam was a football player from urban Baltimore and I doubt he'd ever been to an opera in his life. Sam would use his "folksy" style in ways that caused adversaries to consistently under-estimate him. He wasn't "folksy." He was also far more intelligent and perceptive than many who first encountered him realized. And, he was an absolutely ferocious competitor. Like all CEOs he expected a certain level of personal loyalty, but the primary loyalty Sam demanded was to IBM. And, to winning.

The company Sam inherited from Lou was in far better shape than when Lou took the reins. IBM was profitable and growing, albeit slowly. It was no longer bleeding cash and rife with problem businesses. However, all was not rosy. There were deep and troubling business issues in the core semiconductor technology organization. The services business that had fueled so much of IBM's recovery was badly in need of a substantial infusion of talent and was actually quite weak in some of the most important sources of IT services value and growth. The middleware business IBM had carved out was delivering growing revenue and share gains, but the profit contributions were falling short. The PC business was a perennial money loser. The mainframe business had delivered a near miraculous recovery and was producing fantastic profits and cash flow, but everyone knew that couldn't last forever.

One element of the management system that Sam inherited from Lou was a structure referred to at the time as IBM's Senior Management Group, or SMG. This was a collection of the "top 300" executives in the company. It was not a strict hierarchical list of the "top 300" but rather a combination of individuals in top organizational slots along with individuals whose contributions and influence were crucial to the company. As an example, the top global salesperson on Citigroup might not be in the top 300 based on a strict read of an organization chart, but that person mattered a great deal to the company and had substantial importance. Similarly, the PhDs who were breaking fundamental new ground in semiconductor capabilities were vitally important even if their formal positions on an organization chart didn't reflect that. Lou recognized this and created the SMG as a structure to reflect it.

The SMG only met as a full group once a year, but everyone on the SMG knew pretty much everybody else on the SMG. When Lou or any other top executive wanted to get things done they would reach out directly to the relevant SMG members and engage them in the process. This virtual organization was the collection of change agents Lou explicitly relied on to turn around the business. Appointment to the SMG was a major step in one's career and brought with it substantial increases in annual stock and option grants. It provided a strong, effective overlay to augment the formal organizational structures.

Sam kept this structure intact but renamed it as the Senior Management Team. Sam also introduced four other overlay "teams." This included the Operating Team, the Performance Team, the Strategy Team and the Technology Team. These "Teams" became the primary management structures used by Sam throughout his tenure. The Operating Team was essentially Sam's roughly dozen direct reports with the exclusion of a couple of staff functions. They met every week or two and operated in a way that would be perfectly familiar to any group directly reporting to a CEO. The Performance Team consisted of the top 30–40 executives with direct responsibility for quarterly results, including all major line general managers and geographic sales leaders. As you'd expect given its mission, this team met quarterly to review the final results of the last quarter and make commitments for the following quarters.

The Technology Team and the Strategy Team were different. These were teams of roughly 12–15 people selected from the top ranks of IBM's technical and business communities. The appointment to one of these teams was limited to 18–24 months with approximately one third of the team rotating off every year. The CEO, head of strategy and head of technology were the only three positions with permanent appointments to both teams. The teams met monthly to review opportunities and threats coming from either the technical or business perspective. These were not intended as "decision meetings." They were explicitly intended to provide a forum for thoughtful and extended consideration of the kinds of complex issues confronting IBM. The learnings and conclusions from these meetings routinely flowed into the other management structures driving decisions in those contexts.

Sam used these team structures to ferret out complexities and evaluate different options. They created fora that enabled Sam to listen to complex debates by experts, to review detailed analytics on different issues and for him to evaluate directly the thinking and intellectual skills of his top executives and technologists. Sam also used these to communicate his values and priorities. He might not make a decision in these meetings, but his questions and comments left no doubt about what mattered to him.

One of the primary values Sam communicated both in these team discussions as well as literally every aspect of his management was a focus on profits over revenues. Nothing made Sam more frustrated than what he would refer to as "empty revenue." A business with great revenue and growth, but no profits or no profit growth was a waste of resources as far as Sam was concerned. This clear and unmistakable focus would drive the business throughout his tenure.

As the transition between Lou and Sam began to unfold, there was a strategic vision for the future of IBM emerging. IBM was well along in shifting from a company that was primarily focused on hardware with software and services in supporting roles, to a company that would be primarily focused on software and services. This vision was further refined through a focus on offerings that brought "high value" to "enterprise clients." There were threads supporting this vision throughout IBM, but there were also many things that did not fit. Among them was the reality that a great deal of IBM's revenues and most of its actual profits were still dependent on its legacy businesses, particularly the mainframe server, software, and maintenance businesses along with the IT outsourcing business.

This section is focused on the debates and decisions we wrestled with to resolve these discrepancies and channel our focus and investments toward our vision. Many of these debates began before Sam took charge and some continue to this day. The strengths and capabilities as well as the weaknesses and vulnerabilities that shape today's IBM are almost all rooted in the debates and decisions made during this period. Lou repaired the sinking ship and got it moving again. Sam delivered strong results that set it on the course that Ginni would inherit. Unfortunately, as has happened so often, many of the strengths Sam built on would become weaknesses his successor has had to manage.

MANAGING THE LEGACY CORE

THE SERVER BUSINESS

We'll start the story by reviewing the various parts of the portfolio that didn't quite fit the vision of "high value software and services for enterprise clients." While it might not have strictly fit the strategic vision, IBM was not about to abandon its legacy hardware server businesses. They were still far too important to IBM's financials, culture, and organizational structures, including most of its sales and go-to-market resources, not to mention our clients. Furthermore, this was a period of intense competition in the Unix market with both HP and Sun making major moves. Lou's decision to sustain the mainframe was one of the most important in his tenure, and we all understood how critical it was to ensure we did not lose these businesses.

The mainframe business was still very important to IBM. It not only contributed profits directly from the hardware, but also had substantial software and maintenance streams as well. The business had stabilized to some extent but was still seeing slow erosion. We launched an effort to evaluate whether we could not only stem the erosion, but actually generate new growth. We spent a great deal of time and effort understanding how clients viewed the platform and running tests of price elasticity to see if we could generate incremental growth from price reductions.

These efforts generated some intriguing findings. From the perspective of the overall market there did not appear to be any opportunity for price-based growth. There were a handful of situations where it did appear small amounts of price reduction could be effective, but they were quite narrow and difficult to build into a standard package or program. We also found that the single highest value positioning strategy for the mainframe was as the "most stable and secure *data* hub" for the enterprise. We will see this "data" thread spool out in several studies going forward. At the time, it was a bit of a surprise. We had always thought of the mainframe as the "most stable and secure *transaction* hub." This was still true, but our clients were beginning to move beyond that positioning.

The final result of that work was to tweak some of the positioning and sales strategies and to create special bid centers trained to recognize when and how to use narrowly bounded price actions. Sam also created a matrix management system in which the general manager of the mainframe platform was not only responsible for the direct revenue and profits, they were also charged with ensuring the gross profit stream from the entire stack of mainframe hardware, software and services remained stable. We made the clear strategic decision that this business did not need to generate any growth, but we needed to be able to count on a stable foundation of profit and cash.

The primary competition for the mainframe was the Unix server business. HP and Sun were strong competitors both against the mainframe as well as against IBM's Unix offering. In the eyes of most clients and analysts, high end Unix systems were the natural successors to the mainframe. They could be scaled to capacities that rivaled the mainframe, had superior price/performance, and had the promise of reliability and manageability on par with the mainframe. Other than the price/performance claims, none of these were quite true, but they were close enough in the eyes of many. IBM had famously invented the RISC processors at the core of these systems but had allowed Sun and others to capture most of the early business. By this time, that had changed, and IBM was extremely competitive on every dimension.

One of the major potential technology "forks in the road" was whether to stay reliant on IBM's own semiconductor technologies or to switch to a new offering coming from Intel, the Itanium processor. The Itanium processor was based on an architecture developed by HP called EPIC. HP had teamed up with Intel to produce semiconductors that embodied their architecture. Much of the industry was convinced that Intel was invincible in semiconductors and that the Itanium processor would set the standard for the future of server technologies. Intel was offering generous incentives to any company that would embrace Itanium and we thought it was quite possible others would join HP. If the industry was right, then we could find ourselves at a substantial competitive disadvantage both to HP and potentially to many others as well.

To complicate matters, the fab we had built was beginning to suffer problems from being below optimal scale. The original design for the fab had been carefully sized to deliver optimized marginal costs. As time unfolded and the underlying process technologies evolved, the optimal scale had grown. Intel was building new fabs all the time driven by the enormous volumes from their PC business. IBM was not about to try and build another whole fab and instead worked to retool the facility for each manufacturing process generation. We were making this work, but there was no question the model was under strain.

There was a great deal of internal resistance to the idea, but we knew the Itanium option was a serious possibility that could not be dismissed lightly. We had no doubts about Intel's ability to build fabs and to deliver leading edge technologies from those fabs. The EPIC architecture from HP was another matter. This was a complex architecture. The performance attainable from these systems was very dependent on compiler technology and HP had an early jump on everyone else in the market. After some careful technical studies our compiler technology teams declared they were confident they could match and then surpass everything we had seen from HP. Not only would we not be disadvantaged, but we might actually be able to use those resources to deliver better Itanium systems than anybody else. If the market analysts were right and Intel was able to establish Itanium as a market standard equivalent to x86 in PCs, we might be able to use our compiler teams to achieve a technically advantaged position.

There were internal doubts about these claims, but the far bigger issue was something our leading technologists were just beginning to raise. This issue was around the changing evolution of Moore's Law. Moore's law is one of the most famous and important in the technology industry. It stems from the ongoing evolution of semiconductor technologies. In each successive generation, the transistors on the chips get smaller and faster. In fact, it's the process of getting smaller that has made them faster. Over the years many people had predicted the end of this evolution and at each critical juncture had been proven wrong. The science and technologies of semiconductor production are among the most complex ever achieved by mankind. There are very few people on the planet with enough understanding of all the different aspects of the process to make firm predictions, and almost none of them would stake themselves on predicting a major change to Moore's law.

IBM's technical leaders were cautious, but also quite clear. There *was* a change coming and it wasn't going to be small. The shift was still a few generations out and there were countless uncertainties. One thing that seemed clear, however, was that while circuits would continue to shrink, the associated speed improvements would begin to slow and eventually cease. The only way to continue getting actual performance improvements would be to use the size reductions to increase the number of tasks each chip could process in parallel. In technical terms, each chip would now need multiple "cores" and each "core" would need to be able to process multiple "threads" simultaneously. This meant that ongoing performance improvements would over time be more a function of the chip design than the fab process.

This was a radical shift. It had enormous implications. It was still invisible to essentially everyone in the market outside of the small ranks of high priests who really understood the technology. Most of its effects were still far in the future. In fact, this trend is still unfolding in the market today, with very few who grasp its significance. We knew at the time that it meant the EPIC architecture would reach a dead end. That architecture was simply too complex for a world where chips would need multiple threads and cores to deliver sustained price/performance improvements. It also meant that systems and chips could no longer be developed independently. The system design needed to be in the driver seat. That would be impossible for us if we went with HP and Intel, which made it clear we needed to rely on our own microprocessors and technologies. In the end, the decision was pretty clear. This is a perfect example of how a specific technical insight drove a substantial and widespread strategic decision.

INTELLECTUAL PROPERTY AND TECHNOLOGY STRATEGIES

Having decided to decline the option of relying on Intel we needed to ensure our own semiconductor plans were on solid footing. The business results from that group had been inconsistent. It was profitable, but barely so, and it was consuming a great deal of capital. We used a financial technique to examine the business known as Economic Value Add, or EVA, that specifically includes capital requirements in the evaluation process. The results were not encouraging. The business was rarely returning its cost of capital.

We then engaged McKinsey to help us compare all of the factors driving our costs in comparison to other semiconductor companies. Their findings confirmed our suspicions. The original fab design had been carefully targeted at a scale that would operate at optimal marginal production costs. However, the subsequent technology generations had each required a larger scale to reach that financial objective. We were now far below the scale needed. We had a cost problem that was just going to get worse over time.

We brought the results to a meeting of the Strategy Team. In addition to the usual attendees, the Senior VP's of the Technology Group, the Systems Group and the Software Group all decided to attend. Even though Sam was CEO and was chairing the meeting, Lou Gerstner showed up as well. This was obviously a topic of intense interest.

We went through all the materials and concluded with a recommendation that we needed to consider selling this piece of the business, just as we had done with HDD's not long before. At this point Lou, who had remained silent throughout, took charge of the room. He said, "I came to this meeting because I knew some pinhead was going to do an EVA analysis." (Unfortunately, that was me.) He then announced, "if you do this, I will sell all my IBM stock and I will raise the capital myself to buy the business." He then slowly looked around the room and pointed to the Senior VP of the Systems Group and said, "Shortly thereafter I will make a call on you and explain that I am raising the prices you pay for all your semiconductors." He scanned the room again and pointed to the Senior VP of the Software Group and said, "and, all that work I do with your team to ensure your software gets optimized will now only be done for a substantial fee. If you reject that fee, I will offer the same to your top competitors." He then stood up and left the room.

It was a dramatic moment. His point was obvious. The "business" performance of the semiconductor organization was as much about internal measurement assumptions as it was about actual business contributions. Our cost findings were accurate but taken out of context with the other parts of the business they were dangerous. Sam asked whether the business as a whole, including the systems that used the chips, returned its cost of capital. The answer was yes, and strongly so. We would be keeping this business.

We still needed a strategy to ensure we could sustain our ability to drive those technologies forward. The answer emerged from a major project we did on how to optimize the value IBM got from its intellectual property. Many pundits in the industry look down their noses at IBM's ability to innovate. One can argue the point endlessly, but what cannot be argued is that IBM has the largest patent portfolio in the world. By far. Every year that lead is extended, as IBM files more patents than anybody else as well. The strategic question was how to best optimize the value IBM realized from that patent portfolio.

To understand this topic, we need a bit of background and history. As we've pointed out a few times already, there are countless technologies found throughout the industry that were first invented by IBM. Historically, IBM's focus on these inventions was on ensuring "freedom of action." Essentially, if there were 1,000 patents embodied in a specific offering and IBM owned 999 of them we didn't want to be thwarted by the person who held the one patent we were missing. In addition to our own freedom of action, IBM had realized decades earlier that we benefited from the innovation others brought to the industry as well. We had operated under a principle that put the main focus on using IP to maximize the freedom to innovate, mainly for ourselves, but also recognizing that others shared the same value. In the real world, it was almost never a case where IBM had 999 patents and we were only lacking one other. More realistic is that the thousands of patents needed were owned by dozens if not hundreds of participants and nobody could do anything unless everybody agreed on a mutually acceptable path.

Hence the principle of cross licensing. Under a traditional cross license, two firms would agree to license each other their patent portfolios to enable each participant freedom to use any patent held by the other. In practice, there were always certain exclusions and other complicating terms, but the basic principle was ensuring freedom of action for everybody. It's worth noting how different this is from the popular conception of patents. That notion of an "inventor in a garret" still exists in the real world, but it's actually fairly rare. Far more common is the interdependence between firms either in the invention process itself or in its actual realization in the market.

This collaborative innovation reality is an inescapable aspect of the modern economy. We do not live in a world where innovation is rare. It's constant and comes from everywhere. It comes from businesses in every industry. It comes from government research activities and labs. It comes from academia. It comes from every country in the world. And, it comes from individuals contributing to shared initiatives like open source. Those innovations find their way into the things we make, the materials we use to make them, the tools we use in the process, the way we use those things, and every activity that supports the process as it unfolds. Our mutual interdependence is so pervasive we take it for granted. Yet, it shapes everything we do and everything around us. It is another powerful, though invisible, force in our lives and work.

That invisible force profoundly guides the management of intellectual property. As part of our IP examination we looked at how we managed the patents in our portfolio. We found there were only about 5% where we used the patent in its traditional role where we blocked others from the usage of our patent. These were very important to us but constituted a small part of the portfolio. We found another approximately 10% where we licensed the patent to somebody else who then used it for themselves in the traditional manner of excluding competitors. The vast majority of IBM's patents, roughly 85%, were used for freedom of action. This usage was specifically NOT to block competition. In fact, it was to ensure all involved had equal ability to deliver their innovations to the market.

This realization enabled us to explore a wide range of new strategies to leverage our portfolio. IBM had been active in standards bodies for generations. Those organizations were also focused on freedom of action but were often held hostage by IP owners or those who cynically tried to trick standards into adopting proprietary IP. We realized we could begin licensing our IP to these organizations to give them the ammunition needed to achieve their objectives. In situations where our interests were aligned, why not do so? We also realized we could extract a lot more value in cross licensing deals. There were certainly large organizations with substantial portfolios where a straight up deal was the best we could get. However, in many other situations we could look at the "balance of trade" and demand a fee as part of the deal. That didn't change the essential nature of the deal, but it did bring a lot more concrete value to IBM. We created an organization with the specific mission of finding and executing these types of deals. Over the last 10–15 years you would be hard put to find any other single initiative that has generated as much direct profit contribution as those licenses.

What also emerged was a complicated new business model for semiconductors. We knew we had the skills, resources, mission and, indeed, sheer passion, to continue driving the leading edge of technology. What we didn't have was a financial appetite to manifest that in larger and larger scale fabrication facilities. There were other organizations around the world, like Samsung, who did want to make those capital investments, but who were struggling to stay abreast of the technology complexities. These other organizations also had world leading technology capabilities, just not all of the pieces of the puzzle. In fact, their production process learnings were indispensable for us in getting the complete formula. Similarly, our research activities couldn't happen in an ivory tower. We needed early production cycles to refine our own ideas. Out of all of this emerged a set of partnerships, built in large part around IP licensing deals, that enabled IBM and its partners to not only stay abreast of the technology evolution, but to also drive the leading edge; all while meeting the specific skill and financial capabilities and constraints of each member. We had found the answer to our semiconductor business problem. Few observers thought the model would work at all let alone for over 15 years as it did.

REALIGNING TECHNOLOGY TO THE SERVER STRATEGY

There was another profound and wrenching change needed by this part of the business. As a result of the work on the Itanium decision, we had the strategic insight that server designs needed to drive our technology decisions far more than in the past. Thanks to Gerstner's intervention, we had also sharpened our realization that the business results of the Technology Group were heavily dependent on the value being generated and captured by the Systems Group. Our execution environment was not aligned with these strategic insights.

The Technology Group, TG, was operating as an independent entity with its own business objectives, cadences and management priorities. This would no longer work strategically. In the chapter on aligning execution with strategy I described a logical series of steps through which the execution environment can be redesigned when there are changes in strategy. Similarly, in the chapter on strategic decision making I outlined a logical four step process. Businesses do sometimes work in that clinical a fashion, but not always. In fact, when the stakes are really high, maybe not even all that often.

These two organizations had been at the core of the company for generations. They had long, deep histories. They were quite large, each with tens of thousands of employees. Literally some of the smartest people in the industry, if not the planet had built their entire careers in these groups. They were proud, strong willed and, unfortunately, filled with acrimonious histories toward each other. There was a particular form of organizational disfunction known all too well between the groups. Most new offerings required a coordinated set of technical development roadmaps across the groups. When problems arose, they would engage in a form of "chicken" in which each team would wait for the other to announce they needed a delay. Once that was announced the other team would be let off the hook and could play innocent claiming "no problem here." Both sides knew the game and would hold out until the very last instant. That invariably created countless business problems.

In this environment an analytic based project with polite reviews and discussion would never accomplish any significant change. We needed a different form of intervention. At the time, we had created a senior executive training program administered for us by Harvard University. On roughly a quarterly basis we would take approximately 100 executives up to Harvard to spend three to four days in a form of "strategic workout." We decided to dedicate one of those sessions to this problem. We replaced much of the usual agenda with a program specifically built by my team to surface and deal with the deeper, emotional, and often highly interpersonal issues that had to be confronted.

We flew a little more than 100 executives from across the Technology and Server Groups up to Harvard. The session was intense. The Senior Vice Presidents who led these groups were in personal attendance. But, only because they had been ordered to do so. We gave each of them the opportunity to address the fully assembled leadership team. They took their turns standing in "the pit" of one of the larger Harvard classrooms. Their presentations were short on the need for change and long and passionate on their frustrations and grievances. One of them was so angry his hands were clenched in fists and his body was literally shaking with rage.

We then provided our business and technical diagnosis with all the associated data that pointed to unavoidable changes in strategy. We broke the teams into groups, each with representatives from the two organizations and let them chew on the data. Each team was then brought back to the main classroom to present their strategic conclusions to the overall assembled team. Those presentations started at 6:00 in the evening and ran close to midnight. Every team had come to the same conclusions we had presented in the morning. There was no escaping the need for change.

The next day we had Mike Tushman, an MBA professor from Harvard, and Charles O'Reilly, from Stanford, provide the modules on managing change that we used in all these "work out" sessions. It gave a bit of relief from the emotional intensity of the day before. It also made it clear that to achieve the magnitude of change we needed, every single person in that room was going to need to take ownership. Once again, we broke them up into teams to go off and debate how to accomplish what needed to be done. We were no longer focused on the strategy issues. The focus was on how to realign execution.

The presentations that evening were, if anything, more emotional than the ones from the day before. Many of the long-held grievances were rooted in operational behaviors and experiences. We were talking openly about all of those. As each issue came up, there were accusations and complaints loudly voiced to the whole assembly. But, what was also happening is that the very public venting was gradually giving way to the realization that every team was coming back with essentially the same observations and recommendations. The need for change was inescapable and the specifics of what needed to be done were pretty clear to everyone.

There was a lot of drinking in the bar that night.

By the third day, everyone was emotionally exhausted and quite a few were suffering hangovers. There was still more than a little trepidation, but also a clear realization of what had to happen next. A joint team was identified and given the responsibility of going back to New York and plumbing all the details of what was needed. A rising technical star from the Technology Group was put in charge of the work under my guidance. The two Senior Vice Presidents took the conclusions back and reviewed them as a team with Sam. One of the clear recommendations was to collapse the two organizations into one. One of them had to take himself out of a job he had worked his whole career to achieve. Sam accepted all the recommendations. It took another year before everything was completed.

Real strategic change can be bloody, emotionally exhausting and utterly impossible without leaders who share the deeply held beliefs and values of their teams. Sometimes that means sacrificing immediate personal interests to the larger cause. It's not for the timid.

LINUX–AN UNLIKELY STRATEGIC GIFT

The next potential fork in the technical road was around Linux. IBM had had great success with the open-source Apache project and was eager to explore the possibilities with Linux. Linux was a bit more challenging on several fronts. The IP terms that Linux demanded were not as straight forward as Apache. Our ability to enhance the basic platform and to deliver our commercial IP on top of Linux were limited by their terms. Nonetheless, we saw a great deal of potential value for both IBM and our customers if we could find the right approach. We also discovered, along with our customers, that there was far more Linux activity and usage scattered around our clients than any of us had realized. When clients began to realize this they sought help, support and in some cases just simple reassurances. Our Apache experience had taught us how to become accepted members of open-source communities and through that how to position ourselves to provide some of the support our clients sought.

However, there was a huge complication when it came to Linux. Microsoft had made no secret that they intensely disliked the whole notion of open-source development. They thought it was some sort of left wing, communist conspiracy to thwart their hegemony. They indulged in all kinds of saber rattling, threatening IP lawsuits against anybody who used Linux. Customers asked us and other vendors to indemnify them against any action by Microsoft. We demurred. It was too much of an open checkbook with too many unknowns. We also wanted to ensure that if Microsoft did choose to launch a lawsuit they would have to direct it at a customer, not a competitor. Yes, we were hiding behind customers and putting them in a potential cross fire just as I said we did not want to do. We didn't like it. It felt unstable, but we also were not willing to abandon the open-source pioneers nor those clients who were finding so much value from it.

IBM had an existing IP cross license in place with Microsoft, so we had no IP leverage from our existing portfolio. However, we were able to identify a collection of IP that was coming up for sale in the market and that would be potentially devastating to Microsoft. We were able to engineer the creation of a new company that bought this IP with the sole mission of using it against Microsoft if they ever brought suit against Linux. One of IBM's retirees agreed to be the CEO of this IP shell company and put in place a small staff with the mission of managing their IP portfolio and adding to it as necessary. We let

Microsoft and the market know what had happened. The saber rattling slowly died down and eventually ended.

Just as we had with Apache, we found tons of lucrative opportunities building around Linux. There were lots of services people needed. We could make most of our middleware available on Linux and that opened up many new opportunities. The Intel based server market was large and continuing to grow strongly. We had always had trouble selling our middleware on those platforms when they ran Windows. Now, many of them were running Linux and we had no trouble selling to those customers at all. In fact, Microsoft's ideologically based reluctance meant they were not a competitive factor. They had opted out, leaving the field to ourselves, Oracle and Sun. We liked that equation.

During and preceding this whole process there was a great deal of speculation that IBM might abandon its own version of Unix. We did look at a few different variations on that potential strategy. At one point, we explored a strategy with a company known as SCO. SCO had long been the primary version of Unix on PCs. We were interested in seeing if there was a collaboration or a technical convergence possible between SCO and IBM's Unix. None of that panned out. In fact, at least for a time, Linux looked like it might be a better convergence strategy. In the end, there were far too many development and licensing complexities to make any of those scenarios workable.

However, a different use case did emerge that turned out to be the most lucrative of all for IBM. The mainframe team had looked at Linux and realized they could build an entire virtual environment under the management of the mainframe that could run Linux partitions. It could run thousands of them. Tens of thousands. And, it could do so with a level of flexibility and management that was hard to achieve in any other deployment. We put in place an initiative to promote this use case and, since there was no danger of it encroaching on the existing workloads on the mainframe, we put in place a special set of pricing to go along with it. Mainframe customers loved it. For the first time in decades we actually started to see new workloads moving onto the mainframe. After years of seeing workloads moving the other direction it was an enormous breath of fresh air. Even to this day, the Linux partitions on mainframes are one of the most important drivers of that venerable platform.

Nobody in the market could have guessed that the biggest value IBM would realize from Linux was helping sustain the mainframe.

§

PCS AND CONSUMER MARKETS

Even as IBM was moving toward a software and service focus there was never any doubt about our intent to sustain the mainframe and Unix server business. The same cannot be said about the PC business. In particular, the business of laptop and desktop PCs for use by individuals was a chronic source of disappointing business results. We described earlier how badly designed this business was from the very beginning. We had studied Dell extensively and we felt like we understood what a good business design entailed, but we had made zero progress bringing that to life in IBM.

Dell is obviously and rightly famous for the use of a "direct" model for PCs. This means they sold to their buyers "directly" instead of going through a channel of dealers, partners and distributors. In contrast, IBM, as well as most of the PC industry, sold through those channels. IBM also, in some cases, sold directly to large accounts with fulfillment through the channel. While it may seem like a simple difference to understand, this was truly a shift in business model and it permeated dozens of different aspects of how the business actually worked.

The impact can be illustrated with two simple but profound examples. Let's start with the ordering process itself. When selling distributed technology like PCs to businesses, the normal mode of operation would be for a procurement organization to negotiate an overall purchase agreement that defined standard configurations, prices, duration, volumes, terms etc. The company would then place orders against that master contract. In most cases, the actual orders would be left up to an individual or department manager. This basic process and structure was essentially the same for both the direct and channel models. In practice, however, the results they delivered were vastly different.

In the PC business at the time, at least 100%, if not 125%, of the profits in the business came from all the "add-ons" associated with a given sale. The profit was not in the PC itself. It was in the mouse pads, specialized cables, power strips, cases, etc. Individual orders would also frequently deviate a bit from the configurations negotiated by procurement. These "escapes" as they're known, were also frequently places where profits could be found. There were also potential profits in the services around a given order. Those services might include installation, setup, training etc. In the channel model all of these add-ons, including the mouse pads, configuration escapes, and services, were provided by the channel and, as a result, all of those profit sources went to the channel. Dell, in contrast, was easily able to capture things like the mouse pads and escapes, and over time, developed various ways of capturing pieces of even the services. Their business design gave them access to the profit sources in this segment while ours explicitly precluded us from doing so. It wasn't a matter of understanding or effort, it's the direct result of the business design.

A second example relates to costs and inventories. Few people have any real conception of how a modern supply chain works. The PC business in particular is an "inventory turns" based production business. What that means is you need both volumes and velocity. You have to "turn over" your inventory very quickly, specifically as fast as your competitors. Many things drive this necessity, but the easiest to understand are the dynamics around component prices. In PCs at the time component costs were dropping rapidly—every single day. If your inventory was one week older than your competition you had a cost problem. We had one situation where the PC organization had made a small profit in each of the first two quarters of the year. In the third quarter their profits turned hugely negative wiping out not only the profits from the first two quarters, but also digging such a deep hole there was no way to be profitable for the whole year. The cause? We had allowed our inventory of memory chips to fall behind by two weeks. The direct model didn't eliminate these realities, but it did make it far easier to manage on a consistent basis.

Sam's instincts were clear. For IBM, this was exactly the kind of "empty revenue" he had no taste for. We did an exercise at one point where we added up the total profit contribution to IBM from the PC business over a ten-year period and came up with zero. Ten years of endless work and the earnest activity by thousands of people with literally zero dollars in profit to show for it. Sam was not a hesitant or cautious leader. However, in this instance he did proceed with care. We did several pieces of strategic analysis over the course of many years before reaching our final conclusions.

One of the things we evaluated was the impact of PCs on IBM's brand. The marketing organization was passionately convinced that if we were to exit the PC business our brand would struggle for relevance in the market. They were also convinced that many clients wanted to have a single hardware vendor and if we exited PCs those clients would have no choice but to turn to HP. There were also concerns about supply chain overlap and dependencies between the PC business and IBM's other hardware businesses.

Tangled up in many of these PC specific issues was an industry wide belief that it was impossible to have long-term success in technology without a strong, vibrant presence in the consumer market. IBM might want to focus on enterprise clients, but almost every analyst insisted this would fail because "consumer adoption always supplants enterprise adoption." Or, so they believed. These beliefs were linked to the volumes and network effects of the architectural control paradigm. They were also based on the simple observation that white collar professionals tended to like to pick their own tools and those choices were driven at least as much by their preferences as consumers as they were by business considerations. Many IT organizations had learned to their chagrin that attempting to force a set of enterprise standards on reluctant professionals was not a recipe for a happy workplace.

In addition to the relatively mature PC and emerging mobile phone device markets, there were also a host of internet-based services that were possible avenues for a consumer business for IBM. In the very early days of the web, IBM had tried to offer an alternative search engine to Google, but it had been a total failure. Before that, IBM had explored the pre-internet forms of online communities with Prodigy, another endeavor with nothing to show for it. Like many others, IBM had tested various content aggregation and shopping services. None of these had gained any traction in the market. The various email and messaging services IBM had deployed never reached critical mass and in every case what success they did have was due to corporate adoption, not direct consumer wins.

Companies with success in these consumer oriented services had revenue models that relied heavily on selling advertising and taking consumer credit cards, neither of which IBM had any experience operating. IBM's product and offering managers had little to no understanding of consumer segments, what they actually wanted, nor how to reach them. IBM's technical teams were even worse, building technically sophisticated offerings whose complexities detracted from their value to consumers. Just like our OS/2 experience, the complex capabilities we were accustomed to from the enterprise IT market were at best invisible to consumers and more often a source of problems or uncompetitive costs. IBM's entire culture, history and DNA, were oriented to serving the needs of businesses, not consumers.

The iconic black ThinkPad with the "rubber eraser" pointer in the middle of the keyboard was the last, and arguably only, IBM offering that had achieved any real success for consumers. Those still sold relatively well, but the highly distinctive position they had once enjoyed had passed. IBM had also built a pretty strong track record in advertising, much of which was aimed at the general market including consumers. These activities definitely promoted and enhanced the IBM brand. However, they didn't generate much in the way of actual demand for IBM's offerings and many wondered whether the brand enhancements were in fact more appropriate for a consumer oriented company than IBM.

IBM was suffering the classic issues that arise when there are ambiguities in strategy. We had few offerings really aimed at consumers, little to nothing in the development pipeline that would change that and lots of resources that were partially deployed or dabbling in activities aimed at consumers. None of this activity was organized for success. IBM did have technical skills and resources that could potentially be used to address consumer needs and had shown the potential for putting together consumer oriented marketing activities. But, overall, IBM was ill-suited for the consumer market.

Lou himself had once proclaimed "we are plumbers and should be proud of being plumbers." He compared IBM to Bechtel, making the point that when enterprises in the market need to build and deploy complex capabilities on a global stage, they need the kinds of resources and culture found in every single corner of IBM. This example also illustrates one of the major blind spots among the analysts who track and report on technology. Most of those analysts have little to no direct experience with the kinds of deployments IBM handles every day. They speak from their own perspectives as consumers and the scope of things they consider as "the market" is often fairly narrow. Their observation that devices and tools used by individuals are heavily influenced and driven by consumer adoption isn't wrong. It's just limited to those particular segments of the market.

It was time to stop hedging and make our strategic intent around the consumer market clear. If PCs and phones were going to be driven by the consumer market, that was fine. We made no money from them anyway. If web search and communities were going to be dominated by companies with strong consumer reach that was fine. We had little to nothing in those spaces and a track record of 100% failure in our attempts. If this was going to bleed into the enterprise collaboration market, we didn't like that because Lotus was still important, but so be it. We could find and work with partners who had the skills, culture and business to succeed in these markets. We would focus on our unique value which was addressing the complexities and scale needed by enterprises around the globe.

Sam's basic instinct to exit PCs might have been clear, and our strategic intent to focus on enterprises, not consumers, was also becoming much sharper, but the internal debates were still intense. The PC business might be hollow, but it was big. Some worried that IBM would lose its status as the largest IT company or that it could no longer claim to offer "everything." These kinds of concerns were all part of the "noise" surrounding the decision. We did actually quantify how much other hardware business might be lost to clients who insisted on bundling all their hardware purchases. It wasn't zero, but it wasn't all that big either. The larger issue we quantified was the loss of channel partners, but even there the down side risk was modest.

Sam asked us for one last effort looking at the most "out of the box" ideas we could come up with. The only play we thought might work in the market required a complete, all in focus on consumers as the primary target. We identified a range of PCs and other devices optimized for the consumption of content from music to movies to the web. We contemplated a whole new brand associated with all this multi-media excellence and an associated set of partners and clients. We didn't know it at the time, but we were outlining the playbook Apple would successfully deploy many years later. Our assessment of the market was accurate. What we also concluded was that IBM had near zero chance of pulling it off. There was a formula, but it was not a formula for IBM. Sam had his final answer. It was time to hand it off to the business development team to find a buyer.

Before we move on to the strategies at the heart of the "high value software and services for enterprises" positioning its worth taking a moment to look back over all the activities described in the last several chapters. These were the "less strategic" aspects of the portfolio, yet they generated some of the most innovative strategies of this whole decade; not only for IBM but for the market as a whole. They also generated literally billions of dollars a year in operating profit and cash and freed up an enormous amount of capital from our selective exits and partnerships. As we noted in the chapter on Gerstner, in a company with the scale and portfolio diversity of an IBM there is an absolutely enormous amount of value to be captured through innovative strategies in segments that appear unattractive through a classic strategic assessment. The whole notion of a "cash cow" to be passively milked is badly misleading.

ASSEMBLING THE SOLUTIONS STRATEGY

IBM knew it wanted to focus on creating high value for enterprise clients. Our history, culture and brand positioning were never going to be based on a low-cost strategy. This didn't mean we could afford to be uncompetitive in costs, it just meant that cost would never be our most effective primary selling point. We were also increasingly clear and comfortable focusing on enterprises as opposed to consumers. This encompassed all enterprise sizes in theory, even though we knew we were at our best with larger and more complex entities. Our intent was to be able to "solve problems" and "enable opportunities" for these clients. We would draw from a portfolio of skills, services and assets to address these needs. This was a vision of IBM as an "enterprise solutions company."

We must have commissioned and run hundreds of projects over the years to figure out what we meant by that. None were all that useful. Most tried to focus on how to count things. Was a database license a solution? Was it a solution if it was combined with a consulting service? How about if it was combined with a deployment/implementation service? Was an application software license a necessary part of the puzzle? These attempts to formalize definitions and terms kept staff organizations busy for months if not years and to my knowledge never produced a single actionable result. We knew what we meant even if we couldn't pin it down.

Solutions could be focused on business buyers, IT buyers, or a combination. The offerings included elements of software and some combination of consulting, implementation and operational services. IBM's existing portfolio was oriented mainly to IT buyers. Our software portfolio was primarily in the middleware offerings like transaction processing engines, database management systems, systems management, web servers and other packages that were critical to IT buyers. Our sales organizations were adept at helping IT customers understand where and how to use all these capabilities. We had extensive skills and a rudimentary portfolio of services to help IT organizations with their implementation needs and we had far and away the strongest capabilities in the market to operate a complete IT infrastructure. There were some weak spots here and there, mainly in implementation services, but overall, we had a pretty strong foundation in IT.

PRICE WATERHOUSE COOPERS ACQUISITION
Business solutions were a different matter. We knew this is where the highest value could be found, and we aspired to build the same breadth of capabilities for the line of business buyers in our clients as we did for the IT organizations. There were pockets of capabilities scattered around the world and numerous success stories we could all point to. Unfortunately, almost all those successes were "one-offs" that had not been replicated. We also had a pretty dismal track record in the application software packages at the heart of the business solutions market. Finally, while we had great relationships with our IT friends, we were much weaker with business buyers and often lacked the industry specific skills needed to even have meaningful dialogue.

We had tried multiple times to fill these gaps. We started by just trying to hire people from the market with the right industry and business skills. We brought in a proven "rain maker" and gave him the mission and resources to hire people and build a business oriented professional services organization from the ground up. That effort failed. The few business professionals we were able to hire found themselves surrounded by a bunch of IT geeks and simply didn't fit in. We also discovered that the salary and compensation programs needed to retain these people simply didn't exist in IBM.

We then tried to fill the gaps with a series of small acquisitions. We found and bought a boutique consulting firm in Germany with great skills in the medical market. Within 18 months every single consultant had quit. The environment inside IBM just didn't fit what these professionals wanted. We learned the hard way that acquiring skills is very different from acquiring assets. Assets don't get unhappy and don't walk out the door when they're under-utilized. These highly skilled individuals kept finding themselves brought into client organizations by IBMers whose only contacts were in IT organizations. They didn't fit in and didn't want to stay.

We finally made the much larger move to acquire Price Waterhouse Coopers (PwC), putting Ginni Rometty in charge of integrating the company into IBM. Ginni was specifically charged with doing what we called a "reverse integration." In other words, we would be putting the PwC partners in charge of operating the whole professional services portfolio inside IBM. We transferred the existing IBM services resources we had managed to retain under their control, not the other way around. They knew how to run the business—we did not. Through Ginni, they were given free rein to construct a compensation program appropriate to attract and retain top business talent. They could also create their own sales and go-to-market resources to get at the business buyers IBM had been struggling to reach. They implemented their own measurement systems, engagement methods, quality control and delivery operations.

We all knew that PwC was not a consulting firm like a McKinsey or BCG. That was fine. From our perspective those organizations were often a bit distant from the actual implementation of their recommendations. We wanted to come to the table when companies were ready to translate ideas and concepts to actual implementation. We believed that with PwC we finally had the combination of business and IT skills that would allow us to do that.

THE APPLICATION SOFTWARE CONUNDRUM

The next piece of the business solutions puzzle was software. Our existing software portfolio had a few components that were useful for business solutions, but the bulk of the portfolio was centered on the underlying IT middleware plumbing. We had lost billions of dollars in application software and had pruned out of our portfolio thousands of sub-scale offerings. Now we needed to consider whether we should reenter the market and, if so, in what way.

For a very long time in the world of enterprise IT, buyers believed they needed to write their own application software. The underlying philosophy was that applications brought competitive differentiation and if all one did was to implement a standard package then there was no possibility for differentiation. This had changed dramatically.

One of the less recognized aspects of the quality movement that was famously epitomized by GE and throughout Japan, was the widespread acceptance of the practice of benchmarking. This sharing of "best practices" had been under way in every industry and all over the world for decades. Application software vendors had been systematically capturing these best practices in their software. Companies no longer needed to send teams to far-flung locations attempting to find all these innovative methods and processes. The leading application companies had already done so and embodied precisely those methods in their applications. No company starting from scratch could hope to match all the learnings embedded in that software. What had originally been about differentiation was now a matter of simple competitive survival. Nobody would have labelled this as an example of "collaborative innovation," yet that's exactly what it was. That invisible force had transformed the entire nature of the application software market.

Adding to this was the sheer impossibility of any company to catch up, let alone surpass, the level of capability that application software vendors had built into their offerings. One of the interesting commercial aspects of the software business is that any given piece of code goes through a well understood life cycle. First releases are notorious for missing functions and being rife with errors and instabilities. Over time, those problems get ironed out and the code becomes increasingly stable and reliable. There are times when a given piece of function does become obsolete. But, as long as that doesn't happen, stable code can last forever and eventually takes very little work to maintain. There are IBM software offerings in widespread use around the world where there's been no new development and essentially no maintenance costs for decades. The license fees on those offerings are essentially 100% profit. There are lots of places where stability itself is an important source of value. This is particularly true in the enterprise market, though you don't need to look any further than the consumer backlash against a "new Coke" to see it happens in the consumer market as well. We will come back to this point later when we discuss the latest twists and turns in the value equation.

At this point in our story SAP had emerged as the clear leader in the growing category of Enterprise Resource Planning, or ERP. They were well up the curve on the range of functions and overall maturity of their offerings. There were still tens of thousands of small application providers. Some of those were in tiny niches that were unlikely to ever scale and therefore of little interest to IBM. There were others that had decent assets in specific business functions and that had the potential to be rolled up and integrated into a suite of capabilities to compete with SAP.

This was the route that Oracle decided to take. They began targeting acquisitions that were directly competitive with SAP to build a viable rival. IBM was much more ambivalent. We did acquire companies on a selective basis in areas like retailing and web commerce where we saw the opportunity to enhance the competitiveness of existing elements in our portfolio. Some of these internal plans were quite aggressive and ambitious, but the actual funding and execution was always kept within fairly narrow bounds. Even as we made these moves, we would tell the market over and over "IBM will not compete with application software companies."

One of the "side effects" of all the sophistication embodied in a collection of capabilities like SAP is that it's difficult to deploy. "Difficult" being a massive understatement. Operating systems, database management systems, and many other software categories can be extremely complex, but the vast majority of that complexity is hidden. In the case of application software, all that complexity is not only not hidden, it actually has to be implemented in your business with training, management systems, measurements and everything else that goes with it. Since it literally provides best practice options from hundreds if not thousands of companies you also need to choose which of those options to "activate" for your business.

The end result is that deploying a package like SAP takes literally years, hundreds if not thousands of people, and costs far more to deploy than it does to acquire. This was an absolute gold mine for IBM's professional services business. We still cared about the hardware associated with these implementations, but the hardware business was now being dwarfed by the services opportunities.

OUTSOURCING–WE'LL RUN IT FOR YOU

After consulting and implementation services the next element in the services playbook was to run the operation on your behalf. IBM had built the largest and most successful business of this kind for IT organizations under Sam's leadership in the Gerstner era. The question now was where to go with this. Unfortunately, there was a problem in the very core of the business. We like to think of services as "high value" to clients and the level of responsibility we take on for a client in an outsourcing deal is enormous. We're responsible for the "hearts and lungs" of their business. Any failure on our part, in any aspect of the business can be crippling for the company. Not only must everything run smoothly, but it must also pass regular audits many of which are unique to different industries. And, we must do all of that at a lower cost than the operation we inherit from the client.

IBM almost always sells these deals on the values of lower cost, reduced capital and a promise to bring new and innovative capabilities. The reality of our operations is usually heavily centered on the cost and capital reductions. The result is that the business was actually not that profitable. In many cases, we wondered if we were truly returning our cost of capital. In those situations where we actually did bring new innovations, there was no such question. Far too often the operations executives we put into these delivery roles didn't really do this. In our chapter on business design, we discussed Michael Treacy's claim that companies with a strong focus on operational efficiency are inherently weak at innovation. We experienced precisely that phenomena in our outsourcing business.

There were two initiatives we launched to try and deal with this challenge. The first involved a visit to Toyota to help our service delivery leaders learn how small consistent improvements in operations can lead to fairly substantial results over time. We began embedding the whole spectrum of six sigma management principles in our outsourcing operations. This didn't suddenly make them effective as "innovators," but it did enable us to get more consistent operational improvements and thereby profitability.

More important to the development of our business solutions capability was the exploration of Business Process Outsourcing, or BPO. As the name suggests, BPO involves taking over a complete business process for a client. Many pundits at the time, and even to this day, believe that the reduced transaction costs associated with modern business standards enable companies to be far more aggressive in shifting business process burdens to outside suppliers. A simple example, is the reliance almost every vendor has on companies like UPS, DHL, or Fedex to handle their shipping needs. The hand offs and interactions between the ordering process and the shipping process can be made quite simple and standard. Detailed tracking systems with standard web access also make it easy to satisfy customer inquiries. The fixed costs of the shipping and logistics assets needed can be more efficiently shared by all. It just makes good business sense to use an outside supplier for that process.

As the example illustrates, the provider of an outsourced business process must provide well understood and easily implemented interfaces, including clarity on the business outcomes being committed. They must own or control all the assets needed to complete the process and they must provide some form of economic improvement either in speed, asset utilization, or other efficiencies. Processes that needed extensive and specific capital assets like planes and warehouses were not of interest to IBM, but processes where IT capabilities like applications and data centers were paramount were all worthy of consideration as opportunities for us to consider building.

One of the IT intensive processes that was growing rapidly at the time was in call center operations. As we will describe below, at the time IBM was rapidly growing its presence in India. We seized on the opportunity to acquire one of the leading Indian call center companies, Daksh. When we did the acquisition, we knew their primary economic value came just from labor arbitrage. As we integrated them into IBM we explored how enhanced IT assets might increase that value. The end result was pretty modest. The low cost, labor arbitrage aspect of the business was so dominant that our attempts to introduce "added value" got little traction. It was interesting and informative to have in the portfolio, but not quite what we were really looking for. This was not a path to a higher value outsourcing business.

We then did a comprehensive review of every BPO company we could gather data on. We were looking to understand whether there was a repeatable formula that would generate the kinds of high value solutions we wanted. The result was fascinating and would inform IBM strategies to this day. As we had expected, the BPO companies with strong sustained profitability were indeed very IT intensive. Some used low cost delivery operations as part of their operations but that was not their real source of value. They also all had application software assets that were central to their overall operations, but that wasn't definitive either. The definitive predictor for long-term profitability was the systematic capture and usage of data specific to the process, their clients, and how specific individual situations compared to various benchmarks. It was the data, the analytics, and the insights derived from them that drove the results of the top companies. Our search for differentiated business value in the market had moved from applications to insights. It was another indicator pointing to data as the source of future value.

SOLUTION STRATEGY RESULTS

The net results from all these efforts to build a high value business solutions capability were decidedly mixed. The services enhancements, particularly from the PwC acquisition that improved our consulting and implementation capabilities were enormous. The results in our outsourcing services were more modest, though given the size of that business, even those modest improvements mattered. Our selective participation in application software was pretty hit and miss.

Far and away the biggest single outcome from all this work was the growth of our SAP and Oracle ERP implementation businesses. There were periods where these contracts alone accounted for over 75% of our professional services results. We tended to think of these as "business" solutions, but the reality is most actual implementation contracts were centered on IT organizations. The huge success we had with these offerings did not break us out of our IT confinement.

We also found ourselves wrestling with a set of internal channel conflicts we hadn't really anticipated. At the time of our PwC acquisition it was common to talk about our team of newly acquired consulting partners as "the tip of the spear." We envisioned them in the lead role on our best accounts increasing our access to key decision makers, initiating strategic projects in the account and driving IBM's overall results. We quickly learned that was not going to happen.

Business consultants do not really view themselves as "sales people," particularly "IT sales people." They do have and maintain relationships with their clients and they work those constantly to develop opportunities. They and their teams are measured on billable utilization, so they care a lot about keeping everyone busy. In their minds, they are running a business. It turns out that's quite different from a IT transaction driven sales person. At first, we thought the reluctance we were seeing was just a lack of education on IBM's products. Over time we discovered it was much deeper than that.

IBM's primary sales organization was structured around industries and geographies. The industry leaders of those organizations viewed themselves as thought leaders in their own rights. They didn't work to the drum of billable hours, but they had their own ideas and opinions about their respective industries. Like most sales organizations, these leaders had a fair amount of leverage in their compensation plans. However, even on their best years they got paid far, far less than the consulting leaders. Who did we really want as the "lead" IBM representative on a given account? We eventually created something we called "two in a box" which was comprised of the top consultant and the top sales person. It wasn't really a solution. Nonetheless, variations of that fig leaf exist to this day.

Finally, our ambivalence on application software and our late grasp of the importance of data meant we had very few scalable assets that we could leverage. IBM's research organization was successful in mining the data we had accumulated around our SAP and Oracle implementations. They used this to build an impressive library of assets used to this day by our ERP implementation teams. This was good and is an ongoing source of asset value, but it's a far cry from what we might have assembled over this period. We'll return later to understand more about why we missed these opportunities. The simple answer is that our resources were being completely consumed by capturing and delivering deals and next to nothing was being invested in capturing and building reusable assets. We were under capitalizing the business in ways that would deeply hamper its future competitiveness.

REVIVING THE BELIEF IN VALUES

From the earliest days of IBM's history, the company had a list of three values that were called its "basic beliefs." These were "respect for the individual," "superlative customer service" and the "pursuit of excellence." Both Tom Watson Sr. and Tom Watson Jr. were of the firm belief that these simple values held the company together. By the early 2000s these were in tatters. "Respect for the individual" had been translated over the decades into an implied policy of no-layoffs. When Gerstner eliminated that policy and implemented large-scale, worldwide layoffs, many employees felt a core belief had been abandoned.

Sam set out to fix that with an activity that was called a "ValuesJam." This unfolded over a three-day period and allowed every IBM employee to participate in an "electronic town hall," posting and responding to an ever-branching discussion about the company and its values. Not all those discussions were positive or polite. There were moments when certain grievances threatened to spiral out of control. There was even a brief suggestion the whole endeavor should be halted. Sam insisted on the opposite. He told his most senior leaders to personally join the discussions and help be part of driving them back to productive grounds. The final results were published a few months later, after all of the hundreds of thousands of comments had been digested. Here was the outcome:

- Dedication to every client's success
- Innovation that matters—for our company and the world
- Trust and personal responsibility in all relationships

It's a good list. It resonated emotionally with most IBMers. It matched what we felt and the behaviors we sought from our leadership. The process used generated a very high level of engagement and buy-in. It wasn't dramatically different from the original beliefs, but it had been updated, refined, and had reestablished values as a core part of IBM's culture. The inevitable wallet cards were dutifully published. Those were not and are not what matters. What matters is whether IBM's leaders exhibit those values in the things they do. And, at least for a while, we did.

INNOVATION THAT MATTERS

One of the key initiatives put in place toward the end of Gerstner's tenure was focused on becoming nimbler in responding to new opportunities. This work originated in a note sent to Gerstner by a newly appointed IBM general manager. This GM had just been put in charge of a brand-new organization he had been championing for over two years. His note described how pleased he was about his new job and how excited he was to get his team up and running. He then appended a simple pie chart he had his assistant create that depicted how he had spent his time over the last two years. It made clear how much time he had spent talking to prospective clients and partners compared to how much time was spent in internal reviews and debates. It was not a pretty picture.

Lou sent out a famous missive that went to all his direct reports. It basically came down to, "why are we so systemically poor at responding to new opportunities." The actual note was far more colorful. The last few sentences were in all caps, which was unheard of at the time for a formal, conservative executive like Gerstner.

After the explosion settled down, we went to work looking at two to three dozen different new opportunities we had faced over the past decade. We found pockets of successful examples amidst lots and lots of misses. We brought in consultants who all had their different diagnostics and approaches. Nothing we found really seemed to fit what we thought we needed.

We eventually stumbled across a book titled "The Alchemy of Growth" by Mehrdad Baghai and Steve Coley from McKinsey. This was the first set of approaches that both rang true to us and looked like something we thought we could execute in IBM. We'll describe this in more detail below, but basically the approach begins by looking at your portfolio across three "horizons." The horizon one (H1) businesses are ones that are well established, mature, may or may not have much if any growth to them, but can be counted on for consistent cash flow and profitability. Horizon 2 (H2) are businesses that also have a proven track record, they have dependable growth, and may be net cash consumers. The Horizon 3 (H3) businesses have yet to prove themselves. They almost always need resources and there are no guarantees they will ever produce results. In fact, the vast majority will not. The simple message was to manage the H1 and H2 businesses in ways appropriate to their specific business needs and to realize that special attention is needed to have a healthy pipeline of H3 opportunities.

We realized the learnings we had collected from both our internal reviews as well as all the external sources we had consulted could easily be applied to each category giving us a fairly simple triage to apply in IBM. Within a week we had categorized all our businesses into the three horizons and brought the result to Lou and his direct reports. The percentage investment we found in Horizon 3 varied considerably across IBM's different organizations. The software business was at the high end and the hardware business at the low end. No great surprise. Overall, we had less than 2% of our total investment in what could be considered Horizon 3. We didn't know, or really care, what the right number needed to be because we all agreed 2% was too low.

We quickly set out to address this. The first step was to pick 10 opportunities to start building around. Many readers might assume this was the sort of extensive analysis I've described elsewhere in this story. The opposite was true. Basically, three or four of us got together and put together a list in a few hours. Lou and his directs reviewed the list made a couple minor tweaks and off we went. There was no lack of opportunity and, by this point, a very strong shared set of priorities. We were also united in our belief that the specific list of the first 10 was not as important as just getting the new program off the ground.

We called the program our "Emerging Business Opportunity" (EBO) program. The program was to be managed by the head of corporate strategy, Bruce Harreld. Lou had Bruce report into an executive position that had never existed in the past. The position was Vice Chairman of IBM. The executive put in that role was John M. Thompson, one of the most senior and most respected executives in the company. Here we were taking one of our absolute strongest leaders, putting him in a job that was basically the number two job in the whole company and giving him 10 tiny opportunities to manage, semi-directly. We gave him an appropriately tiny budget to allocate as he saw fit across those 10 tiny opportunities.

Each of these new business areas were placed organizationally inside the group we felt would eventually "own" the opportunity. This made it easier for each of them to take advantage of the sales, marketing, development, finance, legal and other infrastructural elements they might need. While they were "housed" in these organizations they each had their own resources. Their primary reporting and management process was up through Bruce Harreld and John Thompson. That management system was heavily oriented to the commitment of milestones and checkpoints tuned to the specifics of each opportunity. Bruce and John viewed their roles as primarily problem solvers for these small teams. With their seniority and stature in the business it rarely took more than a phone call to solve any internal problem.

The program had mixed results. Some of the early initiatives were great. This was particularly true in those opportunities that focused on clients and industries we had previously ignored. A great example was life sciences. This was and is a large market, but one that IBM had simply never really pursued. Once we did, it didn't take long to begin getting over a billion dollars a year in revenue. Others floundered and were quickly shut down. We were applying one of the core management principles for H3 businesses which is to cut your losses early. Bruce and John were quite effective at recognizing when to pull the plug.

From the perspective of anyone who has tried their hands at venture capital, managing a portfolio of high risk opportunities such as this, we did quite well. In contrast, for traditional IBM executives, the number of "failures" felt very high. There was also a certain amount of resentment that built up over time. Executives who were not part of the program could be heard grumbling "I could do better if you gave me that money and let me off the hook the way you do those guys...." As we went through the transition of Lou departing and John M. Thompson retiring this organizational resistance steadily increased.

Eventually, the original EBO program was shut down. However, within a few years it was resurrected with a new name and slightly less ambitious goals and resources. The biggest difference in the second iteration was to not run it as a program out of Corporate. Instead we told each Group-level Senior Vice President that they needed to run their own programs. They were all running businesses in excess of $10 billion per year so there was no credible reason they couldn't have their own organic innovation programs. We offered help from Corporate on constructing the program, but it was their responsibility. That variation lasted a few years and then petered out as well.

After these attempts the company would resurrect the program off and on several times over the years with slightly different structures and focus areas. The language and understanding of the horizon management principles were by now well understood and embedded in the business. The EBO programs had not achieved the level and depth of cultural acceptance many of us had envisioned, but we had all learned how to recognize when we needed an "innovation intervention" and what form that should take.

As the EBO management program waxed and waned, the head of IBM Research began a program to leverage his organization to find and build new businesses on a more consistent basis. After a few fits and starts he developed a program called the Global Technology Outlook, or GTO. The GTO process starts early each year with IBM Laboratories all over the world nominating candidates from their work for inclusion in that years GTO. The senior Research leaders vet those nominees for their technical innovations, feasibility and potential business impact. Once the nominees are whittled down, the corporate strategy team is engaged to bring further depth to the assessment of the business dimensions.

This process generates a more refined collection of opportunities at which point the line organizations that would need to own responsibility for a given opportunity begin to ramp up their engagement. One of the major points of guidance Sam put over this whole process is to ensure the line engagement stage does not overly shape the outcome. A major goal is to avoid the incrementalism that is so prevalent in any mature business while still ending up with proposals that have reasonable odds of success.

The final step in the process is an annual review by the Research team of their top 8–10 ideas, coupled with a corporate strategy assessment of the potential business impact from each and a line organization's "response" on how they intend to take the idea forward. This is a major review, with the CEO and all of his or her direct reports deeply engaged. The outcome is almost always three to five new business areas that the collective senior team agrees to pursue, with clear ownership and usually the first 6–12 months of milestones. In many ways, the process could not be more different from our original EBO program. However, the details, in particular around the management of these nascent offerings, draws a great deal from what we learned over the years through those programs.

EMERGING MARKETS

From the earliest days of the EBO program we knew that going after new markets that allowed us to draw from the whole IBM portfolio had a lot of potential leverage and could generate useful results quite quickly. Far and away the most important of these opportunities was to be found in those geographies that were experiencing strong economic growth. The whole market was responding to the dynamics of Brazil, Russia, India, and China (BRIC). IBM did as well, and then expanded that to include many other countries in Eastern Europe, South and Central America and Asia. We called That collective set of initiatives our "emerging markets strategy" and it was one of the top two to three most important in Sam's tenure. The growth IBM achieved from these countries literally exceeded all the other growth initiatives combined.

Brazil, Russia, and the long list of smaller emerging countries provided good though sporadic, business results. During the years when Brazil's economy was booming we saw incredible results. When the economy weakened, so did the local IBM business. The same was true in places like Chile and Argentina. There were and are real opportunities to be found but those are dependent on the overall economy and those countries still experience a fair amount of volatility.

Russia is a bit different. The issues there are less about volatility and more about the steadily increased domination of the economy by Oligarchs. Oligarchs can't be counted on to make decisions on business and technical merits and their rise definitely reduced the attractiveness of the Russian market over time.

Which leaves India and China both of which are in a whole different league.

INDIA–THE SLEEPING ELEPHANT AWAKES
Over the last 10–15 years India has become a global powerhouse in the technology industry. They don't produce any significant hardware nor that much in the way of software, although that's recently begun to grow. The domestic market of IT buyers in India is also relatively modest. For a long time, even the larger Indian companies spent about as much on IT as a small to midsize company in the US or Europe. The big deal with India is their role providing technology services for the global market. In that context, they are truly formidable players.

In 2005 Sam attended a conference in India for technology services companies. At the time, IBM had seen some limited evidence of competition coming from India. From our perch in New York they were not really on our radar screen. In this conference, Nandan Nilekani, the CEO of Infosys, stood up and announced that the Indian service companies were going to "do to IBM what

Toyota and Japan had done to GM and Ford." He asserted we were big, slow, clumsy, and expensive. They were lean, nimble and able to operate at cost levels we couldn't dream of touching. They had embarked on extensive investments in delivery quality controls and had reached a point where he claimed they could meet or beat anything IBM could do at a tiny fraction of our costs.

It was a gauntlet thrown in Sam's face in a public setting, with every Indian service company in attendance. Every single one of them believed what had been said. The intensively competitive ex-football player in Sam was not happy. He informed the room that IBM was not GM and that they would learn what it meant to take on the IBM company. In his mind, it was a declaration of war. We had lots of competitors at the time. Many of them, like Microsoft or Oracle, were quite intense. Nothing came close to agitating Sam as much as this very personal affront.

Sam sent an email ordering us to build an aggressive strategy to deal with the threat. He wanted to see the first draft when he landed back in the US. We had a lot of work to do. As we gathered all the relevant data, it became clear that the strong claims made by Nilekani did have a basis in fact. The labor costs were even lower than any of us had expected. The delivery results we were able to get our hands on were pretty solid. Maybe not quite as sophisticated as he had claimed, but still pretty good.

We also began to uncover that they were much more widespread than we had realized. They had perfected a model where they would come into an account where IBM, Accenture, or some other established service company had an existing engagement. They would go to the customer and ask to take over some small piece of the project. After they had proven they could deliver that piece they would expand into some other small, low visibility, low risk part of the project. They didn't try and take on the whole project. They didn't try and act as the prime contractor structuring the whole thing. They entered small and grew ... and grew.... We found several clients where they had actually reached a point where their billings were exceeding our own. And, we hadn't even realized they were there.

The threat was real and far more imminent than we had thought. The strategy we developed was not all that complicated. We needed to rapidly hire our own resources in India to match them on costs. We needed to train those resources and embed them on delivery teams for our engagements around the world. We needed to be far more alert and aggressive in our competitive responses when they tried to carve out a small footprint in engagements that were under way. All of those steps were intended to simply match what we knew they could do. We would then beat them by combining all of these capabilities with our leadership in business insights from our consultants and technology innovations from IBM Research.

The strategy wasn't complicated. The execution was amazing. Numerous IBMers of all levels contributed to our success. That included Sam. His level of personal involvement, his passion, even fury, and his unwavering belief in what IBM could accomplish were among the more incredible examples of personal leadership I've seen in my 35 years in business. Like the earlier story about the Technology Group this was not without its human costs. The changes were rapid and wrenching. They were often heartless. Yet, without them, our services business would have become so uncompetitive as to be irrelevant.

After a short ramp-up period IBM began furiously hiring in India. We were soon bringing on new recruits at a rate that exceeded 10,000 people per month. Think about that for just a minute. How many interviews must be done by how many managers to generate 10,000 new hires per month. We knew we couldn't count on the interview process to ensure all these folks were going to meet our standards. To manage this problem we put in place a series of monthly checkpoints and told the new hires they were being hired on a trial basis. They would not be "official IBMers" unless they met expectations every month and passed an exam at the end of their first year.

We had a lot of folks who didn't make it. For a while the fall out was simply too high. Our hiring rate was amazing, but too many were not meeting our standards and as a result the overall Indian workforce wasn't growing fast enough. At the suggestion of a local manager we put in place a small process change. Just like the other Indian service companies, the vast majority of the hires we were going after were coming straight out of universities. The change was to send a letter to the parents of each of these hires, congratulating them on their child getting our offer, but also informing the parents that the position would only be permanent if their child passed their exam at the end of the year. The failure rate dropped dramatically. Engaging parents like this would have been a disaster in the US or Europe, but in the culture of India it was a master stroke.

Our Indian resource pool was now growing strongly. The skills and delivery quality were also beginning to rise to global standards. The key now was to ensure all that capacity was being used. This was one of those spots where Sam's personal intervention made a huge difference. There was no deal anywhere in the world of any size that was safe from a spot inspection by Sam. Pretty much no matter how many Indian resources had been included in the deal, Sam would declare it wasn't enough and chastise the team for more. Arguments that a client wouldn't accept Indian resources on their project would just infuriate him.

Eventually, the heavy-handed inspection eased as it became less and less necessary. Our teams all over the world had been forced to learn how to use their new colleagues from India. They learned it was not just Sam's wrath they risked if they were delinquent. Creating an opening that let one of the Indian competitors establish a presence was now something they knew to avoid at all costs. The quality and skill of our resources in India were reaching the levels we needed. Delivery processes now routinely included carving out elements to be delivered from whatever location was best for the specific purpose. IBM Research had also steadily expanded its laboratory in India. That lab was now becoming a steady source of innovation in various domains. At one point in 2006, we actually moved one of IBM's regular board of director meetings from New York to Bangalore in India.

This tremendous growth in services from India was not being matched by the business we were getting from India itself. We had won a landmark 10-year outsourcing deal from Bharti Airtel in 2004. At the time, we hoped that would be the first of many such deals. Those did not materialize. Like many emerging markets there are a small number of extended families in India that dominate the local economy. These are similar to the Carnegies, Rockefellers and Fords that played such prominent roles in developing the US economy in the late 19th and early 20th centuries. Winning business in India depends as much on nurturing those relationships as it does on anything else. IBM had such a relationship with Sunil Mittal, the head of Bharti, but few others. That weakness haunts IBM's local sales in India to this day.

It was recently reported that IBM's employee population in India has exceeded that of the United States or any other country. It's a pretty amazing response to that original gauntlet in Sam's face.

CHINA–THE CENTRAL PILLAR OF
THE 21ST CENTURY MARKET

China could not be more different than India. These two economies both have the size, growth and sheer population to be important on the world stage. In the technology industry, India's global importance comes from the IT services companies that grew to challenge IBM and other western leaders. For China, the story is different. Everybody is familiar with the "Made in China" label with all the ambivalent beliefs embodied in that phrase. China is the production center for a vast amount of the technology sold all over the world. Their historic reputation for low quality has long since gone by the way side. Those xenophobic beliefs have been replaced by the current chorus claiming China lacks a culture of innovation. Those claims have no more strategic merit than their predecessors.

Outside its role in manufacturing, China has become one of the largest and most important markets in the world. This is true for many sectors, not the least of which is IT. Chinese companies are among the largest in the world. Like large enterprises anywhere, they have extensive and complex needs. The scale of certain deployments matches or exceeds anything found anywhere else in the world. In addition to simple size, these are also some of the most modern and sophisticated deployments in existence.

IBM's teams in China were well positioned to capture these opportunities, and Sam was quick to realize the scale of the potential. Outside of the world of Internet Services, there were no serious local competitors and many of our global rivals were slow to respond. The IT analysts in Silicon Valley and New York seemed almost completely blind to what was developing. IBM was not.

While the IT demand was growing as strongly as the Chinese economy, there were structural issues arising from the unique aspects of Chinese culture and politics. Hardware was easy to explain, position and sell. It was a solid thing one could see and touch. Software was more challenging. It was invisible. Even those who understood it often had trouble attributing value to its intangibility. It took time for the Chinese market to accept that rampant software copying was theft, not fiscal prudence.

The bigger issue for IBM by far was around services. If there were occasional missteps around software transactions, there were simply no services deals of any scale at all. Some of this was the same issue of the cultural acceptance of value from an intangible asset. More important was the relative availability of low cost labor skills. In most western countries, the timing and availability of a critical mass of skills for a given project are an important part of the value from services. In countries like India and China, where labor and skills are plentiful, this is a much harder sell.

The second services issue was and is around outsourcing. In an outsourcing contract the client turns over its assets, people, and responsibilities to their service provider. This requires a level of trust in the supplier and confidence in the client to be viewed as an acceptable practice. In the early days of outsourcing in the US, it was common to hear European firms assert that "outsourcing will never work here." They felt certain that no European company would agree to turn everything over to a supplier. Then the dam broke and outsourcing flooded Europe. At that point, the Japanese were absolutely firm that no major Japanese firm would ever agree to an outsourcing contract. The dam broke there as well and when it did the market reached a point where outsourcing was not only acceptable but became the norm. We are all still waiting for the moment the Chinese market makes that transition. If it ever does, buy stock in IBM.

The final issue around services in China is the evolution of the market for internet capabilities. China has always placed tight restrictions, including outright bans, on western firms in that segment. The restrictions are mainly driven by the socio-political realities of China and are colloquially known as the "Great Firewall." Much of this is aimed at censoring certain websites and enforcing Chinese laws. These practices have also enabled the development of local Chinese alternatives to Google, Facebook, eBay and Twitter. In the

Chinese market, Tencent, Baidu and Alibaba play the same roles those western companies play elsewhere in the world.

In late 2017 Tencent became the first of these Chinese giants to exceed $500 billion in market capitalization, passing Facebook. In addition to sheer financial scale, there have been several high-profile losses of technical talent to the Chinese, particularly in the field of Artificial Intelligence. None of these companies are household names in the US, but their size and technology capabilities rival those who are. Just as IBM needed to respond to the professional services competition from India, the US based internet services companies are wrestling with their strategies for China both as a market and as a potential source of global competition.

During Sam's tenure, the IBM services issues and restrictions ranged from annoyances to major sources of frustration. We had no real internet services so for us those government restrictions were more theoretical than real. The lack of a market for either professional or outsourcing services was a huge hindrance. These represented nearly half the company and were central to our growth. However, there were no authorities one could complain to. This was up to us to address. If we wanted a break-through in accepting the value of these services in the market it was up to us to find and develop a credible set of references to trigger that market shift.

Meanwhile our hardware and software continued to sell strongly. We cemented the strength of the IBM brand, both with local companies as well as the Chinese government, when we agreed to sell our PC business to Lenovo. Many observers had speculated we might exit the PC market, but almost nobody predicted the sale would be to a Chinese company. Again, the western analysts have traditionally had major blind spots around the dynamics in these countries. The PC business sale included transferring a large coterie of IBM engineers, managers and executives to Lenovo. Almost all these individuals remained in the US, mainly in Raleigh N.C. Many did not last for long in their new roles. However, the combination of a major business being sold to China along with its management and technical know-how raised eyebrows throughout the US political establishment. We were not surprised by this and were well prepared to handle the political challenges that arose. This too, added to our brand stature in China.

THE EPS ROADMAP DENOUEMENT

In the last several years of his tenure Sam began making a classic strategic blunder. He confused his financial targets of earnings per share with the actual strategy. Financial targets are a score card. They define objectives. They are not strategy. At some level Sam knew this all too well. He had focused for most of his chairmanship on the things we needed to do. He reached a point where he demanded others make those decisions while he simply demanded the results.

The result was a focus on financial targets at the expense of basically everything else. The real fat had been trimmed from the business long before. We were now cutting into organizational muscles, bones, and brains. There was a phrase used by Sam and several Senior Vice Presidents that went "if you aren't developing or selling you're overhead." And, that meant you were gone.

When I joined IBM in 1981 there were dozens of IBM HQ office buildings scattered around the lower Westchester area of New York. By the middle of Sam's rein most of that had been consolidated into a couple HQ buildings in Armonk and a campus in Somers, Ct. The Somers campus was large, with four main buildings, a central services building and considerable surrounding acreage. The buildings were designed by I.M. Pei and are great marble edifices. When I worked there in the late eighties it was a vibrant place. In the early to middle stages of Sam's tenure they were packed with people who had been consolidated from other nearby buildings. We had to build extra parking lots and even those were often overflowing. Cars were parked on the verges and in the nearby woods. By the end of Sam's tenure, most of the parking lots were closed and all but the first two rows of spaces in the main lots had been roped off. The buildings were nearly empty. The atriums echoed when you walked through them. It felt like a mausoleum.

Most of those lost people had been offering managers, market and product planners, and the like. They were overhead. But they were also the folks with the skill and experiences to recognize and make changes to the business when needed. Those organizational "brains" were lost and along with them the ability to maneuver. We were executing along our own well-trod paths hoping those still led to good results. In some cases, they were. In many, eventually most, they were not.

Less visible, but far more dangerous, were the hidden losses in the operational core of practically every part of the business. Development resources were dropping below critical mass in many areas. The churn in the sales organization was at a deadly level. Service delivery problems were cropping up all over the place. This nearly invisible erosion would only become apparent when the next set of crises hit and we found ourselves lacking in the critical skills and roles needed to respond.

PALMISANO SUMMARY

Sam's personal leadership had an enormous impact on IBM. He is celebrated for building the services business up from next to nothing. Perhaps his single greatest achievement as CEO can be traced to the success IBM has had outside the US and western markets. The IBM presence in India and China is extremely strong, deeply rooted and highly strategic. Sam's focus on profitability also drove incredible growth in margins and cash flow. In Gerstner's book about his time in IBM he talks about teaching the "elephant to dance." Sam took that dancing elephant to dance halls all over the world.

If the market was static that might have been enough. However, it was about to go through a set of wrenching transitions as deep and critical as any in the last 20–30 years. It was not the time to hunker down and milk the business. That was Sam's biggest mistake and Ginni Rometty would inherit the result.

STRATEGY: THINGS THAT GO WRONG

IN THE BUSINESS strategy chapters I focused on the principles of good decision making, understanding markets, and developing an effective business design as well as its associated execution capabilities. No matter how well those are done, things will go wrong. The market fundamentals around client value, competitive dynamics, and technologies will shift over time. There will be internal changes with new leaders and resource decisions. At several points in this book I have celebrated strategies that endured for more than a decade. At least in the technology industry, I do believe that's a sort of benchmark.

There are three keys to handling the reality of strategic decline—quickly and accurately diagnosing problems when they arise, taking swift effective actions to address the problems and, when possible, avoiding them altogether or delaying their impact.

In this section, I will cover the three most common sources of strategic derailment. In 2008 the Corporate Executive Board published a study they had completed on the root causes of strategic "growth stalls" across 500 companies. The overwhelming majority of cases, 87%, were caused by factors under management control. The top three causes were:

1. **Premium position shifts** – When the sources of value and differentiation in the market begin to shift, incumbent leaders are faced with a whole series of difficult challenges. While the originating source of this derailment category is external, the decisions organizations make in response spell the difference between failure and survival.

2. **Innovation management failure** – Almost all companies have some sort of strategy to drive relevant innovations for their clients and their business, but these programs are notoriously difficult to execute with any degree of consistent success. Depending on the core strategy of the firm, this failure mode can lead to either a slow erosion of competitiveness or abrupt irrelevance in the market.

3. **Premature core abandonment** – Partly in response to our cultural attraction to novelty there's a dangerous tendency to under invest in existing core businesses. Very few case studies or consultant reports include any discussion on the virtues of relentlessly "sticking to one's knitting." The resulting lack of focus on the core frequently leads to a highly predictable and self-inflicted decline.

Each of these common problems will be covered below. Boiled down to its essence the key learnings are first, when markets change, strategies must change. And. When strategies change the execution environment, particularly skills and culture must also change. Secondly, while Innovation is critical, it must not crowd out preservation of the existing core business.

ADAPTING WHEN VALUE SHIFTS

This is the most common cause of strategic stalls across all industries. The problems arise when there are fundamental shifts in the market that impact core elements of the business design. There are countless ways this can occur. The actual buyers themselves can shift. When the market shifts from early adopters to early majority to late majority each of those shifts can be the trigger for a series of associated business design impacts. Similarly, as a market matures it is common for a variety of sub-segments to emerge, all of which are likely to have distinct needs. It's also common for value to shift as well. What might have started as a source of competitive advantage for the customer will eventually become a simple competitive necessity. That's an example of a common form of diminishing returns that almost always occurs at some point in a market's evolution. Any of these changes can arise out of simple market maturation or can be triggered through the actions of competitors.

The first key to addressing these kinds of issues is accurately recognizing them for what they are. The normal assumption when a business begins to stumble is that there is some sort of execution problem. As we noted earlier, when those problems occur it is important to start with the basics.

However, when a business stumble *does* arise from shifts in the customers and/or what they value this is almost always the sign of a deeper strategic issue. Many tomes have been written on this subject. Two of the more useful in my experience are Geoffrey Moore's "Crossing the Chasm" and Clay Christensen's "Innovators Dilemma."

Profound strategic issues arising from basic client and/or value shifts are things we saw frequently. The most basic manifestation of this for IBM was around client concentration. When your client base becomes heavily concentrated, either by industry, size, geography or any other major dimension, then lots of different strategic maladies can ensue. You may find yourself trapped in the cyclicality of a specific industry, or you may find you've enabled concentrated bargaining power, or you may find yourself vulnerable to a competitor or partner solely focused on that specific concentrated set of clients. These issues are common and can often be diagnosed fairly readily.

The trickier diagnostic occurs when the concentration isn't readily apparent in the operational data you track. There's a classic example of this that came out of the differences in the business model IBM used for PCs in comparison with the model that Dell developed. The availability of a range of installation and support services that is a prominent aspect of the channel model used by IBM would appear to be powerful source of value and potential differentiation. Indeed, for clients that value those services, they are quite important. However, for clients that don't want all that "help" they're at best irrelevant and, in many cases, can be a nuisance. This underlying segmentation of the market between those who "want help" versus those who are "self-sufficient" turns out to be extremely important. What we discovered during one of our earliest diagnostics of the PC business is that we were heavily concentrated in "wants help" clients, but that the strongest growth was in "self-sufficient" clients. We had never consciously made this choice. It was a previously invisible side effect of our business model.

Another example comes from Geoffrey Moore's work on Crossing the Chasm. What Moore observed is that there are deep differences in the underlying attitudes and beliefs of what he termed Innovators, Early Adopters, and Early Majority. He further observed that because of these underlying differences, success with Innovators or even Early Adopters can be very misleading about what will drive success with the Early Majority. Things that were valued features for innovators may be viewed as unacceptable complexities or incomplete offerings for those who are later in the cycle. Furthermore, reference clients from one stage may not only lack credibility but may actually impede success with more conservative clients. When an early stage business finds itself inexplicably struggling just when you think it should be ready for takeoff, this diagnostic was often the key. We found this model to be accurate and prevalent across many different stages and technology cycles.

The last example comes courtesy of Clayton Christensen's Innovators Dilemma. Clay's observation is that incumbents, particularly well run, client focused incumbents, are vulnerable to the emergence of new buyers whose needs and expectations are radically different from the current market. The existing clients don't share the needs of the new clients. As a result, when the incumbents focus on the needs of their current clients they often completely overlook and are unable to serve the needs of the new clients. That may not matter all the time, but when those new clients represent the early wave of a new paradigm the incumbents may not even realize there's a transition under way until far too late.

This can be quite difficult for incumbents, particularly market leaders, to perceive and accept. This is the danger we discussed on the over reliance on client advisory councils. Your existing clients are perfectly happy with what you're doing while the ones who would point you in a new direction are people you're not talking to. This also contributes to broad organizational resistance that often dismiss claims about a shift in value because nobody is hearing anything about that shift from existing clients.

When these shifts in market value happen, "trying harder" will not be sufficient. Using our language of business design, its crucial to examine and modify some combination of the target market, value proposition, and sources of value capture at a minimum. These central aspects of the business design are all areas where significant changes in strategy may be required. The tendency for incumbents is to assume they can adjust with only minimal changes and while this is certainly true in some circumstances it can be quite dangerous.

Once a revised business design is developed, the firm must then make corresponding changes to the execution environment. The key aspects of the new design may entail changes to key business processes and will almost always entail new measurement and management systems. Skill and cultural changes are often the hardest part of the transformation for incumbents to effectively change. It can be quite challenging to identify, recruit, train and enable a work-force with key new skills. The old culture will stubbornly persist. Managers often assume these will take care of themselves over time which is a common and substantial failure of leadership.

Only when all these issues have been addressed will the firm begin to effectively adapt. The need to adjust both strategy and execution, with a clear accurate understanding of the shifts that are needed, is what makes these so hard. Companies that attempt to respond simply through execution changes will struggle to compete with those who have recognized the deeper strategic shifts. Companies that proudly announce a new strategy but fail to transform their execution environment will similarly struggle.

IBM is all too familiar with these kinds of shifts. When the market for computers evolved from mainframes to mini-computers to PCs and RISC serv-ers we nearly went out of business. We've described various aspects of those challenges throughout this book. The same sort of market shift is under way again around cloud, mobile, analytics and AI. Once again, IBM is struggling to adapt as we will discuss in more detail in the section on Ginni Rometty.

Building a Systemic Innovation Program

Innovation programs are popular to launch and quite difficult to execute. Let's start with the most basic question—what are the objectives of the program and what defines success? New sources of revenue are a common metric. Others might add an emphasis on profits. Or, the objectives could be less tangible and emphasize brand halos or extensions. The objectives could be constrained to leveraging and enhancing an existing market position or the opposite of establishing a presence in a wholly new market space. Any of these could include specific scale, timeframe, or risk dimensions as well. There are also many different types of innovation programs, each suited to different types of objectives. In some cases, the focus is improving organic development processes. Some of these might focus on "user centric design" or "Six Sigma" design for manufacturability. In other cases, the focus may be on leveraging acquisitions more aggressively. Those programs focus on identifying targets, closing deals and integrating the companies into the business.

Of all the different innovation programs in IBM's recent history, one of the most powerful was actually a focus on the integration of acquired companies. Once we had perfected that process it opened up the floodgates and turned acquisitions from an occasional event to a mainstream innovation program. These days, when IBM begins developing strategies for a new opportunity the first step is usually some sort of "market map" that classifies the various aspects of the opportunity. Once completed, the market map is then populated with two to three possible acquisition targets for each section of the opportunity. That becomes the tool used to guide make versus buy decisions and establishes the eventual integration framework.

Usually the most complex form of innovation management program is the creation of a portfolio of internal "start-ups." This is effectively an internal "venturing" activity and is modeled on how VC's and their start-ups operate. This was the objective of IBM's EBO program. Programs like this need to start with a portfolio management approach that will fit these new "ventures" into the rest of the corporate context.

As we described earlier, the philosophy IBM adopted was based on the horizon management approach described in "Alchemy of Growth." This model makes investing in innovation an explicit responsibility of senior leadership which we felt was crucial for IBM. General managers of existing businesses are expert at dealing with day to day execution issues. Those challenges all operate within existing structures and systems. There are many executives who are world class as long as those structures are in place but will flounder and fail if the structures themselves need to change or need to be invented in the first place. This is part of the challenge of the H3 businesses. They may be small, but they lack proven models and structures. As a result, they actually need a very specific kind of management and leadership to succeed.

When considering launching a venturing portfolio program, resources are probably the first thing most executives worry about. Ambitious, acquisition-based programs will certainly need a lot of capital. However, in my experience, the actual financial resources needed for most programs are surprisingly modest. The far bigger constraint is around talent and leadership time. These are rarely even considered at the outset but have a disproportionate impact on actual results. New initiatives almost always need more leadership attention than expected and that attention needs more experience and seniority in the firm than their scale would suggest. This is one of the many cultural obstacles that trip up so many programs. Most companies think of business scale as the primary, if not sole, determinant of leadership seniority. Since start-up activities are by definition small they tend to be given to low level managers or junior executives. Since they are also usually rooted in emerging market trends, they are often associated with younger executives. What both of these overlook is that the number of unknowns that must be discovered and addressed are far higher than any existing business of comparable size. What is also overlooked is that many of the decisions reached will be counterintuitive to the existing business leaders and securing their confidence in the choices made will need an executive with a strong track record within the firm. In my experience, these leadership issues derail more programs than any absolute funding issues.

Where funding does come into play is ensuring whatever funding is provided can be counted on. Mature businesses are accustomed to the realities of quarterly ups and downs. They have flexibility to overcome that volatility and can manage accordingly. The same is not true for new innovation initiatives. By design, they have essentially zero resource flexibility and any funding uncertainties will directly and immediately create negative effects. This holds true for both funding cuts as well as planned funding increases that happen to get caught up in corporate delays. The key is to provide an agreed total funding pool to the executive with responsibility for the overall portfolio of innovation initiatives and allow that executive flexibility to allocate those resources as needed.

The portfolio, scaling and resource management strategies are three key design aspects of an innovation program. The other key issue to sort out is the organizational context in which the innovation program will be placed. Should it be housed in Corporate or one of the divisions? Should it be placed high or low in the organization. Should it be held in a research group? A development group? A client facing organization? In a business like IBM, with a huge variety of different types of business, one also has to assess which of those is most likely to be useful. As we've described earlier, the business issues that are critical for a hardware offering are different from a software offering which are different from services. Being able to easily access a legal or contractual team is far more valuable if that team understands the types of issues this new business has to deal with. Similarly, drawing from an existing library of relevant software modules or services infrastructure can be made either very easy or a bureaucratic mess, depending on organizational placement.

Leveraging existing organizational infrastructures can also be augmented through the creation of specific resources and capabilities shared across the various innovation initiatives. At its simplest, this could just be a regular monthly forum for the exchange of ideas, experiences and data between the leaders of different initiatives. In some cases, there may be enough common needs across initiatives that it warrants creating a team focused on those needs. Market insight teams are frequently in this category. If many of the initiatives are dependent on a shared outside supplier, it may also make sense to have a team focused on that dependency. As an example, a portfolio of new cloud based analytic services might benefit from a single team focused on the common underlying cloud delivery issues.

Within IBM we created a team focused on building and maintaining relationships with the VC community around the world. This team was used across the business, but its initial formation was to support our original Emerging Business Opportunity program. We found that working with VC's and their portfolio companies brought value on many dimensions. It's a great group of people to test ideas and market insights. Most of them bring only their own anecdotes, but those anecdotes cover a larger and more diverse opportunity space than the anecdotes we tell each other. Some of the companies you meet may well become acquisition candidates. It's also quite common to use go-to-market deals with these companies to explore both their offerings as well as how well they can fit with existing management and cultural aspects of the firm.

Once you've decided on the objectives, how to resource the initiative, where to place it, and what shared infrastructure to create in support, you need to manage the whole process. This includes the processes to select and launch each new initiative, how to track and manage the progress of initiatives individually and for the portfolio as a whole, the criteria used to shut down or redirect initiatives and the process used to "graduate" into the main stream.

There is a classic rule of thumb frequently used to guide the selection process in programs like this. That is to look for new offerings that can be sold to existing clients and/or for new clients that can be targeted with existing offerings. These are clearly the easiest and lowest risk strategies with readily defined scaling strategies. Those were far and away the most successful initiatives in IBM. This simple homily omits one of the more critical learnings over the last 20–30 years. The unfortunate reality is that the highest impact innovations are almost always linked to the creation of whole new business models, not just new offerings or new markets.

There needs to be a place in the portfolio for these higher risk, higher potential initiatives. IBM's initial list included the strategy for Linux. As described earlier, this strategy was highly innovative for both the industry and IBM. And, it proved very, very hard for Microsoft and others to handle. It was highly innovative. Using an open-source asset with complex IP issues as the basis of an enterprise commercial technology strategy was unheard of. I personally handled probably over a hundred briefings for analysts who couldn't understand how it was even possible. I've also outlined how many different execution elements needed to be created or changed.

Yet in some ways it was easy. The commercial IP issues around the asset itself were easily fenced since that's not what we were selling. We were selling things that related to that asset. We do that all the time. In every case, there are IP and contractual issues associated with the non-IBM assets that have to be managed. Yes, we needed new skills in those roles, but it didn't change that fundamentally. There were a few new rules and guidelines we needed to create to avoid certain pitfalls. However, at the end of the day what we were selling were all very traditional IBM assets and resources. We were selling servers, middleware and services, just like always. Customers cared about key functionality and price/performance, just like always. We did find ourselves dealing with folks outside of IT, but we could still direct most of our efforts at the traditional IT organizations. The IBM brand values of security and reliability were actually more important than ever. For the most part, they were just assumed by the customers. The biggest issue, the one that kept tripping up Microsoft, was just accepting that we didn't control major aspects of the architecture. The key to that was our embrace of a core strategic philosophy of value creation instead of architectural control.

We can contrast this with the possibility of IBM launching a multi-media centered consumer strategy around personal devices and content. We talked about this option in the final stages of our decision to exit the PC business. This was the strategy Apple would later deploy en route to becoming the largest market capitalization company in the world. If we saw that opportunity, why didn't we take it? Why isn't that just an example of an innovative business model for IBM? We did see it. We even spent time outlining how to go about it and reviewed it with the Chairman. Even while we were doing that work none of us regarded it seriously. In fact, we were using it to show Sam just how hopeless it was for IBM to try and succeed in the PC business.

This is a great example of a false adjacency. The technical similarities between the PCs we were failing to sell successfully, and those Apple later made fortunes from were not that substantial. Those similarities were largely irrelevant. Every material aspect of the business design and strategic execution environment ran contrary to IBM's genetics. The buyers are different, the value proposition to those buyers are different, the mechanisms used to sell and capture value are different, the types of services used to maintain client interaction are different, the brand value is different, the critical tasks and processes share some overlap, but are probably 75%–80% different, the management and measurement systems needed were the ones we had been failing to implement after years of trying, the skills overlap was less than 50%, and the overall organizational culture could not be more different. Businesses are not just a production and sales process around some widget or other offering. It's the business design of this vast interlocking web of activities, people and culture that make a stategy work.

Once the portfolio is selected the initiatives need to be staffed and launched. The most important early task is selecting the leader for each initiative. In fact, after years and years of doing this work we eventually concluded we wouldn't even bother starting a project until and unless the leader had been assigned. We always kept the early staffing very, very light. This often caught long-term IBM executives off guard. Their first instinct was to surround themselves with people. We would let them have two to three—usually one sales/market oriented person and one technical person. We almost always had all the businesses in the portfolio share a single finance contact and a single legal contact.

For some senior leaders, this was a deal breaker. Others might begin awkwardly but would then find their footing. I remember one executive who was a rising star running a multi-billion dollar organization with thousands of people who suddenly found himself being asked to run a business with zero revenue and two staff, one of whom was temporary. He called Sam that weekend to ask, "what have I done wrong, and what do I need to do to get out of the dog house?" He got over that and found his feet. He actually had a lot of fun once he did because he found himself right in the middle of the action. That executive went on to a very successful career in IBM, eventually retiring after becoming one of IBM's top dozen or so executives. The experience he had with the "hands-on" creation and building of a new business proved invaluable.

The process used to manage these nascent businesses relies heavily on identifying and tracking milestones. Revenues are not useful metrics in the very early days and profits can be kind of silly. We initially left the milestone selection completely free-form, but eventually settled into a fairly simple pattern. Once a small team had been formed to pursue an opportunity they were given three to six months to develop a basic understanding of the market along with a hypothesis of the business design and strategy to go after it. That was their deliverable to receive their first tranche of limited funding. Securing the second tranche required them to have found at least one client willing to commit to a pilot implementation and who also agreed that if deployed they would pay the price that was assumed in the underlying hypothetical business model. We gave teams a lot of latitude to adjust their initial hypotheses to find this fit. The funding provided was just enough to get the market trial to completion. The third tranche required reporting on a "successful" market test. We also gave a fair amount of latitude on what defined success. The key was to capture learnings and adjust the business hypotheses accordingly. From that point on, the milestones became more rigorous and very specific to each business. Some would focus on getting a whole series of client wins. Others would be heavy on technical development and quality progress. Once we knew there was a real potential business we tuned everything to those specifics.

The latitude around the early milestones depended heavily on the judgement of the senior exec running the program. We wanted to focus on learning and adapting not on guessing right in advance. If the learnings were leading us to a business that seemed to have good potential we'd proceed. If the learnings were turning into an interesting academic exercise we'd call a halt. It was always a judgement call about whether a particular twist or turn was actually a viable insight instead of an excuse or wishful thinking. One of the harder things to really test was the actual value clients would ascribe to the offering and their true willingness to pay what was assumed in the business model. We knew it was hard, so we were happy to accommodate a lot of leeway, but we were also insistent it was crucial to establish as early as possible.

Initiatives that couldn't get through these early tranches with all the flexibility built into the process were shut down. We shut down a lot of them. That was a central aspect of the entire program. Once they began to get established and actually start to produce regular results we started talking about "graduating" the initiative into the business. In some ways, this is equivalent to the "exit strategies" that VC's and their companies seek. Since this was all internal to IBM we had the option to graduate initiatives quite early. One of the mistakes I believe we made is to over emphasize speedy graduation versus ensuring a new business was really at the right stage. There can be quite a lot of market activity with clients who are Innovators and Early Adopters. None of that is a guarantee that you're ready to "cross the chasm" to the Early Majority which is where the real scaling takes place. There are many instances where we would have been better served keeping businesses in one of our incubation programs a bit longer to ensure they were really ready to be scaled.

The pressure for early graduation is one of the phenomena related to the critical importance of the overall leadership of these programs. This section started with a discussion about defining the objectives for an innovation program. One might think that clarity on objectives would lead to clarity on the success or failure in achieving those objectives. Nothing could be further from the truth.

There are three distinct areas where organizational and personal realities intervene in ways that make a perception of success highly problematic. The first of these relates to the results of the innovation portfolio versus the results of the overall business. An innovation portfolio that does not actually result in improvements to the business won't be viewed as successful no matter how many internal targets it hits. One can argue about the fairness of this, but it's the reality of human nature and organizational dynamics. What's also true is that even a minor glitch in an existing core business could easily wipe out all the positive contributions of an innovation program. If you find yourself in a heated debate about which has happened, you can bet your program will be declared a failure.

The second has to do with the success or failure of specific initiatives. Every program like this ends up with initiatives that are the personal favorite of somebody in the most senior team. Since many of these will fail, often quite early and often having been given very little resources, these senior sponsors can quickly become major detractors. What compounds this problem are the basic probabilities of success at the level of an individual initiative. In the world of Silicon Valley, a success rate of 25% would be considered a golden touch and 15%–20% would be more the norm. In corporate programs that are able to leverage existing infrastructure, technology and client access this definitely goes up. A 25%–30% success rate would be considered quite strong. In fact, some argue that if your success rate exceeds 50% you aren't doing enough to push the boundary. Any of those numbers would absolutely horrify most traditional executives.

Beyond the simple unfamiliarity with those kinds of odds there are a range of very real personal issues that cause organizational resistance to grow. This starts with the "special treatment" given to these businesses and is further fueled by an underlying resentment to outside interference and meddling. Existing leaders will complain that "I could do great things too if I didn't have to manage to my budget and all the volatility I get from Finance." Others will complain about management interventions on behalf of these startups. Since those will often come from far up the line there's a refrain that begins with "well if I had so and so as my personal sugar daddy...." These may seem petty, but they're quite real and will grow over time.

What may seem surprising is that in many cases the strongest resistance can come from the executives who are leading Horizon 2 businesses. Recall that these businesses have established business models and are almost always hungry for the resources needed to fuel their growth. These leaders will look at what's being given to one of these startups and observe that while the startup has only a 25%–35% odds of success they will happily guarantee 100% odds—and with better results too. And, they'll be right. But, you still won't give them what they want. No matter how much you argue about the long term need to invest in Horizon 3—in fact, no matter how much they already know and agree about that need—they'll still be unhappy.

These are some of the specific issues and complaints innovation program leaders need to deal with. The overarching umbrella though is creating a culture of growth and innovation. This issue runs very deep. All of the usual cultural management tools can and should be brought into play. Public celebrations and recognition events need an explicit place for innovations and growth. A startup that gets through its first three funding tranches in a flash and is already talking about "graduating" needs as much public praise as the biggest contract win of the year. Analyst and PR events need to be peppered with examples of early tests, successes, and, yes, even a few visible failures too.

These all need to flow from the most senior executives including the CEO. There's a story that Sam used to tell about how to recognize a company with a growth culture. Imagine a CEO with his or her senior team sitting in a staff meeting and hearing about a quarterly shortfall. Sam used to say, "watch the CEO and see which way they look in that exact instant. If they look at their CFO it's not a growth company. If they look at their head of sales it is." There were many situations where Sam would tell the leader of a business that was struggling to just "grow your way out of it." What Sam had learned while building the services business was just how powerful growth alone can be in resolving business problems.

MAINTAINING THE CORE

In several sections we've highlighted the importance of sustaining investments in one's core business even in the face of slow to zero growth. We've rejected the phrase "milk the cash cow" that often accompanies strategy efforts that use the classic BCG growth/share quadrant analysis. In all fairness, Bruce Henderson, who is the originator of that methodology, is well aware of the issue and would probably reject that phrase himself. In his 1976 article on cash cows his opening paragraph states "The first objective of corporate strategy is the protection of cash generators.... These are the cash cows." I might substitute the word "preservation" for "protection," but that's mere quibbling.

The original formulation of the methodology was heavily focused on managing a portfolio for growth. Applied properly, as it appears Bruce intended, it certainly has its uses. Unfortunately, the "milk the cow" interpretation is widespread and as noted above its (mis)application is the third most common cause of growth failures.

It is important to properly calibrate investments in these parts of a portfolio in ways that make strategic sense. A massive effort to grow a business that is already in a strong share position and that is operating in a market with no growth or even declines would make no sense. In contrast, investments that ensure the business will be able to maintain its cash contribution should be at or near the very top of the corporate priority list. In the language of the Horizon model, these H1 businesses can be counted on to deliver results. The execution risks of an appropriately aimed investment to sustain them will be much lower than the risks of building something entirely new.

This is exactly what IBM did with the mainframe. The leadership of that business was empowered to invest as needed to sustain their absolute level of gross profit and cash contributions to the business. They were not asked for growth, nor was there even all that much focus on total revenue. The focus was ensuring this core part of the business sustained its essential contributions. There was a brief period, when the mainframe business was being led by a particularly gung-ho ex-marine, that we contemplated a set of actual growth strategies for the business. After carefully looking at the possibilities we concluded that would have been a mistake.

The other observation from IBM's experiences is that mature offerings and brands have far more latent equity than many may assume. Particularly in a B2B context, even quite staid offerings will continue to have customers and sales long after their growth bloom has faded. Customers value their familiarity with these offerings. They are "known" quantities that have been embedded in their own operations and activities. They are stable and reliable. What they may lack in sexiness is more than offset by more humble values. When IBM was near its nadir and Lou was out talking to clients he found a deep reservoir of support. Far from being indifferent, they were pulling strongly for us to rebound.

The dynamic works differently in the consumer market, but the end result can be quite similar. Consumers frequently develop strong brand associations that endure long after an offerings growth phase has faded. In fact, consumers own sense of identity can become entangled with their favorite brands. We all know the "Apple fan-boys" who will participate in endless online debates in support of Apple. These deep affiliations have enormous value that should be sustained.

There are a few internal and external areas that are critically important for leaders to manage. On the internal side, it's important that the people working in these core parts of the business maintain their sense of pride and importance. The legacies, stories and culture of these teams must be nourished. It's easy for an organization to get caught up in the excitement of new opportunities and overlook, or take for granted, teams in the core.

Externally, there are two important constituencies to manage on this topic. The existing customers who are happy with the core offerings need to be reassured by leadership that the company shares their commitment and will sustain appropriate investments. They will fear you may adopt a "cash cow" strategy and leave them stranded. If that sets in they'll start planning an exit strategy. There are lots of tools at one's disposal to maintain the two-way dialogue that helps keep customers engaged. This is where things like dedicated client advisory councils or company managed user groups can be very effective.

The financial markets can be harder to manage. Having a large, proven, profitable cash engine at the core of a business would seem to be something the market should value and there are such investors. For many, however, those businesses are viewed as low growth, boat anchors that dilute the growth value from new initiatives. Imagine a company with two businesses, one that's $90M, profitable, but no growth and the other that's $10M, unprofitable, and growing 20% per year. When combined, the firm is $100M and profitable but growing only 2%. Held apart, the market would assign a low, conservative P/E to the $90M business and a high, enthusiastic Price/Revenue to the smaller one. The total market cap of these two might easily exceed the value when put together. Furthermore, in any period in which the larger business experiences even a slight erosion the combined results could easily have zero growth. The growth dilutive aspect of a mature core can be a recurring complaint from the financial markets.

IBM: The Rometty Years

May you live in interesting times. . . .

INTRODUCTION

GINNI ROMETTY BROUGHT her own distinct style to the CEO position. The most immediate change was a subtle but definitely increased focus on bringing the voice of the client into IBM's top decision processes. Ginni retained all the major management tools that Sam had put in place including the Technology Team and the Strategy Team. She added a new Client Team, which supplemented the various existing client advisory councils, and elevated those inputs to the same level as the internal technical and business discussions. At the urging of the head of marketing, she also began a practice of injecting client stories and anecdotes into most discussions. These had always existed, in fact they were a core part of the IBM culture. The primary difference was that both Lou and Sam understood the importance of ensuring these stories were balanced by actual data. Under Ginni that reminder was often omitted. As we will see, this seemingly minor shift in emphasis was an early warning signal.

Ginni's sheer breadth and depth of client relationships was and is her greatest strength. She is able to hear directly through the experiences of those clients about what is working and what is not. Lou, Sam and, indeed, all CEOs, certainly do the same. With Ginni however, this was elevated to an entirely different level. Ginni had led the integration of PwC into IBM and had spent a great deal of her career leading IBM's professional services and consulting business. The relationships she had developed through those years were further strengthened by her time leading IBM's global sales organization. Not only did she have deep client contacts, she used them on an almost daily basis. Someone did a calendar review that revealed Ginni spent more time with customers in her first six months as CEO than Sam had in the prior two years. It was impressive and had an immediate impact to increase the importance of this long-term pillar of IBM's culture. This too, turned out to be a mixed blessing.

Despite Ginni's highly distinguished career prior to be named CEO, the one thing she lacked was any experience managing hardware or software technology development. Neither of her predecessors had much technology depth either and Sam's experience managing development was limited. Like them, Ginni would need to rely on those on her team who did have both technology expertise and development experience. The technology leaders Ginni inherited were many of the same ones Sam had relied on. They might not have had quite the stature as the team under Lou, but their skills and experience were more than adequate. Trust, however, was another matter.

Trust and loyalty are important factors for any leader at any level. In large, complex organizations, leaders almost always have areas where they must depend on their team's expertise. There was nothing immediately new or notable about this with Ginni. What was slightly different for Ginni was that personal loyalty to her was primary. She would never openly say that personal loyalty to her mattered more than IBM loyalty, but her actual behavior indicated it did. This wasn't something prominent. It was subtle, but it mattered.

On its surface, the IBM Ginni inherited from Sam seemed to be on a roll. However, there were critical issues lurking everywhere. As we noted earlier, for the last several years Sam had been managing the company based on financial targets more than strategy. Those targets were overwhelmingly weighted to earnings per share with a highly public "roadmap" that was religiously tracked on the street. Those same financial analysts were increasingly alarmed that the steady EPS track was not matched by a corresponding revenue track. This reflected Sam's strategic focus on profits over revenue. It also reflected a growing reliance on share buybacks to boost the financial performance above the level generated through operational results. This remains a common practice across corporate America and, on its own, wasn't a particular sign of alarm.

However, it did leave the company open to charges that the ballyhooed EPS track was more a reflection of financial engineering than anything else. Ginni needed to get back to managing the company around an actual strategy and that strategy would need to show results that could be tied to actual revenue growth. As this emphasis developed the true depth of the challenge would slowly become clear.

DEPTH OF THE CHALLENGE–VALUE SHIFTS

As noted earlier, the most common cause of strategic derailment are value shifts in the market. When a company is as large and diverse as IBM, there is some amount of this under way all the time. That same diversity also usually means that other parts of the portfolio are still stable. What Ginni had inherited was a portfolio where almost every key element was being faced with this sort of value shift.

Most of these had been unfolding for years and were reasonably well understood by IBM. The rate, pace and scope of the shifts were definitely under-estimated. The appreciation for the magnitude of the change in IBM needed to respond was even further off the mark. With all the recent focus on EPS, the actual progress in making those changes was outright pathetic.

We were dealing with a paradigm shift. That phrase is used a lot in the technology industry. In most cases it's just hyperbole, or it's accurate but narrow in scope. This was the real thing and it was all encompassing.

As we've seen, IBM's core value proposition is centered on the reliable delivery of mission critical capabilities for enterprise clients. In the early days, this meant enabling transaction processing applications like reservation systems that were delivered from host computers to "dumb" terminals. This was the paradigm that made IBM. In the introductory chapter on Gerstner, we described the arrival of PCs and the shift to the client/server paradigm. That was much more than just a technology shift, and IBM completely misunderstood how deep the changes were in buyers and value propositions. We nearly went out of business as a result. The client/server era came to an end with the proliferation of the Web. This time the key value for enterprises entailed integrating and exposing traditional IT resources to the world of the web. This was the wave that IBM did successfully capture, first under Lou and then continuing under Sam.

The latest era changes yet again, this time with a focus on cloud infrastructure augmenting existing business infrastructure and the use of phones and mobile devices as the primary design point for accessing systems. As we've described in the prior shifts, the changes are far deeper than simply the technologies involved. There are now a whole range of new uses centered on the evolution of collaborative technology to social media and the growing importance of data and analytics. There were clues about many of these deeper value shifts that had been popping out for years. The surprising finding from years ago that the mainframe's distinct value in the mind of customers was shifting from transaction processing to data repository was one of those clues. There were many of them.

It's a perfect example of the most frequent cause of strategic failure. In our earlier discussion on this topic, we highlighted the challenge incumbents have in recognizing these problems when they arise. At some level, that has not been the problem. IBM did see this emerging paradigm and had mobilized resources to capture it. In fact, the whole senior team was well aware that the shifts were under way, and the company needed to respond. At a deeper level, however, very few really understood the depths of what was and is happening. It is eerily similar to the client / server paradigm shift where IBM fixated on the technology dimensions and systematically missed the more profound, strategic shifts in buyers and value propositions. The same is happening now. Like then, the deeply held belief that they *do* understand makes it difficult to realize that they do not. In the eighties that problem was rooted in arrogance. Under Ginni it was rooted in an over reliance on feedback from existing clients most of whom don't really understand what's happening either.

(Mis-)managing the Core

By the time Ginni took charge the hardware portion of IBM's portfolio had dropped to 17% of revenue and 14% of profits. The mainframe was still plugging along, although it had become a completely cyclical business. Each new generation would be rapidly bought up by existing clients creating a short-term surge of results. This would then drop dramatically until the next new cycle. The Unix business was now a real contributor to profits as well as revenue. It was larger and less cyclical than the mainframe. However, this whole part of the portfolio was being hit with enormous shifts in technology, buyers, and sales. The combination was deadly.

The technology shift had been unfolding for years. It might have been nearly invisible to the broad market, but it had been recognized for probably 5–10 years within IBM's technical community. Moore's law, which has featured prominently in both the public imagination as well as the actual evolution of the industry, had irreversibly changed. In a deep way, it had arguably come to an end. As discussed earlier, the key to Moore's law had always been that each generation of semiconductors enabled smaller circuits than the prior generation. These smaller circuits enabled more capabilities to be added to each chip and allowed those chips to run faster. The higher speed was directly enabled by the smaller circuits. The semiconductors now being produced as well as those in the future would continue to have smaller circuits, but for reasons of basic physics they would no longer run any faster.

This reality has been masked for many in the market. Chip designers use the smaller circuits to build many more "cores" on each future chip. Each core effectively runs at the same speed as the older chips but there are now more of them running in parallel. For a great many workloads, this can be rendered essentially invisible. For some, however, it meant that progress was grinding to a halt.

Even more important for IBM, this shift struck at the heart of one of IBM's unique server attributes. IBM's systems, particularly its most differentiated high-end systems, had always been positioned as offering the best performance. This had been achieved through the direct exploitation of the speed improvements in each generation, a formula known as "scaling up." This was precisely the formula that was no longer physically possible. Even worse, our competition had always argued that a larger number of smaller systems, called "scaling out," was a better formula. We could still package up single systems that looked like a "scale up" world leader, but hidden deep under the covers what we were actually being forced to do was employ a "scale out" design.

This was masking the problem. For clients who truly needed the old scale up formula we had reached the end and it was now only a matter of time before everyone would match us. For a lot of clients this wasn't an issue at all. In fact, just the opposite. In the past, every successive generation of technology was quickly consumed by the aggregate growth in demand. As steep as the performance curves had been, demand growth had always been steeper. Across a wide spectrum of IBM's top clients this was no longer the case. Their upgrade needs, including under the new formula, were slowing.

Part of what made this hard to see was related to the second massive shift hitting the hardware business. The actual buyers were changing in a way that was more radical than anything we had experienced. The biggest buyers of computing capability were no longer entities like American Express or Walmart. The biggest buyers were cloud service providers like Amazon Web Services and Google. Those companies didn't even buy systems. They bought components and put them together themselves within their own service delivery architecture. The server "box" was no longer the most important design point. The key for these buyers was the overall infrastructure, not any individual "box."

IBM had known about these buyers for years and failed to make any progress selling them anything. The fact that nothing we had to offer was of any interest was considered an annoyance. There had always been more than enough demand from our usual clients. The shock to the IBM leaders of this business came from an analysis we did of the overall industry demand for servers. The top-level line seemed to exhibit no change at all. The overall demand was rising, albeit at a slow level, but not significantly different from the past. Then we removed the volumes associated with the cloud providers, leaving behind our traditional clients. That estimate showed that overall demand in our traditional market had peaked 18 months earlier and was now in decline. We had no idea.

These first two shifts were based on external factors. We had seen the technical shift ages before. We knew that cloud buyers were growing in importance, but we underestimated the impact so much we missed the fact that our traditional market had actually begun to decline. The third problem was completely self-inflicted and a perfect example of the third most common cause of strategic failure.

This problem began with a first quarter revenue miss for the hardware business. It was nothing that unusual. We had experienced these situations countless times before. The usual process of determining the root cause was more challenging than we had dealt with in the past. There were just many more factors in play. In addition to the shifts noted above there were also some product release issues and worries that our client base had once again become too concentrated. When we were done working through all the details we discovered that while all these factors were real the biggest issue was with sales resoures.

Our sales organization had gone through a great deal of churn over the past few years. We had hired replacements, but the full hiring had been tamped down by the EPS roadmap demands. Our aggregate sales capacity was simply too low to deliver the revenue results in our plan. The situation was worsening and needed immediate intervention. Having worked issues like this in the past we had a solid understanding of sales productivity and learning curve ramps. We knew how long it took to get newly placed sales people up the productivity curve. We knew how much we could rely on things like business partner incentive programs to augment our sales resources.

We modeled the results and developed a sales hiring and replacement plan that would rebuild our capacity to match our plans. There was a ramp, and there would be a shortfall in 2Q, but by year end the sales capacity plan we developed would be enough to deliver the year end results. Ginni rejected the plan. The Senior Vice President in charge of the business asked if we could guarantee the sales results. We told him we could only guarantee the downside. If we didn't fix the sales capacity problem we would miss our year end revenue plan by 20%. That's what we did, and the results matched our modeling almost exactly. It was self-inflicted.

It's easy to be critical of this specific decision, but its more illuminating to think about it in the context of the strategic issues we've been discussing throughout this book. This was part of the core business. It was shrinking in importance and would never again be a source of any meaningful growth under any scenario. It was a business facing substantial changes and risks in both the underlying technology as well as its critical markets. It was profitable, but margins could only be maintained by whittling away on expenses—like the sales organization. In the context of traditional strategic criteria, the decision to not invest in rebuilding sales capacity could actually be considered exactly right.

The contrast with what we did with the mainframe under Lou could not be more stark. Like then, this core part of the business would need investment to recover. The issues the business faced were huge and the risks of failure, no matter what investments were made, were very high. It was already a dwindling part of the portfolio so managing it as a cash cow would seem to make sense. Unfortunately, that strategy practically ensures the business will decline, which is exactly what has happened.

By the end of 2014 we concluded we could no longer maintain the chip fabrication plant we had originally built under Gerstner. The partnership model we had constructed back then had survived longer than any of us had expected. One of those partners was Global Foundries who were willing to maintain the facility and essentially all its personnel. In addition to the physical assets of the plant, we also transferred thousands of critical patents associated with its operations. Finally, we mutually agreed to a long-term sourcing arrangement for IBM's server business. It was a sad day, but it did allow us to maintain our investments in the research and development of these technologies.

Earlier that same year we had made a similar, if less emotional, decision. When we originally sold the PC business to Lenovo we did not include the Intel based servers as part of that transaction. Those servers weren't a great business, but they were important to our clients and were far and away the volume leaders in the overall server market. Back in 2012 we had made a last-ditch effort to improve the business with an initiative called PureSystems. The idea behind that play was to integrate all the necessary elements of a working system including the networking, storage, and key management software. This was the old formula IBM had employed to great success in its midrange servers decades earlier. Cisco had introduced their own version and they appeared to be getting decent traction in the market.

Within six months we knew something wasn't right with our PureSystems offerings. They were not getting the results we had expected. The feedback from clients was not nearly as positive as we had heard from our advisory councils and early installations. We launched an investigation and found to our horror that many of the integrated capabilities we had been discussing and promising simply weren't real. It's not that they couldn't have been done. They just hadn't been. The networking definitions in particular were a mess. Those skills had always been in short supply inside IBM. Still, none of us could remember any prior situation where what was actually delivered was so far from what had been planned and promised. It was a microcosm of the skill erosion that was growing critical.

We struggled for a while to see if the problems could be fixed, but concluded the whole effort was too difficult with too little returns to be worth it. The Intel server business was now fully in question. This should have been a more difficult and complicated decision than the original Lenovo sale. Unlike those client systems the Intel servers did actually share supply chain and part sourcing with other parts of the business. They were also highly important to the thousands of business partners IBM relies on to cover most of the hardware market. They made up a meaningful percent of IBM revenue in both Europe and China. And, versions of those offerings were the systems that cloud providers actually did buy. All of these factors could have affected the exact course of action for this segment of the business. Under Sam, these would have been thoroughly vetted. Under Ginni, little to none of this occurred. We quickly sold the remaining parts of the business to Lenovo. From one perspective that was a crisp decision fully aligned with the overall strategy. From another perspective it was a further step in the abandonment of IBM's historical core.

The core part of our professional services business was also in the midst of a dramatic shift. Unlike hardware, this business was still both a major revenue contributor as well as an important strategic capability. The critical shift was in the market demand for implementing packaged application software, specifically ERP packages from companies like SAP and Oracle. The ERP market was going through a classic maturation process. In its early days, each new release or set of upgrades were eagerly sought by many clients. Functional enhancements enabled existing clients of one set of capabilities to expand into new areas like HR or Sales Management. Over time, these existing clients reached a point of diminishing returns where new functions didn't add that much new value. Even though the base functions were still critically important to those customers the incremental new value was becoming quite low. There had also been a steady progression from early adopters, to early majority, to late majority. By now, most clients who needed ERP capabilities had it. There were still some cases where clients would acquire other companies and want to migrate those companies onto whatever package they had selected. Overall, however, the market was well past its prime.

These projects with their enormous scale, extensive resource require-ments, and multi-year duration had been the bulk of the professional services backlog. That backlog was now draining faster than it was filling back up. We had recognized this strategic eventuality and had declared our next focus to be on analytics. This was a new strategic source of value for enterprise clients and one we should have been well positioned to capture.

Unfortunately, most of these projects had only a fraction of the scale of an ERP implementation and they all required different skills. The skills we needed had to encompass both the technical aspects of analytics projects along with the business insights to understand and sell the value to be derived. Both were in short supply. Technical skills certainly existed in IBM, but, other than things like project management, the needs were quite different from the specific skills used in ERP deployments. Furthermore, in the era of ERP we teamed with SAP and Oracle and their resources often brought much of the business selling skills. In the case of analytics, we were working from our own offerings and we were therefore dependent on ourselves for those business skills. We had very few people who could really qualify and those who did were stretched beyond imagination.

Cloud was also a factor, though not the way most analysts assumed. They thought clients were deploying ERP on the cloud, which was minimal. Or, they thought a cloud deployment somehow avoided all the integration chal-lenges associated with typical ERP projects. If anything, the opposite was true. In fact, there were instances where unfamiliar cloud integration issues were obstacles that impeded our ability to deliver. Where the cloud really became a factor was in our move to analytics. Those solutions frequently had high dependencies on different cloud-based components. In many cases, the client wanted the whole solution built and deployed on a cloud environment. These requirements were technically quite feasible, but once again depended on skills that were sorely lacking in IBM.

We also had many, many executives who simply couldn't believe clients actually wanted to use cloud at all for these analytics projects. The clients they spoke with would routinely assert they would never allow their critical data to be placed on a cloud. These were IT executives who didn't realize or accept that vast amounts of their data were already out in various cloud deployments. When their marketing organizations hired companies to evaluate opportunities or qualify programs they frequently put data in those company's hands, which they then analyzed on cloud deployments. When their sales organization gathered all their prospect information and assigned them to different sales representatives and partners using Salesforce, that data was on a cloud. Cloud services were everywhere and all of them used data. The assertion that would *never* happen was a blind spot for both our IT clients and the IBM executives who listened to them.

Cloud was an even bigger factor in the shifts impacting our outsourcing services. As noted earlier these contracts were traditionally sold with a "your mess for less" value proposition. Unfortunately, this too was reaching the point of diminishing returns. Once we had squeezed out the obvious problems and moved whatever work we could to India or some other low-cost geography it became harder to find meaningful savings. Many of the steps that might have generated useful further improvements required that the client allow us greater control of their existing architectures. That would have enabled us to drive deeper standardization across functions but was rarely accepted by existing clients.

Clients were also demanding that we carve out various functions and move them to a cloud deployment environment. They wanted "hybrid" contracts that included both traditional outsourcing terms and conditions for some of what they did and cloud-based solutions for other components. This made perfect sense on paper but proved incredibly elusive in practice. A major part of the problem was that our outsourcing teams didn't really understand how these hybrid deployments were supposed to work. That might have been overcome by picking and working on a couple of common workloads with good cloud affinity like email. We could expect to find those in almost all contracts and could develop a standard solution for them. This kind of standardized approach flew in the face of the deeply rooted outsourcing culture which prided itself on unique customization for every client. Every attempt we made in that direction floundered.

Far and away the section of the business that has struggled the most with the cloud model is software. For reasons we will describe below, the software team was confused and inconsistent in its approach toward the cloud era. Some of this was denial. Some was rooted in a belief that cloud was "just a deployment model" and had no implications on the offering itself. However, the cloud model was shifting the values and investment priorities in the market. IBM's software business needed to ensure its base didn't erode while it began shifting to more cloud relevant offerings. There was no clarity on just what that meant. As a result, neither the core base nor the potential new capabilities had the right level of prioritization and focus. In that situation, nothing new gets any scale and nothing old gets what it needs to survive. The result was very predictable erosion.

THE GROWTH MARKETS COLLAPSE

IBM's growth from emerging markets over the prior decade had exceeded the growth from all other initiatives combined. When that growth stopped it created a revenue hole as big as all the cloud shifts described above. The economic fundamentals of both Brazil and Russia had stalled. These were macro-economic shifts that simply rippled through the IT industry and IBM. IBM launched significant efforts to build business in Africa. These made some progress, but frankly the market was and still is too immature to drive substantial results. Those efforts were more in the form of strategic investments for the future. In the case of India, IBM was continuing its progress building up service delivery capabilities from India. What was not progressing were our sales into the Indian market. With the exception of Bharti, IBM had very few major contracts or clients in India, and the Bharti deal was beginning to develop issues. All of these created difficulties, but far and away the biggest issue was China.

Part of the "China 2025" plan includes an initiative around "indigenous innovation" whose aim is to accelerate the movement of the country into higher value-added roles in a variety of industries, including information technology. Under this banner, Chinese clients were increasingly focused on driving up the local Chinese content of all their IT projects. This kind of "bidding pressure" is not all that unique in the world. It's usually more of a slight tilting of the playing field than anything else. In China's case, however, the tilted field also came with open demands for IP licensing.

One of the demands that had been an off and on issue for years was for access to source code for IBM's major software assets. This was frequently justified by claims that they needed to ensure neither IBM nor any US intelligence agencies, had installed any "backdoor" access that would enable US espionage. There had been rumors that EMC had been guilty of doing so. We never saw any proof of that claim. Nonetheless, we did find many situations where China used that rumor to demand source code access. We had established a process in which a third party was allowed access to IBM source code and would allow a controlled inspection by the Chinese in a form of "code escrow." The Chinese "inspectors" did have opportunities through this process to learn details about how certain capabilities worked. They did not have the ability to simply "copy" any of the code. This arrangement was cumbersome and imperfect in its protections but was becoming a growing necessity.

The new wrinkle we had to confront was around the design of high end servers. This was an area we knew the Chinese wanted to master. We also knew they had been attempting to extract IP licenses from IBM, HPQ, and Sun for many years. They would often hint that one or the other of us might "crack" and thereby be granted privileged access to contracts across all of China. At one point, they actually made us an offer to pay us a one-time license fee for unfettered access and usage rights to all of IBM's high-end server IP.

The amount offered was ludicrously low. We said "no," and we were reasonably confident our competitors would do the same.

While those rejections may have slowed their progress to some degree there was and is no question about where they are going. The world of High Performance Computing, or HPC, is a specialized sub-segment of the broader server market. These systems focus narrowly on specific types of computing and algorithms, so they're a bit different from the types of computers most businesses rely on. Nonetheless, they're a very important segment and are highly illustrative of the state of the art. There's a regularly published list of the top 500 HPC systems in the world. Almost every entry on that list is a "one-off" usually built for a government laboratory. The US had dominated that list since its inception. Until 2016.

In 2016 China surpassed the US for the first time in both numbers of entries as well as the top two spots. Of particular note is that the number one entry uses no technology from the US. It's completely built on Chinese components. Up until 2015 the Chinese had relied almost completely on components from Intel. The US government blocked that access in 2015. It didn't matter. There are several new US HPC systems that will go into production over the next couple of years, one or two of which are likely to take the top spot away from China. Even if they do, everyone involved in this part of the industry is fully aware China will leap-frog those offerings before very long. Most observers agree that China has now fully caught up with the US. Many forecast they will achieve sustained leadership over the US as early as 2020.

The Chinese attempts at extracting IP licenses relevant to the commercial server market were becoming so severe that sales were grinding to a halt. We needed to find a different strategy and we knew that whatever the strategy was it needed to address their root desire to increase their ability to generate systems IP that could be owned by China. This was one of the primary triggers of what would become the "open Power" initiative.

The idea behind open Power is rooted in the technology trends we described earlier. When semiconductor chips stopped operating faster even as the number of circuits were growing that opened up a new domain for innovation. What kinds of "accelerators" could one add to a chip, using all those expanded circuits, that would allow important workloads to continue to see speed improvements? There were countless ideas and lots of experimentation going on. In most cases the results were minor improvements for limited sets of workloads. Nonetheless, it was (and is) an important new field to be explored. Neither IBM, HPQ, Intel, nor anybody else has figured out a clear winning technology. In fact, it may well be the case that this trend will spawn a widely diverse set of semiconductors optimized for different use cases. For such a technical design strategy to be possible there would need to be corresponding strategies around fab operations.

What had always been a closed, tightly integrated, development and production process looked like it might be ripe for transformation. If we could create an open ecosystem that delivered a rich range of innovations around IBM's Power technologies we might have a whole new business model that would be good for IBM, would be good for clients using Power and could become an "open" playing field that would enable China to pursue its ambitions. China, of course, wanted it "open" on their terms and IBM wanted it "open" on our terms, but that's just how negotiations always begin. Furthermore, for this strategy to work it was going to have to be about far more than just China. It would need to be global.

There are only a handful of companies on the planet that could even conceive of such a complex endeavor. The technical issues are profound and rooted in the absolute frontier of current commercial innovation. The production issues are equally profound and require a level of coordinated process deployment that is rare in any industrial context let alone something as technically complex as semiconductors. The IP development, licensing and usage terms are highly nuanced dealing with literally thousands of patents and copyrights from dozens if not hundreds of institutions. Essentially all of those institutions can be assumed to be operating around a "control" paradigm instead of the "value" paradigm. Trust is in very short supply.

The open Power strategy is still developing with numerous and growing participation. Whether it succeeds is far from certain. It illustrates many different dimensions of the themes throughout this book. This is a glimpse of the growing complexities associated with the leading edge of innovation in today's global landscape. As we will describe below, the innovation frontier and the organizations involved in driving it are about as far removed from the solitary inventor in a garret as can be imagined.

Every major element of IBM's core business was facing major disruption. Almost all of the technology issues had been seen in advance. However, the clarity on specific plans and the actual progress to adapt was slow. With some notable exceptions like the Open Power initiative, what was being done with haste was more geared toward cutting expenses than sustaining revenues. These large core elements in the portfolio were moving toward strategic decline. In some cases, the decisions being made were so severe that decline had become inevitable.

THE NEW IMPERATIVES

If these were the "cash cows" what were the "stars" and what was IBM doing to drive them to success? There was an acronym running around the industry called "CAMS" which stood for Cloud, Analytics, Mobile, and Social. Cynics liked to rearrange the letters into "SCAM," which always got a knowing laugh. IBM added one additional "S" for Security. While everyone joked about our predilection for acronyms, they also pretty much universally agreed these four or five areas were the hottest in the market. These were the key drivers of the new paradigm. Mobile and Social offered transformative opportunities for companies to change how they interact with employees, clients and consumers. Cloud was the new infrastructure enabling seamlessly scalable IT resources that could be readily integrated and accessed by Mobile and Social implementations. Analytics was displacing simple automation as the new frontier of enterprise value. Security was the acknowledgment that all of these were creating new vulnerabilities that were growing in urgency. Looming over all of this was the promise of AI to completely transform society, for good or ill.

IBM understood the technical dimensions of every one of these trends and was working hard to build new businesses around them. That work had challenges as all new initiatives do. There was also progress, with almost all of these delivering consistent double-digit revenue growth. However, the core was eroding faster. It was becoming a race to see if the new, growing, businesses could reach enough scale, fast enough to offset the declines. At a corporate level this portfolio perspective became the de facto "strategy." Unfortunately, in actual practice we were replicating the strategic error Sam had made of conflating these measurement objectives with an actual strategy. Coupled with the failure to strategically sustain the core business it was a very dangerous posture.

CLOUD-INNOVATORS DILEMMA RETURNS

One of the critical new initiatives was around cloud. IBM's strategy for cloud began during Sam's tenure at the end of a Strategy Team meeting. This meeting was held shortly after Amazon had announced a set of recent quarterly results. As always, they had provided verbal guidance on the contributions from their cloud business, but no financial specifics. The scheduled topics for the meeting had been completed and in the midst of the general discussion that followed someone raised the question "is the cloud business profitable for Amazon?" Amazon, to this day, does not share any specifics so none of us had any hard data. The general consensus was that it might be profitable, but, if so, it was only because so much of the fixed costs associated with the infrastructure were being defrayed by the rest of their business. As the discussion wound down, Mike Daniels, the Senior Vice President who ran IBM's outsourcing business for decades, declared that he thought we might be under estimating the profits. His assertion was based on a key learning from his long experience running IT operations of all types and sizes all over the globe. He claimed if they were able to simplify and standardize enough of the management processes their costs might be much lower than we were assuming. Sam told us to go get the answer.

There was very little we could glean from Amazon's financial disclosures. We could put some boundaries just based on simple math, but that wasn't nearly good enough. We began going through a thorough bottoms up analysis of what we knew about the technical and operational details of their infrastructure and what we could deduce about costs from that knowledge. Details were very sketchy, with no single source providing anything like a full picture. We had to piece together disparate elements from various sources. Eventually we felt we had captured enough technical and operational specifics from enough sources that we could have reasonable confidence in our estimates.

The results were astounding. Not only did our calculations indicate it was profitable, they suggested the business was actually highly profitable. This was completely absent any fixed cost leverage from other parts of the business. It was a huge eye-opener for the whole senior team. Shortly thereafter Sam assembled a group with the mission to build a cloud business for IBM.

Problems began almost immediately. IBM was organized around hardware, software, and service groups. The initial staffing for the new cloud business was primarily sourced from the service organization, specifically the outsourcing team. That background gave them a good understanding of the factors that drove operational costs. It did not equip them to understand how to leverage software to change those factors. Meanwhile, the software teams viewed cloud service providers as just a new set of clients with a new deployment model. To them that implied there was nothing they needed to do with their existing offerings other than to get cloud providers to buy them. This was despite the fact that none of those buyers showed any interest in our offerings at all, nor had they ever done so. Finally, the hardware teams were of the firm belief that nothing based on an Intel architecture could be profitable long term and that therefore the whole IBM cloud needed to be based on IBM's Power technology.

These schisms were exacerbated by the terminology used in the industry to describe different categories of cloud services. Amazon's basic service was referred to as "Infrastructure as a Service" or IaaS. This provided basic compute, storage and networking capabilities with associated operating systems, virtualization and management tools. Salesforce.com's service was referred to as a "Software as a Service" or SaaS. The Salesforce service provided access to their sales management application software capabilities. There were few existence proofs at the time, but everyone in the industry assumed there would be a growing class of "Platform as a Service" offerings soon to emerge. This belief arose from the traditional conception of IT as a stack that consisted of hardware and operating systems at one level, middleware platform software at the next level, and application software at the level above that.

The IaaS, PaaS, and SaaS nomenclature was based on the traditional software industry hierarchy we all knew so well. This led everybody to believe their intuitions around that hierarchy should firmly apply to these different categories of cloud offerings. This was a set of beliefs rooted in understanding the value of an offering by itemizing the ingredients going into the service not the actual service itself. It's like assuming the cake my daughter made for her 16th birthday was the equivalent of a three-star Michelin chef, just because they both use flour and eggs as key ingredients. Building on that analogy, my daughters cake would be pretty bland without icing on top. If you project that assumption onto the Michelin chef, you'll completely miss what is possible from an expert chef making cakes with no icing at all. Our teams had deep skills and expertise in their ingredients, but little to none in understanding what value was possible in their actual deployment as a complete service.

Despite the fact our bottoms up analysis showed there were profits to be had from the most basic services, our teams simply could not believe those would be sustainable. Their experiences told them IaaS would commoditize, SaaS would be dominated by thousands of small application software companies and the only sustainable place for IBM would be in PaaS. This meant we needed to build platform services, but nobody knew what that meant other than putting a piece of middleware on a cloud. Which would be like taking that Michelin chef's cake without icing and sticking an M&M on top and assuming the M&M provider would capture all the current and future value of the cake. It didn't make a lot of sense, but the "ingredient" view of value was deeply rooted in IBM's culture.

Just as Clayton Christensen predicted in his Innovators Dilemma, we were also beset by problems coming from our existing clients. They too were struggling with conceptual models that kept reverting to old patterns. On top of that, their normal worries about data security and access controls were on high alert. Certain workloads were declared as ones that would "never" be run from a cloud. However, there were lots of cases where one department in a client put a specific workload on the "never" list at the same time that a different department of that same client had it on the "planned" list. In response to this confusion we created a spectrum of workloads ranging from "cloud ready right now" to "cloud ready in the future" to "probably never great for cloud." Unfortunately for the cloud doubters that analysis concluded somewhere between 70%–80% of all enterprise workloads could be quite feasibly delivered from an appropriately designed and managed cloud service.

The client doubts continued. The senior executives in IBM's software group seemed to encounter more of those skeptical client stories than anyone else. That client input made our software teams hesitant. They really couldn't see how the value of a service could be greater than the sum of its parts. The service teams struggled with the inputs they heard from their clients as well. In their case the issue was focused on what clients would tolerate in terms of standardization and what they would demand be customized to their specific needs.

In reaction to all this client input IBM put an early focus on what was called "Private Cloud." The idea behind private cloud was for individual enterprises to build their own cloud services to be operated and used for their own purposes. For most in the industry this was a huge oxymoron. IBM was not hung up on the ideological purity of the true cloud believers. We did an analysis of the cost scaling curves to figure out where the points of diminishing returns set in and therefore what minimum scale would be needed for private clouds to be viable. Based on those results we concluded that many of our larger clients had enough scale that they could get a substantial percentage of the potential value. Most modern IT operations also operate with some sort of "service model" for their end users. These internal structures and agreements could be modified to reflect the best practices coming from outside cloud vendors. Private cloud was a viable, if limited, strategy and one we knew our existing clients would accept.

We also knew that no matter how much resistance any given client thought they had to cloud they would inevitably find themselves having to interoperate with outside cloud services. This goes to the basic realities of how business processes get broken down into components and sourced broadly from all over the world. It was and is an inescapable truth that some of those will end up having cloud-based elements and many of those will require some level of integration. Hence the need for "hybrid" environments that include traditional deployment models, private cloud models, and multiple public clouds.

All of these were easier steps for IBM to take in large part because they were easier for our clients to take. We were all fully aware that this was precisely the Innovators Dilemma that Christensen warned about. We knew we needed to make more progress on the "true" public cloud service category. After several false starts and failed initiatives, it was time to acquire somebody who had figured this stuff out.

A team set out to meet potential candidates. By this point we felt we knew what we were looking for. After reviewing dozens of potential acquisition targets, they selected Softlayer as the company that could get us out of the ditch. Softlayer was an interesting company. They were definitely in the cloud infrastructure service business. However, their technical and business strategy was quite different from everyone else in the industry and not quite what we had originally set out to acquire. The primary difference was that most of the market used a technology called virtualization to carve out chunks of capacity separate from the underlying bare server metal. This gave those services more flexibility at the expense of the added overhead of the virtualization layer. Softlayer had concluded there was a substantial market that wanted access to the bare metal so that they could use virtualization for their own purposes. Without a server-based virtualization layer, Softlayer relied more on networking technology to handle the scaling and workload variability needs of their clients.

This acquisition finally provided a credible cloud service foundation and the IBM team began to rally around them. Softlayer's sales went up dramatically. The IBM software teams began porting different parts of the portfolio onto Softlayer. The existing IBM cloud efforts developed convergence plans to align around Softlayer and their overall results began to improve. A major strategic focus was to attract outside software developers into building on IBM's emerging cloud infrastructure. The strategy was to make this into a preferred "platform" for as wide a market of developers as possible.

Despite this progress we were still not delivering the results we were expecting. Most of the senior executive team still had grave doubts about the long-term viability of cloud services in general. IBM was not seeing enough revenue from these services, nor were we achieving any sort of acceptable gross profit margins. Nobody was looking for bottom line profits, given the level of investment we were making, but we did expect gross profits that would promise long-term results and those were not materializing. This just confirmed the suspicions and worries of the leadership team.

One of the fiercest skeptics decided to hire an outside consultant to assess whether it was truly possible to deliver infrastructure and platform services on a profitable basis. The hiring executive wanted confirmation for the arguments he had been making for years. This isn't unusual, it happens all the time. The challenge for good consultants is how to handle a client that only wants one answer. In this case, Bain told us what the hiring executive wanted to hear. They concluded cloud services were unprofitable and IBM's poor results were a reflection of that market reality, not flawed execution.

The report was almost completely wrong. Not only were there pervasive execution problems, those issues were not being surfaced in a way that could lead to systematic corrections. The early conceptual challenges we had wrestled with had not been overcome. The vast majority of IBM's critical leadership simply did not understand the difference between a piece of software running on a server and that same software as an element in a service. IBM had indeed ported dozens and eventually hundreds of different pieces of software onto its various cloud services. There was even a broad catalog of software one could peruse. But they were still just piece parts. The ordering process was a mess. Furthermore, there was no way to actually meter and bill for most of what was available, so IBM teams were often just giving access away for free. They planned to bill people once there was a billing system that worked. There were also chronic planned and unplanned outage problems. Both were far too frequent and lengthy for a commercially competitive service.

The service flaws flowed directly through to the financial results. The biggest financial manifestation was linked to another aspect of the cloud business that was both poorly understood and difficult for IBM's culture. Cloud services are sold and billed based on usage. This means the revenue generated takes the form of an annuity stream. In any such business, there are two metrics that matter enormously, churn rate and Average Revenue Per User or ARPU. These are familiar to anyone with a background in the telecommunications business, which follows the same usage-based annuity model. The key to success is to capture clients with small initial deals and then grow the usage by those clients over time. That usage can grow by word of mouth from happy users and/or through the steady addition of new services that are attractive to existing users. Whenever one of those clients are lost through churn they have to be replaced and you have to start the process all over.

A cloud service business that is operating properly will get at least half their revenues and 75%–80% of their profits through the expanded use by existing clients. In the telecommunications world, a churn rate over 3%–5% will generate alarm. IBM's churn rate was frighteningly close to 100%. In other words, we were losing clients as fast as we were capturing them. That churn was directly attributable to the service conception and quality issues. We were flailing like a person who can't swim being tossed into a lake. We weren't drowning, but neither were we making any real progress toward the shoreline.

It's fair to ask how this could happen. We had all the ingredients needed for success. While there were lots of people who didn't understand what was actually happening under the covers, there were also lots of people who understood it perfectly. There were countless reviews and checkpoints. The pressure for results was off the charts. Ginni would have happily funded any plan or recommendation that she trusted and felt was credible. This was not a lack of focus, nor willingness to make hard decisions, nor ability to generate pressure and accountability, nor willingness to invest. However, it was a profound failure of leadership.

The leadership issues were numerous and widespread. Unfortunately, many of them stemmed from the subtle aspects of Ginni's style described in the introduction to this section. There was no leader with a clear compelling vision for the *services* IBM wanted to create. There were lots of competing ingredient debates and posturing, but no vision for the services. That was partly rooted in the lack of insight about the realities of the market. Ginni's predilection for client anecdotes contributed to the problem. The clients we were talking to didn't understand the market any better than we did and the clients with clear understanding of cloud weren't the people senior executives spoke with. This was Clay's Innovators Dilemma in action. Our skills were also misaligned. The teams with the development skill to build the service didn't understand what a service was and those who understood services were abysmal as developers. This could have been fixed, but to do so required a leader that both understood the business and what was happening—and had Ginni's trust. The people Ginni had invested with her trust were all people who played to her desires for personal loyalty and none of them understood or were willing to discuss what was really happening. There was also no focus from anywhere in the leadership team on building a cloud organization with a service culture. When the operations teams took down the entire service on a Sunday night they approached it as just a technical maintenance process. Nobody had the mind-set that they were pulling the intravenous feed on a patient in intensive care. Nobody was focused on reducing churn or putting in place sales resources focused on selling new services to existing clients. The whole service orientation was missing.

The one aspect of leadership that was not missing was persistence. IBM has continued to chip away at the issues with its cloud business. The progress has been slow and is still rarely recognized in the industry. But, there has been progress. There has also been growth. As of 2017, the cloud business as reported by IBM matches the total business from the Asia Pacific region which includes both Japan and China.

MOBILE-NEXT GENERATION BUSINESS SHIFT

The explosive growth of mobile phones isn't news to anybody anymore. It has fueled the meteoric rise of Apple, brought Samsung into a major role in the consumer side of the technology industry and flummoxed both Microsoft and Intel. Industry participants and analysts alike have sought to draw lessons from the parallels between the mobile market and the history of the PC business. That history would suggest there would be a competitive fight over the architectural control points of these devices and that the winner of that battle would capture most of the value over the long term. That is precisely the thinking that caused Microsoft to try to extend their PC experience to the phone and that drives Google's focus on Android. It's also the mind-set behind the attempts by telecommunications companies to "lock" phones to their services and to bundle all kinds of applications that consumers have not requested onto their devices.

The Microsoft efforts have been total failures as have the consumer hostile bundling attempts by telecommunications providers. The growth of Android in the market has been tremendous and the faithful still believe it's only a matter of time before Google begins to exploit this presence. I do believe there are strategies Google can employ that would be powerful, but only if they use that presence to enable genuine value propositions for consumers, enterprises, or service providers. If all they seek is to suddenly begin charging everybody for the basic use of Android that will fail.

The inescapable 800 lb gorilla is obviously Apple. They have no dependency on Google or Android. They have also proven to have a keen sense of what consumers actually want and value. For the architectural control believers, their success is due to control over the Apple operating system, IOS. For everyone else, it's the fact that they make phones people love. One of the savviest moves made by Ginni was the partnership with Apple. She had the strategic clarity to recognize there was little to no downside for IBM from such a partnership and absolutely tons of potential upside. It is, however, an initiative with little in the way of meaningful results. T

For IBM to capture this potential it needs to look not at the parallels with the PC history but rather to the parallel with the evolution of the web. Mobile phones are by their nature devices that connect with services. They have stand-alone capabilities, but the bulk of their value is driven through the services they access. These may be consumer entertainment services like access to music or videos, or they may be business services offered by enterprises like reservation systems or shopping. This is the heart of IBM's world and offers enormous potential on many levels.

The opportunity begins with simply ensuring secure, scalable, reliable access to whatever infrastructure is being used to deliver the service. In the traditional enterprise context, this is equivalent to what IBM did with Websphere to enable the delivery of basic web services. Websphere was a major driver for the growth and profitability of IBM's entire middleware portfolio during the last two decades. An equivalent result for IBM around mobile would be enormous.

The second mammoth opportunity would be helping enterprise clients figure out new ways of interacting with consumers. Mobile devices cannot be thought of as desk bound systems with small screens. They are mobile. They go with you everywhere. They are in many ways as much, if not more, about personal communication as they are about access to systems. They offer the potential to reimagine every aspect of how enterprises interact with consumers. This potential is also enormous and if fully exploited would dwarf what IBM experienced with Websphere.

Both of these opportunities have been elusive for IBM. There has been progress helping enterprises with tools to enable the development and delivery of secure access to their infrastructure. However, most of this has been very narrow and limited in scope. Part of this comes from fears that Apple or Google will eventually displace anything IBM puts on a phone. Part of this stems from the general failure to understand the role cloud services play in this world. IBM has been highly ambivalent about both of these central aspects of the paradigm and as a result has achieved results that are tepid at best.

The bigger failure is to seize the opportunities for completely reinventing the experiences enterprises deliver to consumers. This failure stems from the weak and fragmented skills IBM has on industry specific strategies in general and consumer oriented strategies in particular. This has been a long-standing challenge for IBM. One might think that with a corporate strategy focused on delivering high value solutions to enterprise clients, industry skills would be everywhere. Unfortunately, those skills are scattered between the consulting services teams and the sales team and neither really has the depth and breadth needed to fulfill IBM's core vision.

ANALYTICS AND DATA–NEXT GENERATION OF VALUE

Probably the largest and most valuable opportunity for IBM over the next decade is the industry wide evolution to analytics, data and AI as the new sources of enterprise value. The AI opportunity, which will be covered in the next chapter, is actually dependent on a rich "big data" foundation. In fact, there are many pundits who lump the two together. For our purposes, we will keep them separate, but they are closely related. We began to realize just how much potential existed in this arena back in the early 2000 period when we were studying the business process outsourcing opportunity. As we discussed earlier, that analysis revealed that the best predictor of long-term profitability was the leveraging of insights that came from capturing and analyzing the data exhaust coming from the operations of the process services. There was clearly a lot of value hidden in all that operational data.

We also knew that the value clients were getting from new transaction processing systems, professional productivity solutions and even many web-based marketing solutions were entering the land of diminishing returns. It seemed obvious that the next generation of value would come from mining all that data for new insights. The industry was rife with entertaining anecdotes. One of the most famous, and probably apocryphal, was the discovery that placing six packs of beer next to diaper displays was an effective merchandising strategy. The story goes that young fathers running out for diapers could be tempted to buy beer. After a while, most clients got tired of these stories. They were hungry for something more concrete.

The critical step to get beyond funny stories about beer and diapers is to find "actionable insights." For an insight to be actionable it has to be both relevant to the business and sufficiently timely that the potential action can be executed while the insight is still relevant. An insight about a desirable feature of a new electric car might be readily addressed in the design cycle of the next vehicle. An insight about the best advertisement to put on a mobile phone might need to be generated in milliseconds. Actionability also depends on the specifics of individual companies. A complex market analysis that achieves its optimal results through dozens of sub-segments might be perfect for a web marketing company and utterly useless for a company that creates whole divisions around each segment they try to serve.

Like almost all of these imperatives, IBM had realized the significance of this trend much earlier. The general manager of IBM's Database Management System (DBMS) offerings had realized in the mid 2000 period that the long running competitive battles with Oracle had reached a stalemate. In any given year, IBM would secure a handful of major wins, but would also lose a similar number. Neither side was gaining any ground. He decided to change strategy.

The new plan was to simply hold ground on the DBMS category while shifting resources to the adjacent analytics category. Not long after, in 2008, IBM acquired Cognos and then SPSS in 2009. These became the anchor tenants for a series of acquisitions over the next several years that fleshed out a new analytics middleware portfolio.

Analytics would become the second largest growth driver for the latter stages of Palmisano's tenure. Unfortunately, all of these acquisitions needed fairly substantial investments to achieve their intended integration plans and we were entering the period when EPS was beginning to rule supreme. Many of those plans were never fully funded. The integration plans were not completed and before long several of the key assets were losing ground in the market. IBM was not alone in recognizing the growing importance of analytics. In fact, the market was exploding with big data and cloud-based offerings. IBM was staying abreast of this wave through continued acquisitions, but the integration shortfalls and lack of cloud skills were substantially hindering our leadership goals.

Software and professional services have been the primary focus of the analytics strategy. However, there is a potentially much larger business area to pursue as well. The business of providing data to enterprises has been around for a very long time. Dun and Bradstreet has existed for longer than IBM. There is a whole industry dedicated to capturing and selling basic data about consumers, markets and companies. Almost all analytic projects rely to one degree or another on these data sources. They provide the context against which the unique data of each enterprise can be compared. This traditional industry is being radically transformed through an absolute explosion of new data sources and new uses of that data. Web based consumer services like Google, Facebook and Twitter all capture and produce enormous volumes of data. Similarly, the growth of mobile and all the services in support of those devices create their own incredibly rich and dynamic streams of data. The emerging field of "Internet of Things" or IoT promises to expand the range and scale even further. Data is exploding. The value derived from that has an equally explosive potential.

The world of web marketing has been on the frontier of many of these efforts. This is fueled by the advertising delivery strategies adopted by companies like Google, Facebook, and Twitter. All of those companies tout their ability to deliver specific ads to whatever segment a marketer wants to target. They provide those marketers access to things like search data, Likes, Tweets, and social connections. All of those can be combined with traditional consumer data from companies like Axciom as well as the data owned by the client. The IBM partnership with Twitter was intended to specifically mine Tweets for a wide variety of consumer insights.

Those web services are all household names. The giant iceberg under the surface that very few people have heard of or understand are the companies that support the world of mobile advertising. Companies like Lotame, as an example, have data volumes every bit as deep and rich as any of the other sources we've mentioned. What they have that nobody else has is timely location data. The GPS systems in cell phones make it possible to track their location with high precision at all times. These companies have the ability to evaluate where you are and what you're doing and then select and place an ad on your phone in literally milliseconds.

The next huge wave of data is coming from the Internet of Things or IoT. In this emerging paradigm, everything we interact with will be capturing and transmitting data. That includes your car, refrigerator and appliances. It includes the stop lights you pass and highways you travel not to mention culverts and storm drains. It includes the subway or train you ride, the planes you fly in and the boats you sail on. Almost every conceivable device you encounter has plans to become "smarter" and connected, which basically means it will capture and transmit data. When all of that is aligned with your cell phone location, not only will the device providers know about the workings of their widgets, they will also know who used it and when.

When IBM acquired The Weather Company (TWC) there were three key strategic assets we were seeking. First, was access to the weather data itself. This data was more precise than any other source, enabling analysis down to a city block. Second, was a cloud infrastructure designed from the ground up to pull data from thousands of weather oriented IoT sources. This same infrastructure gives IBM the ability to pull from literally the whole world of IoT.

Third, was a data platform that was specifically designed to gather all forms of geo-spatial data into a consistent structure for analysis.

These examples indicate the direction the industry is heading. There is a rapidly growing body of services that will enable access to almost unlimited data about people, places, companies and things. All of this data will be updated and accessible in real time. In IBM we often spoke about two major types of data. There is relatively static contextual data, like demographics, which is where most of the traditional information industry has focused. Then there is data with real-time embedded signals. Twitter is rich with potential signals as is weather data. When you can extract relevant signals from that real-time data you can trigger actions. Signal embedded data is one of the keys to getting the next generation of actionable insights.

There are many aspects of this opportunity that align with IBM's strategic intent. This is unquestionably where the next major generation of value for enterprise will be centered. There is also no question that the providers of actionable insights that can be effectively integrated with new and existing business processes will capture a great deal of value. Most industry analysts fixate on the data that companies like Facebook control. There's no doubt that will be a valuable piece of the puzzle. However, the full story will come when that data is combined with all the other sources I've described and there is nobody yet in a position to deliver that kind of capability. Ironically, the widespread concerns about privacy could also work in IBM's favor. The IBM brand carries a great deal of value associated with issues around security and integrity. It is easy to see this extended to consumer concerns about privacy. It's also easy to see IBM assert that the very fact they do not do business with consumers means they can be trusted to manage access to sensitive data about consumers. The overall strategic fit for IBM is excellent.

However, as we have seen, every aspect of the new paradigm has been difficult for IBM to execute. This opportunity requires exactly the types of cloud skills, industry specific innovation and consumer knowledge that have been lacking in our prior examples. It also requires sophisticated business negotiation skills to find and structure the right kinds of data partnerships. Everyone knows there is value in data and nobody is going to relinquish their unique data without appropriate compensation. Despite these challenges this is an opportunity IBM sees clearly and should eventually be able to capture and potentially lead.

COGNITIVE/AI–DR. WATSON, I PRESUME

Shortly after Watson won at Jeopardy I got a call from Ginni asking me to figure out what to do with this marvel. It was an exciting time and more than a little unexpected. Part of my normal role was to work with IBM Research to help assess and prioritize work based on commercial possibilities. As a result, I was intimately familiar with almost everything Research was working on. I had monthly formal reviews and probably exchanged some number of texts, calls or emails with researchers literally every day. I knew nothing about the Watson work in advance. The work had been under way for years. They had charted their progress and knew they had reached a point where they would be competitive with the top Jeopardy players, but nobody could predict with certainty that Watson would win. And, then it did.

The news swept around the world and moved artificial intelligence back as a serious topic for discussion among technologists. Every client that every IBMer met with wanted to know more about this wonder. It dominated conversations. Even in the most senior internal meetings the executives would share endless stories about all the questions and inquiries coming in from clients. None of us could remember a time when there was so much direct interest in an IBM capability and we knew we needed to capture that energy before it faded.

This would be a bit tricky. At this stage Watson was a classic example of an "underground" Research project. It made use of very few commercial IBM products and those it did use could have been chosen by a dart board. The code was filled with miscellaneous sections written by Research, open source, and academia. The training data was heavily weighted to Wikipedia and other open Internet sources. It had been developed with a "cost no object" philosophy so absolutely no attention had been paid to any operational efficiencies. There were several tools the developers used, but most of those were chosen based on whatever the researcher liked to use. There was no coherent set of tools for the management, maintenance, tuning, operations, or error recovery. It worked and had won, but it was a far cry from a commercially supportable offering.

On top of the technical gaps we also needed to worry about the individuals who were the brains behind this amazing invention. Within days of the victory announcement all the key members of the team were getting recruiting offers from competitors. We moved quickly to ensure we had both competitive compensation as well as extensive support, recognition and access to and from IBM's very top executives. We showered them with love and managed to hold off major defections. At least for a while.

We set up the team as a Research housed incubation project under my direction. They began teaching me just how this thing worked as a basis for figuring out a vision and strategy. My last experience with AI had been 15–20 years earlier. Back then the AI philosophy was to interview experts on a topic and capture their knowledge in the form of rules. It was hoped that these collections of rules would encompass the range of situations this particular AI system would encounter and enable it to respond based on all the wisdom of the experts who had contributed. As we will discuss in a later chapter, essentially all of these efforts ended in failure. The few successes were usually more dependent on brute force evaluation of many more paths than any human could handle than any real depth of acquired knowledge.

This was not the case with Watson. Instead of rules, Watson relied on a combination of statistical linguistic analysis and a whole host of different machine learning techniques. When the head of IBM Research first spoke to me about the system in private he told me in a hushed voice "the damn thing learns!" It got steadily better with time and exposure. Each iteration of the technology had limits, but the team had pushed those limits steadily in every direction needed to enable Watson to win. When Watson was exposed to an "answer" it immediately developed hundreds of possible interpretations which then spawned thousands of possible responses. Those were then passed through a collection of evaluations that had been developed with different machine learning algorithms. There were whole structures devoted to things like the concept of "Up" versus "Down," or "East" versus "West." Watson had extensive libraries of these machine learning modules that were used to assess and score the probability of correctness for each of the thousands of possible responses the system had generated. It could then surface its top recommendations along with their associated probabilities. That then was the basis for deciding whether to buzz in with a response.

The structure had a lot of flexibility. We could swap in different modules trained on different topics. The parallel evaluation of hundreds or thousands of possibilities meant the system would, by design, avoid many of the most common human reasoning errors. We envisioned multiple variants each trained with a combination of standard concepts and domain specific concepts. The ability of the system to learn through the ingestion of standard literature seemed to promise an incredible ability to scale the learning process. Unlike prior generations of AI, we would not be dependent on the tedious process of interviewing experts. It seemed amazing.

The first hint that all would not be that easy came when we examined the actual training process. Every rebuild had to start from scratch. It didn't retain any learning from one training session to the next. The entire corpus had to be rebuilt. It took on average three days. In other words, if you wanted to update Watson with a single new article from the medical literature it would take three days. Of course, if you wanted to update Watson with a thousand new articles from the literature it would also take three days. It was very much a "batch" oriented learning process. We hoped this was just an artifact of the Research stage and not something inherent, but we weren't completely sure.

Another problem was around how two or more Watson systems could interact. We had visions of Watson systems being able to exchange corpuses in a federated model. If Watson A learned a number of concepts and Watson B learned a different, though related set of concepts we wanted them to be able to exchange that learning. The Researchers assured us this was technically feasible, though they admitted they didn't know how to do it immediately. We logged it as a key future enhancement. It's still on the list for some future date and is probably far more in the future than we originally hoped.

We developed a vision in which we would host domain specific "master" instances of Watson in an IBM Cloud. We would then deploy client specific instances of Watson either on that cloud or on the client premise. All of those client instances would share learnings with the cloud-based Master instance. The Master instance would then propagate learnings out to all the client instances. The vision included a shared learning process that would scale with time and would deliver systematic improvements as the corpus of knowledge steadily improved. Each client would have their own instance of Watson and could control their own data, but all instances would share in the steady improvements of Watson's learnings.

The vision was powerful but dependent on two key unknowns. First was the actual federated learning process. The technologists said it was possible, but we didn't really know the details. Second, there was a tacit assumption that the machine learnings captured by Watson were assets that were distinct from the data used to train it. In our vision, our clients would own their unique data and IBM would own the machine learning weights and structures. Nobody had ever tried to build a commercial relationship with those distinctions. It seemed plausible but needed to be tested.

One of the clients we met with was in the pharmaceutical industry. They were potential providers of clinical trial and other data we wanted to include in the medical version of Watson. We met with their CEO and most of their top executives. As we described our vision, they were fascinated by the notion that Watson would learn and propagate knowledge across the industry. We sold this idea as a vehicle to generate interest and demand for new drugs. Once Watson had been trained on how that drug could be used and on all the clinical trial data it would begin generating recommendations for the drug. After lots of questions the CEO finally blurted out "you mean Watson will study our data and then use that to make drug recommendations?" We affirmed that was the vision. He turned to one of his team and whispered, "we have to stop this. We can't let this happen." I doubt he knew we had overheard his comment. It was quite telling. Needless to say, they never agreed to share any of their data with us.

The other aspect of the vision was that we would at least partially shield clients from the actual operational costs by putting as much as possible into the IBM owned cloud instance. Costs were still a central concern. We knew they would come down, but we had no idea by how much or over what timeframe. It was quite possible we were going to need to absorb some of those costs for an extended period. That didn't bother us at all, but we didn't want our clients having to confront the problem.

The cost concerns made us focus on use cases with the greatest financial leverage we could find. We believed that even if the costs never came down very far we could still generate enough value that we could come up with a business model that would work. This led us to investigate the healthcare space and the financial services/hedge fund space. The Research team had been doing their own tests on healthcare problems, so we already had a partially trained corpus. The finance industry solution would need to start from scratch.

We began selecting clients for interviews. This process was unlike anything any of us had seen. Instead of us having to recruit clients, we needed to decide who we were going to have to disappoint. They all wanted to be the first. None of them really knew what they would be signing up for, and few of them cared. We knew this was going to be a longer and harder process than they were anticipating so we were careful to try and manage expectations. At least one of the health insurance clients we picked announced that outcome to all their members and their board of directors. This was big news.

By the end of the first year we had made enough progress getting the business organized, finding initial clients, and setting up milestones that we decided to move Watson out of its "incubation" mode and into a line organization in the software group. This next phase was dominated by cleaning up the offering to make it actually viable in a commercial context. The oddball code scattered throughout was replaced by standard IBM commercial code. Those all came with associated tooling and support modules. A major milestone was when we were able to implement workable error recover methods and tools.

The team had grown substantially. Instead of the two dozen people we had started with we now had hundreds of technical resources that were rapidly climbing the Watson learning curve. We had lost a few of the original team, including the overall leader, David Ferrucci. That loss was disappointing, but overall, we felt pretty good about our skill retention and development.

The best news was that costs were dropping faster than even our most optimistic projection. This opened up all kinds of new potential use cases. We no longer needed to rely on curing cancer to create enough value to cover our costs. We had solutions under way for Watson to help make recommendations for wealth advisors in the banking industry. We were actually looking at solutions in call centers. These were obviously very low-cost operations. These use cases were only made possible by the dramatic drop in Watson's operational costs.

We also had a much better understanding of the things Watson was going to need as the business expanded. There were a number of very specific capabilities we had identified which became the "shopping list" for potential acquisitions. We met with many different potential targets and acquired a small handful, each of which brought a particular capability we needed. One of them was a small company called Alchemy that built their own extensive library of AI functions. They had tracked Watson's progress intimately and were eager to add their assets to the growing pool.

The biggest need, which unfortunately was not progressing, was access to the right training data for Watson on the right terms. Lots of discussions had been initiated, but almost none were closing, and most were headed in unproductive directions. We spoke with companies that had the copyrights on textbooks used in medical schools all over the country. We wanted to use those textbooks to help train Watson. A fair amount of work would be needed to annotate and mark-up the texts, they would then need to be edited and converted into workable cases that could be used as training data. At a minimum, we were happy to pay a license fee for access to the textbooks. In a best-case scenario, we would work with them, their authors and editors in a collaborative process to reshape the text in ways that would be more practical for machine learning training.

Every publisher loved this thought. And, then they got dollar signs in their eyes. They began to demand royalties on all future sales of Watson. They were happy to scope their demands only to the domain they were helping to train, but they expected a share of all Watson sales in that domain. Even if all they provided was the raw text with no partnership on the actual usage of that material for training they demanded royalties. Most of those demands were impossible to meet. There were similar demands from the periodicals and journals that published the most recent findings and materials. Data sourcing and training was clearly becoming a larger hurdle than we had expected.

Every client we dealt with had their own data as well. They were particularly keen on having their unique data be used to train their specific instance of Watson. They were also crystal clear that all machine learning from those instances would be owned by them, not us. Every client engagement had to start from scratch. It also meant that the vast majority of the potential value was at risk of slipping from our grasp. If IBM owned little to none of a "trained" system, then IBM didn't own the value, it just owned the tools to create it.

There's a particularly ironic aspect to all of this. There were literally hundreds of data sources used in the original Watson. However, far and away the primary source was, and to some degree still is, Wikipedia. I well remember when my step daughter was in middle and high school that the local school policy was to forbid students from using Wikipedia as a source. It's a common policy all over the US. The reasoning at the time was the untrustworthy aspect of publicly edited content. I argued with the school that rather than banning Wikipedia, I'd prefer they taught students to recognize entries that looked suspicious. I wanted them to teach the importance of checking multiple sources and applying good judgement. Here we had Watson relying heavily on Wikipedia, simply because it created few licensing burdens. It's an example of how access to open data can be a critical enabler of these emerging technologies. It's also a caution on the need to ensure the quality of those sources.

This backdrop set the stage for the third phase of Watson's evolution which was to shift to a cloud-based platform strategy. In this vision, IBM would provide access to all the underlying tooling used to create Watson. Anybody who wanted to use those tools could use them to create their own Watson-based, learning system. The domain they chose and data they used to train the system would be completely up to them. The revenue and profits associated with whatever they created would be theirs as well. They would simply pay a fee for the access and usage of the Watson capabilities. Since those were based on the IBM cloud which still didn't have a workable billing system it meant you could use them basically for free, though we were clear that eventually that would change.

Lots of people, teams, universities and companies had fun playing in the AI sandbox IBM provided. Few if any were aiming at any substantial commercial opportunity let alone actually on a track to build such volumes. A close inspection of the API's would also reveal that most of them actually came from Alchemy or one of our other acquisitions. The original Watson code base was somewhat difficult to render into general purpose API's.

Meanwhile the underlying capabilities of Watson were still advancing. A major focus was the construction of systems that could ingest and understand images. Needless to say, the medical industry is filled with X-Rays, MRI's and other visually oriented data. None of this had been needed to win Jeopardy, but there was no way to achieve our intended objectives in medicine without a robust capability to understand image based diagnostic information. Having learned how awkward it was to find workable content licenses, the team also set out to acquire a pair of companies that would address that aspect of the problem. The acquisition of Explorys finally gave us a solid foundation of medical data directly owned by IBM. Truven complemented that with the largest repository of medical image data. We now had a solid foundation of both data and tools for the medical opportunities we were pursuing.

At this stage, many years had passed since the original Jeopardy win. Progress had been made with many, though not all clients. In all cases, it was taking far too long for clients to see the benefits they were counting on. We were still finding it extremely difficult to develop offerings that could be replicated and scaled across clients. There had been no progress on the original vision of a federated learning model across instances of Watson. Yet, despite these difficulties, there was still an incredible appetite in the market for all things Watson.

One of the strategic issues we had debated from the earliest days was just how much to leverage Watson as a brand. We had no doubt the brand itself was powerful. There was a temptation to make everything "Watson," even though we all knew that risked destroying everything that made that brand so powerful in the first place. The stories of rabid client interest were still quite prevalent. Certainly not like the early days, but Watson as a brand still carried an aura IBM cherished even though we struggled to deliver.

The first cracks in the dam occurred when we did an internal organization change that pulled a number of initiatives together under the umbrella of "Cognitive Solutions." Most of those had nothing at all to do with Watson. In fact, the basic structure and types of data used in many of them had little to no basis in modern AI, nor was it even possible to use with Watson. It was just a matter of time, however, before everything from that group would carry the Watson brand.

Broken Pillars of the Temple

The Rometty era has clearly been problematic. The core business has been allowed to erode. It's debatable whether that erosion could have been avoided or slowed with more aggressive investment. The new imperatives have been clearly selected, identified and funded. However, they have all struggled with execution and their ability to close the revenue gaps created by the eroding core have consistently fallen short. There has been ample pressure and urgency from senior leaders and enormous amounts of time and effort expended from across the company and all over the world. Yet the results keep falling short. I've pointed out some of the specific issues with each of the imperatives. However, there are also deep issues with several of the core pillars of the company. These issues are all linked to the need to adapt to the changes in the marketplace.

If there was a single tap root that has fed IBM's success since its founding, it would probably be its sales organization with its attendant culture and client relationships. As often happens when there's a paradigm shift in value, many of the core strengths of this organization have fallen out of step with what's important. As we've noted several times in this book, IBM's primary relationships with most of its clients are with the IT organization. When IBM sales representatives think about the needs of their clients and how to position the value of their proposals they think about IT. Many, if not most, actual IBM proposals are centered heavily on cost savings in technology and related support activities. When these same individuals attend a conference to enhance their skills or participate in social activities its almost always in the context of IT.

The new imperatives IBM is pursuing all have roots in technology. However, the ability to identify the value of these initiatives is almost completely rooted in improvements to the client's core business. Furthermore, this value is almost always industry specific and requires business creativity and insight. IBM does have individuals with those skills, but they are few and far between. IBM rarely has any significant presence at events in industries other than technology. IBM's thought leadership always begins with a technology and then seeks examples where that can apply to a business rather than the other way around. What this generation of imperatives actually needs are sales people who start from a business issue or opportunity and then draw from a range of technologies to craft a creative approach.

IBM knows this and has for years. There has been some progress. Many of the acquisitions in the healthcare space have brought in these types of skills. Similarly, in the field of digital marketing there have been a number of acquisitions focused on the business and creative skills IBM has lacked. None of this has yet delivered at the scale IBM needs.

One of the other major characteristics of the IBM sales organization is its focus on large transactions. IBM sellers are "big game hunters." The culture is centered on the celebration of winning large deals. As we described in both the cloud and analytics sections, what is needed now are "farmers" who plant seeds and then grow them systematically over time. It's hard to overstate how radically different these two sales cultures are from each other.

My first awareness of this schism happened very early in my career when I was a young Systems Engineer assigned to a large account. It was November and we had a mainframe sale scheduled to ship and install in December. I was working day and night on all the plans related to this installation. I was in charge of the weekly briefing for the branch manager on our status. It was my singular focus and the only thing anybody anywhere in management wanted to talk about. The lead marketing representative on the team was a grizzled old veteran who had been selling computers for IBM since the 1960s. I came across him one day poring over a large printout and asked him what is was all about. He showed me the listing which was our backlog of other transactions for the rest of the year. It was nearly a hundred pages of tiny little items like printers, copiers and terminals. I couldn't understand why he was spending so much time on such trivial items particularly when nobody else seemed to care about them. His answer was simple. He showed me the total at the end of the printout. It was double the size of the mainframe sale I was working on. The mainframe sale would generate recognition and probably an award, but it was all the little items that would actually make our numbers for the year. After two highly successful decades in sales, he knew what was important even if seemingly nobody at any level of the management around us did.

The other critical institution in IBM is Research. Other than Bell Labs at AT&T, IBM Research is one of the only commercial research organizations that funds basic research in pure science and mathematics. The organization can boast of six Nobel Prizes, 19 National Medals of Technology, and five National Medals of Science to name just a few of its honors. Almost every major technology at the core of the IT industry can trace its roots to IBM Research. Watson is a fantastic example of how IBM Research has contributed to the new imperatives. Unfortunately, it might be the only example.

In the area of cloud, research has offered very little. The people with skills and knowledge about systems and servers have traditionally thought very little about how those boxes get assembled in a functioning infrastructure which is at the heart of the cloud innovations. IBM researchers invented almost all of the key technologies around data management. Yet, they have offered very little insight on analytics. The core issue for both analytics and mobile is that the most valuable innovations from those technologies require industry and business skills. These are not strengths of IBM's research organization. In fact, many of the business ideas they bring forth are so naïve they can be painful to even discuss.

ROMETTY SUMMARY

Lurking over all of this was a gradual erosion of the cultural core of the business. The values we had originally developed under Sam had weakened substantially.

Some of this can be laid at his feet, but Ginni was responsible for her share as well. Ginni's personal embodiment of the commitment to client success was enormous. However, down in the trenches, the number and frequency of delivery problems in services were not healthy signs. The relative importance Ginni placed on personal loyalty was also having subtle impacts on the value of personal trust. All large organizations have politics and fiefdoms. Under Ginni, many of these took on a personal dimension that was corrosive. Ginni's lack of experience in managing development, coupled with numerous bad examples like PureSystems, had led to an almost perverse attitude toward organic development. Ginni had reached a stage where almost any acquisition would take priority over any internal development efforts. We were no longer comfortable being the source of "innovation that mattered." Our leaders still talked about it, but rarely backed that with the resources needed to make it real.

What has not eroded is IBM's passion to make a difference in the world. When people choose to work at IBM they almost always do so out of a desire to have an impact on things that matter. IBM's unique raison d'etre is its ability to help large companies, governments and institutions tackle the hardest problems and largest opportunities. It was IBM that teamed with NASA to put men on the moon. It was IBM that developed the first workable airline reservation systems. Watson really is being used to help cure cancer. These are definite points of pride for IBMers all over the world.

The business has been making some progress as well. The Strategic Imperatives have been growing strongly for several years and will soon reach a size that could move the whole company. Frankly, if IBM had been able to stabilize the core parts of the business to avoid their erosion the entire recent history might have been written differently. Unfortunately, many of the deeper skill and cultural issues continue to persist. Business skills and creativity remain scarce. The core conceptual understanding that cloud services are more than the sum of their parts is still absent from the senior team. Big game hunting continues to dominate the sales culture. The crucial growth markets of China and India remain in low gear. The problems are deep and widespread, but they are also solvable. The challenge for this generation of leadership is to step out of the financial driven mind-set and get back to what really matters in the market.

STRATEGY: THE
MODERN FRONTIERS

THERE'S AN APOCRYPHAL Chinese curse that says, "may you live in interesting times." The current world of business strategy certainly fits both the literal and implied meanings of that phrase. The technology industry is going through another one of its paradigm shifts. In addition to the impact on that industry, it is also opening up wide ranging and powerful new sources of competitive advantage in every other industry. Clean energy, battery, and electric vehicle technologies are also reaching important inflection points. Genetic data capture and analysis has become enormously powerful and economically viable for widespread usage. The global business phenomena we've discussed in the IBM chapters has reached the point where it is becoming a driving factor in many industries and product categories. The combination of all these trends will reshape the economic landscape in more ways than any of us can fathom.

Every aspect of the strategic business design template we've been discussing is now open for substantial overhaul. Mobile and data technologies are enabling far more sophisticated market analysis, targeting and service delivery capabilities. The rise of China and India to economic parity with the US, Germany and Japan has dramatically expanded the range of potential markets. That same trend will bring new competitors, just as we described in the IBM experience around the Indian service providers. All of these new markets and segments will offer new opportunities for value creation and new challenges.

The very nature of the value propositions that will lead in the future are under-going substantial shifts. Later in this section we will introduce the notion of competing on "experiences." This is an area that has been forecasted and discussed by strategists for well over a decade and is now becoming a practical reality. Predictive insights from data and the emergence of artificial intelligence are enabling the identification and creation of value in ways that might have seemed like science fiction only a few years ago. Most of this book has focused on information technologies, but it's worth noting that the world of electric vehicles is ready to emerge from its "innovator stage" cocoon and promises an incredible range of as yet untapped design and capabilities to explore. Similarly, clean energy and battery technologies have reached points where they're ready to begin playing ever increasing roles.

Almost every conceivable offering from every industry will have a digital element somewhere in its makeup. Even today, many auto mechanics will tell you they spend more time using an IPad or some other electronic diagnostic aid than they do a wrench. More and more companies that used to make all their money on products are now deploying associated services. Just as IBM experienced in the computing industry, these services will grow and, in many instances will become the primary source of value capture. The digital world has also whole-heartedly embraced the principles IBM pioneered around the use and leverage of free and open-source technologies. This distribution of free and open technologies has created an ocean of open-source software and data that every modern business can and must exploit. Failure to do so risks competitive obsolescence.

The combination of global developments and reductions in transaction costs, have enabled every input factor and operational process to be open for new sourcing possibilities. The business design "scoping" decisions can be much leaner than ever before. Every business is becoming a virtual network of participants. In many cases those participants will come from literally the other side of the world. Businesses are not defined by their boundaries. They are defined by their connections and those have no discernable "edges."

Finally, the strategic design elements that enable sustained competitive advantage are becoming more and more dependent on unique intellectual property. This is creating new stresses on the global world of IP law which is already in serious need of a substantial overhaul. The critical assets of the future are increasingly digital. They include data, insights, and trained artificial intelligence systems, none of which have traditionally been thought of as "central." These technology frontiers are all now at a stage where every business needs to begin incorporating them in their strategies.

Amidst all this globalization and technology driven change there's another monster iceberg looming. The tip of this iceberg is quite evident in many sectors of IT, but there are signs it goes much deeper. Simply put, as offerings become more mature and as their economic life-spans increase, their value to customers begin to evolve. This is another of those value shifts that can be so disruptive to incumbents, so it's important to understand and track.

I will illustrate this with a couple of examples, starting with a hypothetical word processing software package. When someone buys the first release of that package it gives them great value. The next release may have several new features and improved stability, making it an easy sell as well. After a while, the software becomes pretty mature. By this I mean, the features most of the market wants are all in place and the code is perfectly stable. When new releases focus on something like spelling correction in Swahili it may well be valuable, but only to very specific segments. Most of the market won't care. When the provider must resort to new releases that offer something like "Japanese to Swahili language translation for Haiku poetry" you're well past the point of diminishing returns. Since digital assets don't wear out, this means at some point the market stops buying even though it still has enormous value. There's just no value in buying "more" of it. What also happens during the course of this evolution is that all of the competitive alternatives tend to converge on essentially similar capabilities. This exact pattern has already happened in many sectors of the software industry.

Non-digital goods obviously work a bit differently. They do eventually wear out and need replacement. However, the whole globe has been working on six sigma quality improvements for decades and the economic life span of many hard goods has become quite long. An automobile with 100,000 miles on it used to be nearing the end of its useful life. These days with reasonable maintenance it might be only half or even a third of the way. Tesla asserts their Model 3 is designed to last a million miles with one or two battery pack replacements. Even if the original buyer of an auto decides to move on, the car itself will enter a well-established used marketplace where it will find ample buyers. In fact, the markets of used, refurbished, and consigned items which used to be filled with rubbish are now primary sources of top quality goods. Counterintuitively, this is particularly true at the high end of the market where the inherent quality of the original item enables this extended life.

These trends are triggering the exploration of creative new business ideas. Most of these are aimed at creating an enduring "subscription" model of some sort. The idea is to separate the value capture from the item itself, but the trick is to ensure the value also resides at least partially in the subscription. In the digital realm, there are plenty of consumers happy to subscribe to a music service that allows access to nearly unlimited songs instead of buying each one. Nobody has yet found a formula quite as successful as that for digital books but it's not for a lack of effort. In autos, Porsche recently introduced a "subscription" service for their autos. For a regular annual fee, you can draw from a variety of vehicles, basically on demand. If I want a sports car for the weekend I just pick it up. If I want to shift to a sedan on Monday morning, I can do so. When I'm ready for a long road trip I can take a big SUV. The subscriber gets access to multiple vehicles that they can use whenever they choose.

I do not see these as just entertaining examples. I believe they're rooted in a deep shift in value that will play out over several generations. The era of "planned obsolescence" is far behind us. The distinctive value in more and more categories are rooted in digital assets with nearly unlimited economic life spans. As more and more of those assets are based on machines that learn they will evolve as value evolves. Paradoxically, the very fact of the enduring nature of modern "things" means that more and more value must come from their ephemeral surroundings.

We're at a new frontier in business strategy. Every key business design element is in the midst of substantial technologic and global transformation. The three most common causes of strategic derailment are all in play everywhere in ever industry and every geography. Value shifts are already under way and will accelerate. Innovation pipelines are more important and more encompassing than at any time in recent history. And, as we've noted more than once, it's still critical to maintain your core business amidst all the excitement.

IP–Building on the Shoulders of Giants

There's a famous phrase from Isaac Newton that says, "If I have seen further it is by standing on the shoulders of giants." That phrase captures an important aspect of modern business in general, for intellectual property, and particularly for digital IP. The modern world is incredibly complex. Innovations occur throughout the globe and throughout the supply chains that encircle the globe. Every business seeks these out and must do so to remain competitive. We are constantly using and building on the innovations from the past and from others all around us. And, more and more of those valuable innovations are coming from China.

In the world of software, an amazing phenomenon has happened over the last 20–25 years. The open-source movement which was considered highly controversial in the mid to late 1990s is now simply part of the modern economic fabric. The starting point for any software project now includes a review of the available open-source components relevant to the project. The resulting inventory could easily comprise well over half, if not three quarters, of the total code needed. Some of that open-source material may be rarely used and of questionable quality. However, the components with heavy usage will almost always be robust and will provide solid foundations on which to build. The fact that mature software requires little to no maintenance and never degrades, has turned age-old sourcing assumptions on their heads. Far from a "tragedy," the digital commons has become an amazingly rich reservoir of incredibly valuable resources. As more and more businesses increase their reliance on digital assets and services this is becoming a major "invisible force" shaping our businesses and economies.

Those same 20–25 years have been among the most tumultuous in the history of intellectual property in general. The emergence of "perfect copies" through the digital realm has challenged the basic foundations of copyright-based businesses. Setting aside the open-source phenomena, the incredible dynamics of the software industry overall has raised issues around the role of patents on software. The sheer possibility of patenting business methods when embodied in software, has become a substantive debate. As analytics grows in importance, basic algorithms and mathematical constructions have become critically important business assets that beg for protections.

Amid this turmoil, we have all watched as the music and publishing industries flail about damaging themselves, their partners and their clients in the process. An entire industry category of "patent trolls" has emerged. Unscrupulous companies have tricked standards groups into accepting technologies with hidden patents enabling rapacious licensing models. Emerging markets have ignored or violated IP rights pervasively. Much of this has been "off stage"—of interest to those in the middle of the turmoil but not top of mind for most.

These are stresses on a system of laws that are in many ways hopelessly out of date. The basic provisions for patents and copyrights were established in the early 17th and 18th centuries, respectively. Both sets of laws are intended to create a legal framework to incent the creation and advancement of innovations. In the case of patents, the basic social contract is the granting to an inventor of a limited monopoly in return for sufficiently specific disclosure that will enable usage by anyone after the expiration of the monopoly period. The inventor is able to capitalize on their monopoly while it lasts. Other inventors and society as a whole will gain unlimited access to the invention once the monopoly is over. That's the essence of the deal. With some tweaks and refinements every few decades or so, the system has held up reasonably well over its first few hundred years. However, that is no longer the case.

To unpack the deeper issues on this topic let me first describe a few of the key foundations of current IP law. The first point is that "facts" and "natural laws" are not subject to either copyright or patents. Knowing the mass of the earth and Newton's physical law of gravity is valuable, but not IP that can be owned by any entity. If nobody else has calculated the mass of the earth, I can keep that a secret, but once it's out in public I have no protection for that data. If I create a Fancy Tee-Shirt with a creative picture of earth, a falling apple, and Newton's formula, that "expression" can be copyrighted. However, the protection is just for the creative picture, not the concepts it represents. Anybody else is free to create their own expression, using the same elements. If I invented a method and tool that precisely "snipped" the stem of a young apple in such a way that when it fully ripens the force of gravity alone will cause it to fall from the tree, that could be patented. The key underlying elements of the invention rely on data about the mass of the earth, of ripening apples, and the application of Newtons law, none of which can be patented even though my hypothetical invention can be.

In the last few decades it has become increasingly difficult for those few categories to deal with contemporary realities. The rising importance of software and the associated IP rules illustrates the problem. Copyright alone is insufficient to encompass the scope of innovative value coming from software. Conversely, allowing patenting of every piece of unique software could violate the basic principles of patent law prohibiting patents on mathematics or natural laws. Application software that is basically an encoded representation of a business process, may or may not be innovative and worthy of protection. This confusion led to an explosion of software and business method patent filings many of which eventually needed to be rescinded. The current rules for software have evolved through a series of precedent setting decisions that have helped clarify many situations, however there remain an enormous number of gray areas. This situation is about to become much worse.

One of the emerging IP issues that is increasingly complex and fraught with uncertainties is around data. The commercial world has realized that the data in their possession is a potentially highly valuable business asset. Companies are careful to treat this data as confidential and to take security measures to prohibit unauthorized access. From an IP standpoint, that's equivalent to treating data as a trade secret. That worked fine when the data being protected was something like a 19th century merchant knowing a secret trade route or when Coke protected their secret recipe. For today's world of data, it's a model that is fraught with problems at many levels. The most basic issue is that the value of data is only realized when it is used, and the basic process of using that data will often include its disclosure, which makes secrecy problematic if not impossible. Furthermore, when data is used to train a modern AI system it becomes an inseparable component of the invention itself. One could argue the innovations in those systems derive as much from the training materials and processes as any piece of software.

In some ways, the deepest most fundamental breakdown can be traced simply to the era when these laws were originally developed. There are still examples of the solitary inventor in their garret, but those are rare birds and should not be the central assumption behind our legal structures. Ideas and inventions do come from individuals, but they almost always arise out of their collaboration with others and almost always include elements of ideas and inventions from others. As we've discussed elsewhere, innovation is much more of a collaborative process than a solitary "eureka" moment. There are contributions to the final results coming from participants throughout the process. Adding to the challenge, those participants may live and work anywhere in the world. This is part of the incredibly messy backdrop behind trade conflicts with China which will be covered in much more detail in a subsequent chapter. Finally, it's worth noting that even those inventions that can be cleanly attributed to a single individual are almost always owned by the company that employs them. The notion that patent laws act to protect the economic interests of solitary inventors is basically historical fiction.

DATA–A PRIMARY STRATEGIC ASSET

One of Ginni Rometty's favorite phrases describing this new era is "data is the new gold." It's a tricky phrase. The notion that data has substantial value, like gold, is completely accurate. So too, is the notion that data is a particularly valuable raw material. Unlike gold, whose use as a raw material is fairly limited, the uses for data seem unlimited and nearly universal. Also unlike gold, data is something where the value only exists when it's used. Even while it demands security, it's not something to hide in a safe.

In the modern digital economy, data is emerging as one of the principle sources of competitive advantage. Even companies that don't think of themselves as "digital" are beginning to discover that the same can be true for them. For data to realize its potential value it has to be actionable. For those actions to be competitively unique, the data, or more often the insights derived from the data, must be unique. Which is why my catch phrase is to focus on "actionable insights." The second key is scale. As we will discuss in the next section, one of the most important emerging uses for data is the training of machine learning systems. These systems all improve as the volume of data available for training increases. In that domain, size matters.

Most companies start their data journey with a focus on improving marketing and/or sales. The basic assertion is that better targeting will yield a higher response rate which yields higher sales results. It's obvious, intuitive … and, not quite true. The dirty secret of marketing is that almost all of the complex targeting analytics companies like Google tout produce actual response rates that are not significantly better than the archaic methods used by direct mailers looking at nothing more than magazine subscriptions. The actual big marketing improvement over those old methods is simply reaching a larger audience so that the total volume of responses is higher even though the *response rate* is no better. It seems clear that better insights on targeting, while a necessary step, are not sufficient.

Improved targeting may not be enough, but it still is where everyone starts. To better understand how the value of data is evolving beyond simple targeting we need to examine the various means used to assemble data, how that data is managed, and how it is used. I will illustrate the stages by describing how a hypothetical apple selling web commerce company might proceed.

Let's begin at the point where a consumer comes to the company website and decides to sign up as a customer as part of their first purchase of apples. When that happens, the company will collect data entered by you about your name, address, and credit card. At the same time, they will capture data about which apples you bought, what day you bought them, when they were promised to ship to you and how much you paid. You may not have given those details any thought, but it certainly is no surprise and would not bother you that they have done so. Unbeknownst to you, at the same time they've gathered this data openly, they've also examined your PC or phone and logged every other site you've visited, as well as when you did so. They've also logged key identifiers about your other devices so they can "follow you" no matter which of your devices you happen to be using. You may or may not care about this, but you are certainly not aware of it nor its extent.

At this point the company knows enough about you and how to reach you that they can begin placing simple ads on web pages you visit from your phone or PC. There's a fair amount of insight they can glean from your web visiting behavior, they know you made at least one purchase from them and what that was and they know how to find you. They use this to improve their targeting and to decide what offers to provide you and when.

The company has now begun to build a profile about you. In the next phase of our example the company goes out and licenses data from a number of third parties. The data may include general demographic information, statistical data about apple buyers, data about where you live, data about the seasonable weather patterns in your area and hundreds of other factors. We did a study at one point in IBM where we looked at the data warehouses we had built for over a dozen different companies. On average those projects involved integrating over 200 external data sources. When our fictional company licensed all that data there was nothing that explicitly "connected" any of that data to you. Establishing all those "connections" across all these sources is work done by this fictional company or, more likely, by a analytical services organization they have hired. This profile now has a great deal more data about you than what was present in your initial moment of purchase.

This is the point where the basic targeting can start to get much more sophisticated. It starts simply by having a richer set of data about you. That probably includes some amount of financial data as well as a great deal more demographic data. The company's segmentation analysis will be much better grounded and more likely to have relevance. Some of those external sources may have included Facebook, Twitter, Instagram or other social media companies. That data is noisy and notoriously difficult to analyze. They may also have included a great deal more geographic data from your cell phone. These are the kinds of sources that provide both contextual insights as well as "signals" that can be used to trigger actions.

The company's analysts begin looking for patterns across all the data that will be useful for the promotion of their apple sales. Let's imagine they discover that clear, sunny autumn days increase the likelihood of apple buying in the area where you live. They may also discover that apples show up in pictures you posted to Facebook about a recent picnic. The combination of weather related context and the inclusion of apples in your picnic basket gives our company opportunities that go beyond a simple ad placement. Many upscale hotels in leisure destinations will often put together picnic baskets for their guests. Our fictional apple seller now has enough insight to begin exploring partnerships with grocery stores to promote picnics on autumn days with baskets that always include apples. These promotions will build on and use the targeting from the earlier stages but are now enriched with a potentially more compelling offering. This is obviously a hypothetical example, but we will describe an entire emerging class of strategies that follow this basic pattern in a later chapter.

In the world of data, for the example above, both you and the apples you bought, the "nouns," are referred to as "entities." The weather and picnic observations are referred to as "events." A key part of transforming simple data into a strategic asset is to connect entities and events both within a given data source and across data sources.

This connection process is technically challenging. One data source may refer to me as "Joel Cawley," while another uses "Cawley, Joel" while another uses "jcawley." Sometimes these are predictable variants. Sometimes they reflect simple misspellings or coding errors. Sometimes they may be deliberate attempts to camouflage my identity. There are similar challenges with the "apple" entity. Some sources may be referring to the fruit while others are about the company. Some sources may use more specific names like "Gala," or "Golden Delicious." The tools used to understand that these two terms are members of the apple family are called taxonomies and can be extremely complex. One of IBM's early acquisitions in support of Watson was Blekko, a company with extensive taxonomy libraries. The ability to distinguish between a gala "event" and a gala "apple" often requires some understanding of the context.

Data professionals have known for years that there is great potential value when multiple sources can be combined. Most companies focused on just merging data from across all their internal sources. Banks would like to realize that the bank account, credit card, and mortgage you carry with them are all related to "you." The industry went through a phase several years ago where many companies launched projects to achieve this integration. At the time, these were referred to as Master Data Management projects, or MDM. Many, if not most, of these failed. The problem was that everyone believed that if a little integration was valuable then integrating everything would be even more valuable. However, company databases contain a lot more than just entity and event data. A record that has an identifier for your name may also contain hundreds of other fields of data, some of which may only relate to internal processing needs. That same dataset may be joined with other internal sources increasing the data by orders of magnitude. The early MDM projects tried to match and reconcile all of this. The complexity quickly spiraled out of control.

One of the major developments enabling the creation of strategic assets out of the explosion of data are the technologies and methods that address these challenges. Entity analytics tools have become extremely powerful, capable of addressing both inadvertent as well as deliberate attempts at confusion. Companies all over the world have constructed taxonomies across countless industries and categories. These technical advances have made it possible to construct extensive collections of data with explicit entity and event connections. Companies have also learned to only go beyond that stage when a specific use case requires it. Many of the big data and machine learning tools won't actually need any additional structure. That makes it possible for individual companies to build these strategic data assets. It also is making it possible for multiple companies to exchange data to reach levels of scale that would otherwise seem impossible.

One of the more prosaic drivers behind the need to connect all this data is the reality of the quality of any individual source. Many data sources are quite incomplete and sparse. There may be numerous errors and / or inconsistencies between sources. Some data sources have great data, but its embedded in a ton of "noise" that must be filtered out. This latter problem is pervasive in the world of social media. When a company is able to combine data from lots of sources these issues can often be surfaced and either ameliorated or avoided.

Reaching beyond the simple entity data to include related entities and events like our picnic example, can be extremely valuable because it is almost always the case that data must be put in context to be of real value. In some cases, this is simply through the comparison to a reference or benchmark. The more interesting examples are based on your immediate context. For example, if I tell you it's 50 degrees Fahrenheit outside you have a piece of data. That simple metric in and of itself may be of very little value. If I also tell you it's the middle of summer in south Florida, you will know people will be wearing heavy coats and complaining. They will have no interest in picnics. On the other hand, if I tell you it's the middle of winter in New England you know people will be outside in shorts and tee-shirts tossing a ball or going for a walk and might well be up for a picnic.

The absolute temperature was important to know, but its interpretation was highly dependent on its context. What this example also illustrates is that the contextual factors often have an immediacy that requires nearly constant tracking in order to trigger some sort of action. This is a very common situation. The data you intend to use as a signal for a business action can only be triggered if it is connected to all of the relevant and immediate contextual information. It may seem like the signal is what you care about most, but absent the context, the signal itself can be useless.

In our hypothetical example, we assumed the company sold to consumers using a website. Part of the power of that model of commerce is the ease with which useful data can be assembled. For businesses that don't fit that profile the data gathering step may be a bit more complicated, but it's still a crucial first step. Every company should have an explicit strategy for the assembly and connection of data about their customers.

One of the biggest challenges to this process historically has been the intermediation of sales and distribution channels. Typically, it is those firms that are positioned to capture the customer data and they will usually be very reluctant to share. Companies can often circumvent this problem by creating and delivering some sort of digital service to the end customer. Even when those services offer little in the way of direct revenues, their strategic value as a means to engage customers and gather data can be considerable.

In the world of B2B the situation can be even more complex. Companies themselves are rarely single entities. Much more often there's actually a need to create a taxonomy of entities spanning all the internal organizational and functional structures of a business. The data gathering is also frequently more problematic. Companies will routinely refuse to allow access to the kinds of business metrics that would be most valuable for the establishment of performance benchmarks.

One of the most important tools to overcome all of these issues is to instrument everything possible. Even in a B2B context, instrumenting and metering to enable maintenance and other services will almost always be allowed. More importantly, the instrumentation will generate vastly more operational data than any of the pure transaction oriented sources. This is rapidly becoming one of the primary use cases for the Internet of Things (IoT) deployments.

Most of the focus for these discussions has been on customer insights. However, the principle of "instrument everything" applies far beyond customer data alone. Every operational process should be examined for opportunities to capture and collect detail data from IoT based instrumentation. That data gathering process should also consider the relevant contextual data. Weather is a classic example of contextual data that frequently is a major driver of retail sales, or maintenance intervals for anything located outdoors. When the weather data itself isn't available to your instruments, capturing date, time, latitude and longitude will enable you to combine your data with external weather data sources.

An area of considerable potential importance as well as one loaded with potential issues is geo-tracking data. With the advent of modern phones with embedded GPS systems it is now possible to track people 24 hours a day, seven days a week, and 365 days a year. It's not just possible. It's happening right now. Every mobile phone service does this today with no permission request or company disclosure. Mobile phone applications have the ability to tap into this stream of data as well. Fortunately, right now the accepted paradigm for mobile apps is to request permission from the user to track their movements. Some people routinely allow this and others equally routinely do not. I suspect most people aren't quite sure exactly what they are granting in either case.

One of the mobile applications that users almost always approve for tracking is the weather. We all want to know the weather where we are and an app that keeps track of that just makes sense. What it also means is that entities like The Weather Company have mountains of data that trace the movements of all of their users. This can be amazingly powerful and equally unsettling. I have seen demonstrations by companies who can send text messages to car salesmen telling them that the client sitting across from them, who hasn't even opened their mouth, has been looking at four different vehicles online, checked Autotrader for prices on two of them and just came from the competitors' lot down the street. This isn't some futuristic vision, it's happening right now.

Geotracking has another unexpected attribute. Data scientists have discovered that our routine movement patterns are extremely accurate identification tools. They may not be as distinctive as fingerprints, but they are much easier to capture. This illustrates another deeply vexing problem with consumer data. Most efforts at restricting undesirable data disclosures focus on the existence or absence of Personally Identifiable Information or PII. PII can take many forms including simple names, but also includes things like social security numbers, drivers license numbers, passports and the like. The idea is that companies can collect all the data they want as long as there are no associations with any form of PII.

All the companies involved in these consumer data trends take great pains to follow this practice and regularly assure everyone that they do not store any Personally Identifiable Information. This is more than a little disingenuous. I have personally met with many companies who know what time you get up in the morning, where, when and by what route you go to work in the morning, what you do on your lunch break, when you come home, what TV programs you watch, what websites you frequent, what news sources you rely on, what car you drive, whether you own that car, etc. etc. They can also distinguish between you, your spouse and your children. They have built cloud-based systems that are incredibly capable of combining and integrating data about individuals from thousands of external sources. When they sell all that data to marketers it takes the marketer no time at all to match all that data with your name and whatever customer identifier they use. The theoretically private, non-PII associated, data is in reality an incredibly detailed open book. Just be sure not to tell anyone.

There are other issues with the notion of PII as well. Setting aside secret agents with multiple identities, its actually fairly common for everyday people to have multiple personas. We may use one email, phone and name at work while operating with a completely different email and "handle" on social media, and yet another with close friends and family. As our worlds of work and society get more complex these tendencies are likely to increase. There is obviously an "actual" person behind these three identities, but that person may not want their various identities revealed or connected. What's more, for many use cases the best identity for a company to analyze is the situationally appropriate persona, not the "true" person. It is the relevant context of work, social or family activities that will define the individual's motivations and behaviors.

In addition to the data that has been gathered through all these processes and instrumentation, and all the data that's been licensed from others, there's an entire class of data that arises from a company's own analysis. The most common form of this is the addition of segment identifiers. This need to connect the strategic insights from segmentation analysis with the operational data that drives actual usage has been a chronic problem. Traditionally, the best data for segmentation was impossible to map to operational data and the operational data provided a very poor basis for strategic segmentation. There can still be problems making these connections, but the types of extended and enriched entity and event data I've been describing enables far more effective connections.

The business drivers behind these data trends are incredibly powerful. The technical issues are steadily being overcome. The business potential of the artificial intelligence systems that can be built from the data is unprecedented. However, there are still a number of issues and challenges to be navigated. The most immediate of these are around IP and licensing rights and consumer concerns about privacy and usage. There's also a very uncertain overlap between these two sets of issues. To what degree do consumers get to control how data about them is captured and used? Are they participants, even owners, in the debates about IP and licensing?

Let's start our examination of these issues with the IP fundamentals using our hypothetical apple seller. The basic data collected about you, including all the non-obvious data from your device can be considered as "facts" and therefore not subject to any form of IP ownership. The only protections for this data are confidentiality and secrecy. This creates some immediate issues. Since I shared my basic data with you openly that is an implicit disclosure and therefore cannot be considered secret any longer. The data associated with the sale can also be considered as "disclosed," at least to you. However, I may want all those "facts" kept secret between us. For a long time, companies considered this data as "theirs" and its further disclosure or usage completely at their discretion. That's changing, and most sites these days will have some sort of privacy policy available that lets consumers know what the company will and will not do. From an IP standpoint, the crux of the matter is that these are "trade secrets" whose only protection is confidentiality. What happens when the consumer wants to make this data available to another apple seller? Is that their right, or is it your secret too?

The data hidden on my device may not have been consciously disclosed by me, but for those who know how to find it, it's actually completely public. This lack of awareness means that consumers are unwittingly revealing secrets about themselves every day. Since these would all be considered "facts" their only form of protection is secrecy. When that protection is forfeited by the consumer, companies will simply exploit the data. While consumer awareness about these vulnerabilities is growing, so too are all of the unexpected data sources and unwitting disclosures.

The process of licensing data from companies and then connecting that with your internally gathered sources introduces another set of complexities. Many of the different sources will have licensing restrictions that limit how the data can be used. The limits can be quite complex. There are whole categories of data that cannot be used by business for decisions about issuing credit or loans. Many countries stipulate that data about their citizens must only be housed within their geographies. A common limitation centers on the use of data in aggregate, which might be permitted, while no individually identifiable usage is allowed. The limits may even include what data you are allowed to connect to each other. In the US judicial system there are a number of criminal data sources that prohibit connections with general consumer data, and in healthcare there are similar data usage and disclosure requirements.

For the most part, these realities reflect operational challenges rather than legal ones. However, adhering to the maze of licensing complexities is so onerous that the data industry is notorious for being bogged down in lawsuits. There are many cases where the actual provenance of a piece of data is unclear. If a license has been cascaded through multiple stages, which often happens, the details on usage rights and restrictions need to be maintained and often are not. When errors are discovered at any stage, the process of generating and propagating corrections can be enormously disruptive. What seems like a simple set of terms to administer can easily get out of control as the scale of the data sources and their mutually conflicting terms escalates. And the scale is exploding.

Returning to our example, the discovery of the insights about apple buying behavior might be patentable, as long as they were truly nontrivial and as yet undiscovered. It might seem that these are just other "facts" and not capable of protections. In truth, the resulting output of the analyses probably are "facts" that must be kept secret to be protected. However, the algorithm to generate that output could be a quite complex form of invention, precisely what patents are intended to protect. The question becomes what rights does the company have to license the results of their patented algorithm? To license the "facts" that they alone are able to create. Is that subject to the limits of any of the individual sources of data? If the data about apple consumption has been mathematically subsumed in the algorithm that predicts picnic behavior, is the picnic predictor subject to the apple terms? If the picnic predictor was based on data about apple consumers in Germany, can it be used in North America? It may seem these are academic arguments, but I have personally been in negotiations where all of these issues were important.

When the company begins connecting all their data with the hundreds of external sources this can be considered a form of "expression" that could potentially be protected by copyright. Like our Tee-Shirt example, each source is presumed to be unprotected but the particular collection of sources and the interconnections the company has created between them could be a unique piece of IP. Other companies are free to draw from the same sources and put them together in whatever form they choose, so long as it's not an exact copy of what our apple seller has done. To my knowledge this has never been tested, but it seems like a plausible path based on traditional IP laws.

The massive, interconnected data structures I'm describing are being assembled by thousands of companies all over the world. In the past, these data assemblies were built by companies in the business of selling data. Nowadays many major companies are engaged to some degree in this process. Their primary objective is to make use of the data, not sell it. Very few of these projects have really grappled with the complexities that are lurking. When they do, we may begin to see the kinds of "freedom of action" oriented cross licensing that is routine for technology patents. If the technology industry had not adopted that pragmatic approach, it would not exist as we know it today. Under the right circumstances this could be a similarly tremendous aide to the innovations these companies are trying to pursue. On the other hand, if every company fixates on tight control of their data it could end poorly with a small handful of companies maintaining monopoly or oligopoly control of the primary resource needed by 21st century innovation.

One of the interesting and less visible trends is the growth of "open data." This is data made freely available, usually by governments, with essentially zero licensing issues. The model is similar to the open-source movement in software. As we've discussed, that once controversial practice has now created a vast set of valuable resources. The open data movement has a similar promise. One of the more creative and potentially valuable initiatives under the Obama administration, was the publishing of guidelines urging far greater availability of this kind of data. Essentially, they concluded that anything that could be made available should be made available.

Some of this is new. Some of this has been around for a long time. In the US, the National Oceanic and Atmospheric Administration, has made weather related data and forecasts available for years. This has not prevented the creation of businesses that focus on either enhancing that baseline data or on providing value through distribution and interpretation of that data. In fact, it's the open availability of the NOAA data that makes those businesses viable.

These licensing and usage issues have historically been between companies, but as hinted above will increasingly involve the general public. Those complex structures are not only vulnerable to unintended unlicensed exploitation they are also targets for data thieves. This raises the potential legal exposures significantly. In general, the responsibilities associated with the ongoing stewardship of this data need as much attention as the focus on rights. The lack of legal clarity around these expectations has been and will continue to inhibit its full development.

If the commercial complexities are threatening to spiral out of control, we've barely begun to deal with all the coming consumer issues, particularly around privacy. Many individuals may assume they have some sort of "right to privacy," but the actual legal structures to support that assumption are for the most part narrowly confined to specific types of data, situations or geographies. The EU is actively trying to come to grips with some of the major consumer related issues. Despite several years of work and considerable focus I would describe the overall state of affairs as "nascent." It might seem obvious that at some point we will need to develop a set of principles that at its foundation ensures that each of us is in control of the data about us. However, as we've illustrated in several places, the amount of "hidden" data companies are capturing from mobile devices as well as the growth of IoT applications means that more and more of the devices we encounter every day have embedded data capturing and transmission. As a general rule, in the future no consumer anywhere can be assumed to know all the different hidden data capturing that's occurring all around them. Unintended disclosure will be rampant, implicit and beyond the control of individuals. We're still a very long way from the kind of societal awareness and consensus we will eventually need.

The consumer expectations of a general right to privacy may be currently incorrect from a strict legal perspective, but they are quite real. They are also hard to pin down. Part of the problem is the lack of clarity throughout the market on all the different types of data in play, the potential value of that data, the degree of personal "exposure" associated with that data, and exactly who has what rights and what responsibilities from the outset. Most people would agree they would not want their detailed medical history intermixed with a collection of marketing and sales data. Many, though not all, marketers might agree with that sentiment. However, the medical professionals will tell you they desperately want as much "lifestyle" related data as they can gather to supplement their analyses.

This leads to the next factor which exists for all data but is particularly thorny when it comes to consumer data. What is "truth" and where and how should it apply? This may seem like an issue that's more important for philosophers than business strategists, but in certain situations it's actually pretty important. The first part of addressing this issue is ensuring that the data that has been captured and connected together is accurate. As we noted above, most purchased data sources are rife with errors, omissions and sparse data. It is in every companies interests for this data to be cleansed and rendered as accurate as possible. It's also in the interests of most consumers, most of the time to do the same. But, not always, and therein lies a well-known problem. Consumers are often the best and only entities capable of identifying and correcting inaccuracies about them. When they are so motivated there is no better way to improve the accuracy of your data. When those motivations are in question the path is more complicated. There are legal frameworks and precedents to help with these situations, but in practice this can be a significant issue.

The question of "truth" begins with accuracy, but in many cases, goes further. At the outset we should caution there are severe limits on how far society can go in imposing any standards for truth beyond the accuracy of facts. However, when there are well known patterns of mistaken analysis, and when the application of that faulty analysis can cause material harm, the societal need arises to establish certain base lines.

Every analyst is taught that correlation does not imply causation. Yet this error happens every day. Similarly, popularity or election results do not establish "truth," nor do solemn proclamations by experts. Yet, people behave as if they did every day. Many of these error modes are present in the police practice of "profiling" which obviously has substantial potential for material harm to citizens. Even worse, there is an AI based system known as COMPAS, which is widely used by courts around the US. That system has been shown to consistently recommend longer prison sentences for blacks than whites even when all other data points are equal. These are erroneous assertions of truth with material consequences. At some point, citizens and governments will demand accountability for those consequences.

When these kinds of errors just impact a marketer's targeting accuracy, society does not need to care. If their errors are too egregious they'll just go out of business. The market will take care of it. However, as in the police and medical examples, when there are material societal consequences we do need to establish baselines either on "truths" themselves or acceptable practices toward getting the truth. The easiest example for this is the role the US Food and Drug Administration plays in establishing the "truth" about drugs. The standards they establish and enforce around clinical trial results provide THE independent conclusions for the trials. Complaints about this are persistent and I'm sure there are improvements that could be made to the process. However, some sort of certification process cannot be avoided and the self-interested parties most directly involved cannot be trusted to provide it.

At the other end of the "truth spectrum" is the data coming out of social media. These sources are riddled with "noise" and even the most basic indicators must be used with caution. Probably the most common example is the field of sentiment analysis which attempts to interpret comments as being either positive, negative, or neutral. This might seem simple, but distinguishing trolls and irony is a serious problem. The standard practice is to use something known as "triple encoding" in which three different humans review each comment. This is almost all done by low cost delivery operations out of India, so you can add uncertain language skills into the mix.

Despite these challenges, social media analysis is an important area to explore. These sources are quite rich with observations about people and the endless topics they find interesting. A few years ago, I was sharing a stage with Chris Moody who at the time was the leader of the data group at Twitter. Chris had a rotating globe on the screen with dense flashes of light popping up all over the planet. He asked the audience to guess what those flashes represented. Nobody came close to the truth. What they actually represented was an extended global discussion of soft drinks that Chris had captured a few nights earlier. People never cease to amaze and we truly do live in a global age.

Most of this discussion has centered on the state of the market in the US and to some degree the European Union. As you look around the world it becomes ever more complex and problematic. Some countries have established very strict regimes regarding the handling of data about their citizens. Others, like China, have made it extremely difficult for outside commercial entities to collect and gather any data at all about their citizens even while they amass that same data on an unprecedented scale and scope. There are also restrictions and debates around how citizen data can be shared and moved around the world. While these strategic data structures are often housed in the US or EU, a great deal of the encoding work is actually done in India. The global dimensions of this topic are far from sorting themselves out.

I will close this discussion on consumer data with one additional caution. For the most part, we take for granted that the data we're working on is about individuals. We noted the multiple identities people assume in different contexts, but even in those situations we're still dealing with a person. Unfortunately, we cannot always make that assumption. The reality of automated "bots" surfing the web has been around for a very long time. In recent years, 50%–60% of all the traffic on the web was actually not connected to any human at all. It was just bot traffic. Some of those bots are performing legitimate tasks, but roughly half are malicious.

That problem has become much, much worse. There are now criminal entities in the world that focus on the creation of fake people, fake companies, and fake activities among them. They have been known to spend years creating sufficient traffic across all digital environments that these fake people are very hard to distinguish from an actual person. There have been demonstrations where these fake people have been granted access to US Department of Defense events intended solely for certified contractors solely on the apparent strength of these credentials. These fake entities have unleashed an unprecedented potential for fraud in every industry.

One of the subtler forms of this fraud is to trick search engines and social media sites. These are essentially indistinguishable from real people so all the algorithms that rely on links, referrals, likes and the rest can be manipulated. Those algorithms are incredibly widespread and highly vulnerable to this form of deception. There's an entire field of marketing services known as Search Engine Optimization or SEO. None of the companies I know in that field would use these types of fraudulent methods, but they are all well aware of the potential impacts. We may yet see unscrupulous entities using these fake people to mount "dirty tricks" campaigns against competitors. Absent any specific fraud, it's not at all clear what sort of legal protections might be used against this.

These fake people can also be used to distort political processes. There have been numerous reports on how Russia used some of these tools to amplify differences between factions in the 2016 US elections. Less well known is how pervasive they have become in distorting the "open comment" periods used by public institutions to directly gather information from citizens on proposed policies. In recent studies, there have been tens of thousands to hundreds of thousands of comments provided that were proven to come from fake people or real people whose identities had been stolen. Fake people have unfortunately become real factors in our society.

ARTIFICIAL INTELLIGENCE–MACHINES THAT LEARN

This complex world of interconnected data is just the beginning. It is one of the key foundations for a series of technologies that are poised to transform our societies. The companion pillar is Artificial Intelligence. Yes, it's real. It's probably not what you think, but it is real. The rapidly developing world of AI is creating incredible new opportunities and strategies for business. It creates a new set of conundrums for our beleaguered IP system. It is also opening a wide range of public policy issues for society as a whole.

AI has been through major hype cycles in the past. The modern version is a bit different, with both greater opportunity and several new, unforeseen issues. To understand what's different we need to start with a brief history of the topic. The early versions of AI were often referred to as "expert systems." The basic idea was to interview a collection of experts to capture their insights into a set of "rules." These rules were usually formed as a set of "IF xyz, THEN DO abc." The theory was that if you gathered enough of these rules from the right experts that would generate a system that would behave like they do.

None of those efforts worked very well. Gathering the rules was incredibly laborious. The amount of generic knowledge required was a swamp that needed to be avoided, but often could not be. The resulting systems were "fragile" in that even minor changes to either the problem being solved, or the expert rules frequently resulted in complete breakdowns. The once hyped systems often devolved into simple collaboration tools that did little more than house white papers and host discussions. They had become systems used by experts, not systems that acted like experts.

When IBM's Deep Blue beat Gary Kasparov at chess it was heralded as a major milestone on the journey to "true AI." It certainly was a major accomplishment. The computing world had long wondered when, or even if, a computer could beat a world champion at chess. A great deal of work had gone into its development, capturing volumes of history on opening theory and classic end game situations. In truth however, what it really amounted to was the brute force power possible with leading edge computing at the time. Deep Blue did not "out think" Kasparov, it just looked at thousands more possible moves than any human could imagine.

Deep Blue was important, but not the major breakthrough the field needed to really advance. Meanwhile an entirely different technical approach to AI was slowly making progress. This technique took its inspiration from the structure of neurons in the brain. Neurons take in simple signals from other neurons and, depending on the patterns of those signals, either trigger their own signal or remain quiet. The idea was to electronically simulate such a structure and then connect a number of them into a web. One end of that web would be connected to a set of stimuli, usually from the outside world. The other end would be connected to some particular action, like recognizing a face. A structure like this is referred to as a "neural net."

Once your neural net is set up, the system then needs to be "trained." This involves a process known as "backward propagation" in which the system is "shown" a series of training cases and then allowed to adjust the weights associated with each neural input to get a correct result. After a few thousand such examples, the systematic adjustment of the weights on all the inputs eventually produces a system that behaves as it has been trained.

Systems with this basic design were quickly discovered to be vastly better at recognizing images than any prior method. The training process was also substantially more manageable than the process of trying to interview experts. There were a few issues. More than a few, actually. Training data itself was hard to find, cleanse, and annotate. Then there was the uncomfortable fact that even the best neural net developers often could not quite explain how their systems worked. The systems were statistical in nature. They operated on probabilities, not hard rules. They were "trained" for their task not "coded" for their task. But, they did work and the exploration of both suitable problems as well as a wide range of structural variations has opened a new world for computer science.

Over the last few decades the underlying mathematics and technologies associated with these methods have advanced enormously. Problems like facial recognition were a form of classification system, while problems like movie recommendations were predictive. Each spawned whole libraries of underlying statistical methods designed to ingest and process the relevant data. Analysis of different classes of data revealed their own structures and relationships that became the basis for other modeling techniques and associated libraries. Systems were developed to ingest completely unstructured data, like natural language input. The original version of Watson could ONLY ingest natural language data. A table of statistics actually had to be translated into a series of sentences. The training process itself spawned half a dozen different methods each of which can be tuned or optimized in different ways.

This description is obviously highly simplified, but it allows us to illustrate some of the key aspects of modern AI. All of these systems are designed to learn. The data used to train them is a critical part of the process. The choices of statistical methods, tools and modeling structures are incredibly diverse, reflecting the wide variety of underlying problem structures. The behavior of the resulting system is probabilistic, not deterministic. This last point can make the systems appear more "human," but does not mean they're actually "thinking," at least not as we usually mean when we use that word. It also means they make mistakes.

The excitement is growing because they are making things that were once considered impossible now seem realistic. A well-known example is the development of self-driving vehicles. Setting aside for the moment the question about whether this is desirable it is unquestionably remarkable. Driving a vehicle safely on open, public streets, with no human oversight would have been regarded as an entertaining fantasy not long ago. The challenge of hard coding every possible instance of every situation that occurs on a road is so cumbersome it's basically impossible. In contrast, systems that can be trained to recognize all those situations and respond appropriately have already been built. The difference between systems that are "trained" versus those that are "programmed" is enormous.

One highly revealing example takes us back to chess. The brute force method used by Deep Blue still exists. Of course, computers these days are vastly more powerful than they were back then, which means the brute force algorithm is vastly stronger. These days there are several chess playing engines that are essentially unbeatable by humans. The current world champion is an open-source program called Stockfish that anyone can download and run on their PC. A world leading grandmaster will get a few draws and maybe even a victory or two against Stockfish but has near zero chance of winning an overall match. In fact, there are now tournaments held strictly between chess playing engines. No human is qualified to even try and compete.

A surprising twist to this story happened recently. Google had set out on their own marquee AI project with AlphaGo, an attempt to build a system that could master the game of Go. Go is vastly more complex than chess so when they were successful it was an important landmark. Far more stunning was what happened when they taught an updated version of this system, known as AlphaZero, to play chess. They did not go through a complex, "chess optimization" process. They just programmed the basic rules and allowed it to play games against itself for four hours. After which they had it play against Stockfish. The Google system achieved 72 draws, 28 wins and zero losses. After only four hours of self-driven training.

The result has stunned chess players, not just because of the comparatively tiny amount of training required, but also because of the games themselves. Like humans, the Google system has a distinctive style of play. It's strategies and move selection are quite unlike that of any existing chess engine. Under the covers, it was actually analyzing literally an order of magnitude FEWER positions than Stockfish. It's not just better than the best, it is quite measurably "smarter."

The underlying mathematics, modeling methods and tools have become incredibly rich. As we saw in the prior section, the potential data sources are exploding. A number of leading edge proof points have emerged and are beginning to make their way out of the labs and into the world. What does it imply for jobs? What does this imply for businesses? What are the unique issues businesses will need to navigate?

The self-driving vehicle may make it seem like AI systems will be used to replace real humans. There are certainly situations where that is likely to happen, but many AI systems are actually used to augment human intelligence, not replace it. We always envisioned Watson as a member of a care giving team, not the lead MD. We envisioned an interaction where Watson would suggest possible treatment paths and be able to explain why it was making those suggestions. Watson would be the team member who had always "read" the latest journals, that nobody else had time for. It would also be the member who was the most open to a wide range of potential diagnoses and possible treatments. It might not have the best bedside manner on the team, but it would be a consistently valuable contributor. The final decisions would always rest with the humans.

The risks and liabilities in medicine make this the obvious model. However, we found the same basic pattern in everything from investment recommendations to call center management. To a greater or lesser degree, Watson was always intended in an advisory role to a human expert. In contrast, there are many current machine learning solutions for things like manufacturing quality control where the AI based systems are specifically designed to replace a significant number of human workers. There are still humans overseeing the process, but far fewer are required and the overall results are often vastly superior.

These two examples give some sense of the range of possibilities from AI. Any company with a strategy based on client intimacy should be looking for ways to enhance this value through AI. One of the most famous current examples is the recommendation engine developed and used by Netflix. This is a fully automated process for highly customer specific engagement. The Watson augmented financial advisor illustrates the same client intimacy only with a human remaining in the equation. Companies that rely on operational efficiencies should examine any and every role currently played by humans to see where they can be replaced or significantly reduced, all while increasing quality. The most recent Chinese government plans include an explicit focus on the union of AI and manufacturing as part of its "Made in China 2025" roadmap.

The driverless vehicle offers some additional perspectives on the value potential of AI. Many people envision using these as a virtual chauffer. The system drives while you read the paper. That would be an example of innovation leading to a whole new experience of car travel. It could also be used by fleet operators of buses and other vehicles to reduce or eliminate labor, representing an operational efficiency. Uber and others envision using this technology to bring vehicles to drivers and allow them to take over from there. It's essentially a highly distributed rental fleet that will dispatch vehicles to customers wherever they need. That vision could change societies entire perspective on vehicle access and ownership at least in urban areas. We are truly at the very beginning.

The various unique characteristics of AI systems we listed earlier bring with them some unique business issues and challenges. The fact that these systems are trained instead of being coded raises issues right at the heart of the technology. This makes the development and testing process more a matter of experimentation than the normal IT process. It also means most testing is done on the entire completed system, not piece by piece. That reality greatly increases the complexity and risks that arise as the systems increase in scope and scale. It also means there are always elements of uncertainty about how the system will perform when confronted with situations that go far beyond its training set.

The training sets themselves are becoming one of the most crucial assets. While data in aggregate is exploding, very little of that is currently suitable for use in AI training. The data preparation steps needed to produce good training materials are not simple, nor are they easily automated. A break through on this front would dramatically accelerate the evolution of the field.

The needed data will often come from multiple sources that require some form of licensing. These licenses have already become quite complicated. There are extensive debates about how to properly reflect the contributions of differ-ent parties to the value of the system. For example, if the data I'm providing you is only used during the training stages, what should be the proper basis of the fees you pay? Is it just the limited use as a development tool? Or, is it a core part of the operational value and therefore tied to the commercial results of the system? When the provider of medical textbooks used to train a system like Watson believes the medical skill of that system is directly a result of their text-books, shouldn't they expect compensation for every medical deployment? Or, would that be like asking medical students to remit a portion of their lifetime professional earnings to that same textbook provider? IBM has encountered all of these in real world negotiations.

There's another tricky issue that has existed from the very beginning. It is still far too difficult to understand exactly how these systems actually work. It's one thing to adapt the development process to an experimental process. It's a whole other issue when that same lack of clarity and certainty exists once deployed in the real world. The first, obvious issue is how to handle matters of liability when things go wrong. In any such situation, understanding what hap-pened is a crucial starting point. If the provider of the AI system cannot explain why it did what it did, they will be open to all kinds of lawsuits. If they attempt to place the blame on the provider of the training data they will need to be able to clearly link an action by the system to a particular training source, some-thing not generally possible. When AI systems are used to augment human experts, it is essential that they be able to provide some sort of explanation for their recommendations. In the case of Watson, we tried simply pulling out journal citations only to discover that often led to even more confusion.

There's a far more subtle issue lurking underneath this problem. Harken back to our original description of the social contract around patents. In return for a limited period of monopoly, the inventor must provide a disclosure with sufficient detail that others will be able to replicate the invention. What does this mean for systems like this? There is no question we are dealing with truly amazing innovations but what exactly is being patented? Is it the problem decomposition, and associated methods and training techniques? Is it the par-ticular collection of training data? Is it the system that arises from that training even if the inventor isn't quite sure how it works or why it does what it does? If the training data is omitted, then the system cannot be duplicated which violates the basic social contract of patents. Does that imply a license to that data once the patent expires? What about examples like Google's AlphaZero being taught the rules of chess and then playing itself? It might seem obvious that the Google patents would be found in the construction of AlphaZero. What then is the added IP that coverts AlphaZero to a chess grandmaster? Is there any?

All of these questions will eventually be sorted out. However, they illustrate yet again how ill-suited our current institutions are for the future unfolding all around us.

EXPERIENCE BASED STRATEGIES–SHIFTING CONSUMER VALUE

There's an enormously important shift in value that is slowly spreading through the contemporary consumer market. We are moving toward a society that values "having experiences" more than it does "owning things." Joseph Pine and James Gilmore predicted this evolution to what they called the "experience economy" almost 20 years ago. Recent studies of millennials have found that generation to be particularly focused on experiences. The same is true for Boomers and Gen-Xers as they grow older. People do still want "things." Many will also still prefer "new things." However, the world is awash with very high quality used, refurbished, and consigned goods. And, the reality in most markets is that many, if not most, of the "new things" are now deep in the realm of diminishing returns. That means the "new things" aren't really more valuable than the "old things." Buying used, which might once have been confined to the lower end of the market, is now everywhere. High end autos, fashion, jewelry and watches are only a few examples. All of these goods can be confidently purchased used or refurbished from reliable sources at a fraction of their original costs.

This creates an enormous challenge for companies that want to charge a premium for their "new things." The "things" themselves have reached the point of diminishing returns on new features so they need new strategies. The potential power of experiences to provide that kind of differentiation has been known for a long time. However, companies and brands have struggled to find scalable, repeatable ways to deliver on these strategic ideas.

Part of the challenge can be found in Pine and Gilmore's original Harvard Business Review article. They observe that memorable experiences are inherently personal and exist in the mind of each individual. In order to build a strategy around such an experience the marketer must have insights around these somewhat ephemeral and highly personal motivations

Adding to the challenge is the reality that each of us will seek different experiences at different moments in time even when we're dealing with the same product or offering category. This need, to align experiences with the very specific expectations and desires of individuals in a specific context, was described brilliantly by Jill Avery, Susan Fournier and John Wittenbraker in their HBR article "Unlock the mysteries of your customer relationships." Their article focuses on relationship styles—only one aspect of an experience—and they observe there are times when each of us wants a quite different style. For example, there are times when we want the interaction of a warm and compassionate friend and other times when we want a human exchange that is very light, fast and efficient. They have identified over a dozen different relationship styles that vary depending on context and which are all potentially relevant for different types of experiences.

To understand these ideas, we'll begin with a focus on fundamentals. Every company has some variation on a customer journey that includes processes for awareness, evaluation, purchase, ownership, and disposition. Most companies also have some degree of ecosystem in place across these stages and across their offering categories. The ecosystem partners could be in marketing, sales, support, offerings, financing, etc. In order to build an experience strategy, companies need solid fundamentals across these disciplines. If there are glaring defects in the purchase process or ownership experience, for example, those will make it difficult if not impossible to build effective experience strategies. Similarly, as target experiences become clearly identified, companies will need to assemble offerings across all these stages, many of which may depend on partners in the ecosystem. As an example, some product experiences may depend on specific underlying delivery or financial services. Experience strategies build from these fundamentals, so a key step is getting the basics in place.

There are many categories, processes and companies where just working on these fundamentals in a disciplined way, and from the perspective of the end customer, can yield substantial value. Paying close attention to the full aspects of the ownership experience from the eyes of the customer can reveal many untapped areas, such as the aforementioned transportation and financing.

To reach the more powerful types of experiences envisioned by Pine et al, we must first understand the various motivations underlying all of our desires. One of the more promising methodologies uses a framework of character archetypes and stories. As a species, we love to tell stories, either to others or just to ourselves. Those stories capture memorable experiences. When we're thinking about a major purchase like a car we tell ourselves all kinds of stories. We indulge in fantasies and dreams about what we'll do and where we'll go. Those stories reveal our desires. We all know this. What's less understood is that there is a substantial body of work on the structures found in stories, the recognizable and repeating emotional patterns and the characters that populate them. That work can be used to organize and operationalize investigations into the experiences customer's desire.

Scholars have studied the structure of stories as far back as Aristotle. Over the centuries a great deal has been learned about what makes a good story. Joseph Campbell studied the myths and stories found in cultures all over the world, from the most primitive to the most advanced. A particular focus for him was on those elements, themes and characters that showed up everywhere he looked. In every culture, at every stage of development these "archetypes" could be found. In his work, he was able to connect these archetypes to work done by Carl Jung on the patterns of the unconscious mind that manifest in dreams.

Psychologists and HR professionals have evolved this work to create diagnostics useful in their respective professions. Many of those tools focus on the "darker" dimensions of human psychology and have been tuned for use in a clinical context. In contrast, Carol Pearson and others have taken the scholastic work and evolved it to help brands develop marketing and advertising strategies. Both of these approaches seek to place an individual into the collection of archetypes they most frequently experience or seek, and both refer to the archetypes as "personality archetypes."

One way to think about using these archetypes in a strategy context is to contrast them with the classic needs-based segmentation approaches we discussed earlier. In the classic approach, some form of quantitative research is performed to gather data on a large, demographically diverse population. This data is then analyzed statistically to identify clusters of common patterns. The archetypes can be thought of as predefined clusters that have been proven to exist across cultures and time. They bring a rich variety of examples from literature and popular culture that reveal subtleties and nuances that would take many years if not decades to develop around statistically derived clusters. They also bring well understood expectations for both marketers and customers about the roles they play in stories and how they react to various events.

One framework that I have found useful is based on 12 archetypes which are consistent with the ones Carol Pearson has used. When used as a basis for experience strategies these can be thought of as "motivational archetypes" because the focus is on how these motivations drive people to desired experiences. Here's the full list:

ARCHETYPE	SELF-VIEW	MOTIVATIONS	EXAMPLE	ICONIC BRAND
Explorer	I find	Discovery Stimulation Freedom	Indiana Jones (Raiders)	NASA
Creator	I make	Innovation Creation Realization	Storm (X-Men)	Lego
Rebel	I break	Disruption Energy Unruly	Wolverine (X-Men)	Harley Davidson
Sage	I know	Facts Proof Explanation	Obi Wan (Star Wars)	H&R Block

ARCHETYPE	SELF-VIEW	MOTIVATIONS	EXAMPLE	ICONIC BRAND
Magician	I sense	Mystery Spiritual Inner journey	Gandalf (LOR)	Oprah Network
Companion	I relate	Intimacy Connection Commitment	Counselor Troy (Star Trek NG)	Winnebago
Leader	I lead	Control Power Team	Michael Corleone (Godfather)	Apple
Warrior	I save	Courage Competition Strength	Four (Divergent)	Fedex
Jester	I laugh	Fun Playful Chaos	C3PO (Star Wars)	Geico
Caregiver	I nurture	Protect Compassion Generosity	Sam Gamjee (LOR)	Allstate
Everyman	I fit	Belong Ordinary Popular	Freddy Corleone (Godfather)	Budweiser
Innocent	I trust	Faith Optimism Dreaming	Kate (Godfather)	Ivory

In my experience, I've found that even the most market driven firms have blind spots that this method reveals. Brands either have no focus at all on customer motivations or only consider a very limited range. As an example, when we showed a leading fashion retailer there were significant examples of the Caregiver archetype in their customer base, it opened up a range of new marketing ideas to tap into the deep emotional triggers associated with that archetype.

The next component of the analysis is the use of emotional metrics to understand the story genres associated with a customer's journey. Like the archetypes, story genres have been studied for centuries. There are consistent patterns and structures, particularly around the emotional stages that engage characters and audiences. By understanding the types and intensities of emotions and how those evolve throughout a customer's journey the most relevant story genres in the category can be revealed. This diagnostic reinforces and enhances the understanding of the archetypes. Different motivational archetypes can be activated and engaged by specific story genres while others are left cold. As any actor will tell you, in order to understand a role in a story one must first understand what motivates that character.

The experiences customers seek fit within the context of the story genres relevant to the category and the motivational archetypes that resonate for them as characters in that story. The combination of story and motivation provide the tools to enable a brand to focus on the experiences most likely to create powerful emotional engagements with customers. These point directly to the experiences that can propel a brand to leadership.

It's important to note how powerful and universal this approach can be. Joseph Campbell's original work was focused on those archetypes that were found everywhere. People admire heroes and leaders regardless of whether they're American, Chinese, or Brazilian. The cues that trigger these motivations may well have distinct cultural nuances, but the underlying drivers are universal. This need for global applicability is both a major element and major challenge for modern strategies. The archetypes offer an incredibly powerful tool to meet that challenge.

Customer interests and desires can change from one situation or moment to the next. Consequently, any compelling experience for a customer must fit into their specific immediate context. There are many different ways to approach this, but by far the most useful in my experience is to focus on two simple, intuitive dimensions.

The first dimension is around novelty versus familiarity. Sometimes we want experiences that are new for us and sometimes we want something very comfortable and familiar. We've all experienced both desires. Some of us have motivational archetypes that are energized by exploring or creating new things while others find those experiences to be stressful and want far less of it. In an outdoor recreation context, as an example, some people are constantly seeking a new park or new trail while others go to the same spots over and over again. The potential sources of novelty depend on the category as well as the history for each customer.

The second dimension is around solo/independent versus group/social. Sometimes we want experiences that are just for us and sometimes we want a party. Again, we've all experienced both, but some of us are much more inclined to one or the other. Sticking with our outdoor recreation example, sometimes we want solitude by a lake and sometimes we want a big church barbeque/picnic. It's important to note that while I use the word "solo," in practice this often includes couples or very small groups of close friends.

When you put these two dimensions together you come up with four simple quadrants that are easy to describe and yield very different experiences. In practice, these two questions are often all that's needed to guide a sales or service individual to the kind of experience a customer is seeking. Here's the resulting framework:

New / Solo	New / Group
Type of experience: A personalized adventure enabling self-discovery, creation and expression.	**Type of experience:** A stimulating group or team adventure that allows everyone to establish their role
Familiar / Solo	**Familiar / Group**
Type of experience: An opportunity for contemplation of oneself or companion or to apply one's skills and knowledge.	**Type of experience:** A fun, safe good time where everyone shares in the joy.

To illustrate how this framework can be used let's consider a fashion context and the kinds of experiences a brand might want to create for each quadrant. For those looking for a New/Solo experience the brand could provide a private session with a stylist and a range of looks that stretch the customer's boundaries. As an added frill, capturing photos of the looks and enabling easy sharing helps deliver on the desire these folks often have for expression. In contrast, the Familiar/Group experience is a big fashion show with familiar brands and looks and a charitable contribution from the proceedings. The New/Group experience could be a girl's night out with a stylist, some unique brands, and maybe tickets to a show or club. The familiar/solo could be a private session with the designer or creative director from a favorite brand. These are simple examples. The range of possibilities is enormous.

This classification of experience types is greatly enriched through the use of the archetypes and story genres. Some archetypes are strongly engaged by specific types of experiences. For example, the Explorer archetype craves new experiences and tends toward the solo version while the Leader archetype also craves the new, but almost always wants a group to lead. There are definite patterns of associations that enable "first order" mapping of archetypes to experiences.

The basic alignment of experience quadrants and archetypes can be used to develop a set of experience strategies. Harley Davidson started as the quintessential Rebel brand. They expanded that to include the wider range of archetypes in the New/Solo quadrant, embracing the Explorers and Creatives while not distancing themselves from the Rebel roots that gave "street cred" to their riders. But, the big lift was connecting all of that with the fun, safe group experiences of rallies and club outings.

As the Harley and fashion examples illustrate, brands can leverage many or even all of these types of experiences and archetypes. That leverage can take the form of a strong brand association with an archetype, like the Harley rebel, or it can take the form of specific experiences developed and delivered by the brand like the Harley outings or our fashion examples. Building the strategy has to start with understanding how customers view the category, the brands and themselves in the context of the archetypes and the types of experiences customers associate with the brand and category.

There are several technologies helping make all this much more practical than in the past. The analytic structure of the archetypes is the starting point. Using that requires the kind of real time contextual "awareness" I've been discussing. Using archetypes and stories as key training strategies for AI systems based on that data is rich with untapped possibilities.

Returning to our outdoor categories there are numerous examples of experiences across all four of our quadrants and customers who associate at different times with every one of the archetypes. The brands in these categories have worked diligently to establish images of quality, ruggedness and adventure. Many of them also organize outings, rallies or events of various kinds.

A truly notable example is REI who offers climbing walls in many of their stores and regularly organizes a wide variety of outdoor events. In fact, REI introduced two distinct lines of business centered completely on the creation and delivery of unique experience. REI Adventures organizes trips to a variety of destinations and REI Outdoor School offers classes in outdoor activities and techniques. With 19.4% and 28% growth respectively, these are two of the fastest growing elements in the REI portfolio. REI reports the users of these services are among their best customers. With overall sales growth of 9.3% and same store sales growth of a whopping 7% in 2015, REI is among the most successful retailers in the country.

The REI example highlights the power and potential of what happens when companies build experiences for their customers as explicit elements of their strategy. Properly packaged experiences become direct sources of revenues. Experiences become the stories customers tell others and become the basis for relationships between customers and employees. Those customer stories can become the living, beating heart of the brand's story.

GLOBAL MARKETS–21ST CENTURY REALITIES

The evolution of today's globally connected market over the past 20–30 years has been staggering. The changes are so deep, subtle and profound that even for those who've been closely involved it's sometimes hard to realize just how different the world is today than it was in the late 1970s or early 1980s. Those who haven't been in the epicenter of change can be forgiven a certain level of bewilderment. The world simply no longer works the way most people's internal mental models assume. For most of the post World War II period it was perfectly fine to think about a world where US companies compete and sell to buyers and consumers in the US and around the world. Today this mental model is riddled with erroneous assumptions and at some level is no longer even conceptually accurate.

One of those inaccuracies is the assumption that US firms rely first and foremost on sales and production in the US. I described earlier how critical the Chinese and other emerging markets were to IBM's business results in the 2000s. Those sales dwarfed all other growth initiatives combined. They weren't the largest source of revenue, but without their growth contribution IBM's market capitalization would have suffered mightily. Equally prominent are the Chinese results at GM. GM owns many brands with deep histories including Buick. Many people might guess that Chevy was the original GM brand, but it was actually Buick. The Buick brand languished in the US for many years. However, it has been incredibly strong in China. Over 80% of Buick's revenue actually comes from China and those sales remain critical for the ongoing health of GM as a whole. When US and European auto sales collapsed during the 2008 recession, GM was in serious trouble. The company was saved by a combination of a US government bailout and their sales in China.

As we look back at economic development over the past 100 years we find three distinct stages in the evolution of global trade. The roots of our modern trading systems were put down in the aftermath of WWII. Those practices evolved considerably in the 1980s and beyond with the emergence of what many refer to as "the Washington consensus." The third stage was triggered by China's entry into the WTO in 2001. Each of these periods have left their mark on our current environment.

THE POST WWII ERA

Leading up to and through the end of WWII the US, under Franklin Delano Roosevelt's leadership, set out to completely redesign and rebuild our economy in the wake of its mounting failures in the 1920s and eventual collapse in the early 1930s. Banking and finance laws were rewritten to provide the kind of capital stability needed by the growing industrial sector. The government established a program of supply and demand management along with subsidy programs for agricultural that halted the tidal wave of bankruptcies caused by the growing productivity of that sector. Minimum wages, the 40-hour work week and enabling the formation of unions brought enormous improvements to industrial sector employment practices. The combination of those two put the demand side of the economy on a healthy and sustainable trajectory. The nation's infrastructure was built to enable coast to coast economic development. Roads, bridges, airports, electrical and water systems were built across the country. In support of the war, massive government capital was deployed to build up the production infrastructure of the nation. By the end of the war over half the total industrial capital stock of the country had been paid for by the US government. Finally, the GI Bill opened up possibilities of home ownership and funded training and education opportunities for millions.

Following WWII, the US, Europe and Japan all began a remarkable process of rebuilding their national and global economies. In addition to the famous Marshall plan with all its associated reconstruction, there were rapidly developing principles and standards for trade. With the creation of the International Monetary Fund (IMF) the conference at Bretton Woods in 1944 established the foundations for the handling of currencies all over the world. This was followed in 1947 with the creation of the General Agreement on Tariffs and Trade (GATT) which later evolved to the World Trade Organization (WTO.) This began to formalize the necessary economic and legal foundations for interconnecting trade among companies and nations around the world. For those who adopted the rules, the opportunities were enormous.

The economic development that emerged was explosive. It propelled the US to a level of unprecedented global economic leadership. Europe grew right alongside the US, though no single European country could match the sheer economic scale of the US made possible in part by FDR's policies. Japan, South Korea and Taiwan were a bit slower to develop, but once they began to embrace an export strategy they too experienced incredible growth. Those who rejected the necessity of trade under the new rules found themselves in an economic backwater.

The primary economic philosophy behind these initiatives was the Theory of Comparative Advantage which goes all the way back to Adam Smith's original Wealth of Nations. It was later refined by John Stuart Mill in 1848 with the publication of Principles of Political Economy. This theory puts its focus on understanding the economic pillars of nations, specifically the sources of distinct *comparative* advantages between nations. The key conclusion from this theory is that national economies are optimized when they prioritize the areas where they have advantages, while relying on goods and services from other nations when those sources have the comparative edge.

§

When the major elements of this theory were first articulated in the 18th and 19th centuries, the world economy was in transition from agriculture, raw materials, and craftsmanship to the early phases of industrialization. In that context, "comparative advantage" often meant little more than access to raw materials or shipping and transportation centers. There were specific cultures noted for various forms of craftsmanship as well, but a great deal of the focus in reality was securing, extracting and shipping raw materials. Western colonialism was largely fueled by this set of economics. The colonial system relied on controlling raw material sourcing through the projection of power from the west in a variety of forms, but primarily through the military. The "comparative advantage" of the colonized country was either seized or economically subsumed by the colonizers.

With the end of WWII that era of colonialization came to an end. The former colonies were now free to establish their own government and economic systems. This transition was fraught with difficulties. In many former colonies the notion of "comparative advantage" was laughable. Their strongest industries and companies were often owned by foreigners while the remaining sectors of the economy were essentially undeveloped. This led to two common strategies—the nationalization of key economic companies or sectors and the pursuit of import substitution policies. Both of these were aimed at capturing and shielding domestic industries to enable their development. Energy and raw material sectors were frequent targets of nationalization initiatives, in many cases simply to throw off the legacy of colonial rule. Banking, telecommunication and transportation sectors were also nationalized in many countries as these were viewed as essential to the overall support and productivity of the economy.

The inward focus of the import substitution policies reflected the need to develop greater overall economic strength and the fundamental need to diversify their economies. Unfortunately, the subsidies, tariffs and quotas used to achieve these aims often served to reduce incentives for capital investment and led to countless corrupt practices. Over time it became clear that while there were circumstances where those policies were needed, it was essential that they be balanced by policies aimed at stimulating export growth. It was only through a rapidly growing export sector that these developing nations could achieve global competitiveness and thereby attract global capital.

Over time these learnings led to a generally understood pattern. In the early stages of economic development, when the domestic market is still immature, countries need to focus on exports and the attraction of foreign direct investments to bring needed capital into the market. The workforce then evolves, migrating to urban areas and gradually shifting out of agricultural roles into manufacturing and services. This migration needs to be supported by transportation, housing, education and employment investments and regulations. The nation's growing financial capital then needs to be steered toward investments that systematically improve the productivity of this growing commercial workforce. Government policies can further aid or impede this overall development trajectory through investments in research, development, education and infrastructure along with regulations on taxes and tariffs that are reasonably consistent with global norms. Foreign investors need enough confidence in the rule of law and currency stability to know that contracts and property rights will be respected and enforced. Finally, the whole economic system needs to operate without excess corruption interfering with the movement of goods, services, labor and capital.

In parallel with these public policy understandings, the best practices of commercial entities were also evolving. Simple international sales activities began to transform into multi-national businesses. These firms sourced both sales and key production processes from multiple countries. Some of these "off shored" activities were admittedly pretty superficial, but as companies evolved their international sourcing could become quite complex. As an example, through the 1970s IBM's World Trade organization accounted for roughly

40%–50% of the company's revenue and was organized as an integrated business reporting directly to the Chairman. At one point IBM had over 100 factories around the world and well over half of those were outside the US. Based on fears that some countries might decide to nationalize their computing industry, IBM's manufacturing policy at the time stipulated that all non-US factories needed to be dependent on some set of critical US parts. While the workers, engineers, sales, support and most management positions were held by local nationals the most senior executive positions were US assignees.

This multi-national phase gradually gave way to a true global structure. Sourcing policies became less oriented around political worries and based instead on cost and quality fundamentals. The senior executive slots were increasingly held by locals who were both more effective as internal local leaders and better connected with local clients. Similarly, IBM's non-US research and development facilities evolved to encompass the full range of development and innovation activities from all over the globe. IBM was still headquartered in the US, but every aspect of the business from basic research to development to manufacturing to sales and support were scattered all over the world. IBM's assets including patents, factories, parts, warehouses, sales and support centers and the full range of financial assets, were equally distributed.

Among large enterprises there was nothing particularly unique about IBM. It was obviously more difficult for small and midsize companies to participate outside their home geographies. They often found themselves having to compete locally with companies that had both local and global resources at their disposal. The types of industries and businesses engaged in these global dynamics also evolved. Industries focused on the extraction of raw materials had sought those materials all over the world from the earliest days of trading. This evolved to include manufacturing and eventually services industries. Today's global trade is based 18% on agriculture and raw materials, 58% in manufactured goods, and 24% in services.

WASHINGTON CONSENSUS

That steady evolution of business practices was matched by the evolution of the rules and norms defining the structure of global trade. In his book,

The Lexus and the olive tree, Tom Friedman called this combination the *Golden Straitjacket*. When originally developed the formula was primarily aimed on attracting foreign investment and as such the overwhelming focus was on the drivers of global capital flows. These drivers include things like reducing inflation, eliminating restrictions on foreign investments or capital flows of any sort, having a convertible currency, and allowing citizens and companies to make investments and pension decisions that include foreign run financial institutions. These evolved over the years to include factors related to global production, marketing and sales, including rules demanding the reduction or elimination of tariffs, quotas and local subsidies. Finally, the formula also includes laws on contracts, and property rights, including intellectual property, with the latter being a near continual source of friction and failed promises.

Over time these economic mandates have been joined by a number of political dictates. These reflected the growing US and European belief in a neo-liberal school of economics and include making the private sector the primary economic engine, shrinking government bureaucracy and ensuring balanced budgets, privatizing state-owned institutions of all kinds, promoting competition within domestic markets, and eliminating all government subsidies. In many instances, the demands for these policies have been more about dictating politics and propagating neo-liberalism than about actually enabling free trade.

The "deal" offered to nations all over the globe was if you do all of the above, we, the controllers of access to global capital, will actively invest in your market. If you do not, if you hesitate or equivocate, we will withhold investments. For nations trying to leave behind a painful legacy of colonial exploitation many of these "rules" seemed more like the latest in a long history of formulas for exploitation. The overall formula was sometimes referred to as the "Washington Consensus" a term that could only be liked by citizens of the US. There certainly was a consensus that a market-based global formula was the best way to enable economic development, but there was no consensus about that being dictated from Washington. In fact, as China now breaks every prior economic growth record there has been a rising chorus suggesting the "Chinese way" may be a superior model for most developing nations.

When Friedman originally called this a "golden straitjacket" he was explicitly referring to the awkward trade-off emerging nations needed to address. They needed to surrender a certain amount of local sovereignty and political control in return for investment and growth. If they did not agree to those terms the global economic system essential for the health and growth of their country would be shut off to them. This realpolitik was almost always shrouded in arguments that it's "in your own best interest." It amounted to a massive collection of invisible forces that shaped the development of much of the globe. Other than US interventions in Latin America there were very few situations where it was matched with the sort of overt military threats common to the colonial era. Nonetheless, it was not particularly flexible, nor were its adherents interested in local historical or cultural legacies. It was very much an invisible iron fist in a velvet glove.

CHINA ENTERS THE STAGE

I suspect future generations of historians will highlight the year 2001 as one of the more important years in the economic development of the world. It won't be based on any "space odyssey" nor on the tragic events in September of that year. It will be the year a new invisible force began shaping the planet through China's entry into the World Trade Organization (WTO.). With that step they followed India who had embarked on their own economic liberalization initiative in 1991.

These two gigantic nations are now well into their economic development journey. Comparing economic metrics around the globe has some tricky aspects, particularly around normalizing for different currencies. There are two primary methods, simple currency conversion and Purchase Power Parity (PPP). The Purchase Power method reflects the reality that the difference in the prices of goods in different markets can be substantially greater than just the differences in currencies. To capture this, purchase power comparisons normalize values to match prevailing prices in the US. Under this measure, China has now passed the US to be the number one economy in the world, with the US now second. India comes in third, followed by Japan and Germany. Using the more common currency conversion method, the US is still the largest economy followed by China, Japan, Germany and India, in that order. Whichever measurement is used, the US and China are three to five times the size of the other members of the top five and are only matched by the size of the full European Union.

This is just the beginning. Before long we can expect China to surpass the US economy on many different metrics. It may take quite a bit longer for India to reach that point, but the odds are high they too will eventually surpass the US. To understand why these statements are true, we need to understand what drives economic scale and take look at a handful of key statistics. Any nation's GDP can be mathematically defined as the size of the work force times the productivity of that work force. There's nothing ideological about that. It's just math.

In the case of both China and India the total population and overall workforce is three to five times larger than the US and 10–12 times larger than Japan or Germany. Furthermore, in the US, Germany and Japan you only find 1%–3% of the population engaged in agricultural production while China still has 28% on the farm and India has 47%. As those two economies continue to mature, much of that labor will become part of the industrial and services work force.

All that labor is currently operating at productivity levels that are 1/3–1/5 that of the US, Germany or Japan. However, the Chinese and Indian economies are making capital investments to improve that productivity at a rate that is two to three times the share of GDP being used for similar investments in the US, Germany, and Japan. The productivity levels in China and India will continue to rise as the overall capital stock in those markets reach the levels of their more mature peers. That rising productivity is also likely to manifest itself in the continued growth of a middle class with disposable incomes to fuel a strong local consumer market. As their productivity begins to converge with that found in the west, their economies will begin to dwarf the scale of any western market. China's economy is now on a path to be three to four times the size of the US in the decades to come.

A major contributor to the economic growth of both China and India stems from another invisible force first articulated by Ronald Coase in his Theory of the Firm, published in 1937. This theory is focused on understanding the forces that determine which activities are performed by a firm versus which they choose to source from outside. The principle conclusion of the theory is that the "transaction costs" associated with securing, using and managing a business activity are crucial to determine its sourcing. The more transaction costs can be driven down, the more options a firm has available and the more likely they are to conclude someone else is better positioned to provide that capability. These are the "scoping" elements of our business design template.

There are many factors that drive transaction cost assessments. Processes that are poorly defined or constantly changing are hard to source externally. This is particularly true if the inputs and outputs exhibit high variability. Processes that have complex interdependencies with other processes are constant management challenges. A process that is completely unique may be essentially impossible to source from the outside. As I covered in the chapter on business design, processes at the heart of a firm's unique value proposition are important to control even if there are elements with external dependencies. These control dimensions can sometimes be built into contracts, but always increase transaction costs. Many firms will also worry about maintaining tight management control of processes that might negatively impact the firm.

The global quality movement arising from the success of Japanese auto and electronics firms had a substantial impact on many of these factors. Companies all over the world began applying more rigorous and disciplined approaches to their key processes. These disciplines drove better definition of every aspect of every business process. This included formalizing inputs, outputs, process steps, management processes, measurements, quality and other control mechanisms.

In addition to the improved process definitions, companies also began extensive benchmarking activities that led to widespread adoption of common best practices. The growing prevalence of a given best practice across an industry both reduced transaction costs and created a market for those who wanted to build a Business Processing Outsourcing (BPO) company based on that best practice. I described earlier how this trend enabled the maturing and growth of the application software industry. The clarity of definition on inputs, outputs, measurements and management made it possible to create easily implemented business and information process flows, metrics, management systems and contracts based on all those definitions.

These can all be thought of as instances of de facto standards for business processes. Standards drive down transaction costs and global standards have been exploding. Standards around sizes, shapes, colors, and weights not to mention the electrical, structural and chemical properties both of goods themselves as well as their quality and production attributes have all been growing rapidly over the past several decades. The global agricultural standards that have existed since the 19th century have expanded significantly over the past 20–30 years. All these offering standards have been complemented with the kinds of process standards described above. They've also been complemented with things like standardized shipping containers. These standard "modules" allow everything from warehousing to shipping to trucking and railways to interchange goods freely. Even the exceptions like refrigerated or bonded goods have developed their own specific standards. What might once have required unique packing and shipping can now be placed in a standard container and then handled by anybody.

All of these trends have been occurring at an accelerated pace. The result is a dramatic drop in transaction costs across every process, industry and geography. It is now possible to build a company in which every individual process is atomized down and sourced from anywhere. This is not only true for a firm considering these choices. It's also true for the companies they're considering sourcing from. It is the completeness and robustness of the process and management standards that makes this "cascading" and true "atomization" of sourcing possible.

These increased sourcing options have created enormous new opportunities for developing nations to insert themselves into global economic activity. Those dynamics, which were once completely dominated by the flow of raw materials and capital, now include every business activity. China's growth in manufacturing and India's growth in IT services were both put on rocket fuel as a result of this invisible economic force. The tremendous growth in outsourced manufacturing was driven by standards, not malevolent Chinese planners.

Obviously, both of these nations do have their share of issues many of which stem directly from their large populations. The overall infrastructure in India is abysmal. Environmental conditions are similarly disastrous. There are a handful of extended families that control an enormous share of the overall economy. This is a recipe for corruption and it has stunted progress for generations. Meanwhile China's urban areas face comparable environmental nightmares as in India. China also has its own problems with corruption and the civilian censorship and regulations related to the communist party are social wild cards that could explode and derail progress at any time. Their respective paths to world economic leadership are not guaranteed, but they do have the right ingredients and enough proven success to date that nobody should bet against them.

The one crucial economic ingredient I haven't covered is innovation. One of the common tropes used to dismiss the progress of these nations is a claim that they are "copycats" and unable to generate any repeated pattern of innovation. The charges of essentially unfettered copying, often in direct violation of intellectual property laws, certainly have considerable truth. Anybody with any significant experience doing business in either of these countries has encountered the issue. For a long time, these concerns tended to be discounted, denied or dismissed by government officials as a fringe problem.

It's easy to forget that when Japan, Taiwan and South Korea were each following this overall development path they too were accused of rampant IP theft in their early stages. Once their local businesses started wanting and needing their own IP protections their overall body of laws and enforcement evolved as well. All of those nations now operate with the same level of integrity and rule of law found in the US or Europe. There are no guarantees that China and India will do the same, but there's no real reason to expect otherwise.

It's also important to note that while IP theft has certainly occurred, most of the true IP transfer has been done openly with the full agreement of all parties involved. The Chinese had their own "iron fist in a velvet glove"—access to the largest and fastest growing economy on the planet. The Chinese "deal" was simple. You want access to our market and we want access to your technology and know-how. That economic exchange was usually accomplished through joint ventures, but as my earlier IBM example illustrated, there were many mechanisms developed over the years.

GLOBAL MARKETS IN THE 21ST CENTURY

China and India are very much focused on what's coming next and they fully intend to be undisputed leaders in the economic landscape of the future. This includes an explicit intent to be the principle sources of innovation not just production. If one only considers the events of the 19th and 20th centuries this might seem the height of hubris on their parts. However, both of these cultures have thousands of years of history. Many worldly Chinese and Indian citizens view the last couple hundred years as an aberration resulting from the European colonial period. In their minds, their "manifest destiny" is to lead the world culturally, economically, and technologically. Their recent history may have earned the label "copycats," but that's not their roots, nor their intent for the future. China's rise to parity with the US in the field of High Performance Computing is an example of what will come. When they reach the level of consistent superiority the stakes will be even clearer. There are many technologists in the field of AI who believe China is poised to leap ahead of the US in that critical field. Eric Schmidt, the former CEO of Google, has predicted a "sputnik-like" national shock when this occurs. Not only will China be two to four times the size of the US they will be the dominant source of innovation in many, if not most, segments of the global economy.

China and India are obviously extremely important. They've already reached a scale that makes them unavoidable players on the world stage. In the early 2000s they were often grouped with Brazil and Russia in the famous acronym "BRIC." Those two countries are still relevant; however, they have both dropped considerably in importance. In Brazil's case the government's corruption and gross mismanagement of the economy is the principle culprit. In Russia, it is the break-down of the rule of law and the rise of the kleptocratic oligarchs that are the issue. If you're in the ruling elite in either geography you have few complaints. However, the overall progress of broad economic development in both nations has stalled.

The same is not true across southeast Asia. Indonesia, Malaysia, Thailand, Vietnam and others are all evolving at a rapid pace. They've all seen the formula unfold and are eagerly following the path. Just as China "hollowed out" the manufacturing elements of many western firms, Vietnam is now aggressively doing the same thing to China. Thailand is already a crucial part of the global supply chain in the technology industry. Malaysia and Indonesia are more diverse economies that have the same kind of potential population driven scale leverage we've described in India and China. We can expect continued rapid development and evolution across the entire region. In fact, this region is likely to be the most important region in the world for the next several decades if not the entire 21st century.

The other region that needs comment is Africa. This incredible continent has struggled for hundreds of years. There are examples of progress, but as a whole this is still a very troubled and poorly developed part of the globe. I noted earlier the combination of socio-political factors that must be in place for economic development to proceed. There are very few, if any, places in Africa that have put that formula together and held it long enough to be effective. The vast majority of the continent is still trapped in the tragic state of throwing off colonial era history while failing to adopt the proven successful paradigms that would enable sustained growth. The overall population level is enormous, but so are the levels of poverty and income disparity. Essentially every aspect of a modern infrastructure from roads, rails and ports to electricity and communications, have endured decades of neglect. These economic development issues have been enormously compounded through endless civil wars and the slow steady demolition of the local agricultural economy caused by global climate change. The tragedy worsens with every day.

Despite these enormous problems the continent remains highly rich in natural resources and has enormous human capital potential. There are still very few western companies or nations making any substantial investments in Africa. This is not true of China or India. Those two nations have established partnerships and investments in every aspect of the economic development of Africa. It will take a long time for these to mature and there are certain to be numerous failures. There are no guarantees this early engagement will lead to eventual success. However, this is an example of how those nations are focused on the future, willing to accept risks, and not something to bet against.

NEW INVISIBLE FORCES

The Washington consensus that drives WTO regulations encompasses a great deal. However, it also has many crucial omissions. As an example, most production process attributes including things like pollution, CO_2 emissions, and energy efficiencies have generally been excluded. There has also been very little focus around labor management issues including protections for children, working conditions, anti-slavery, and a wide variety of health and safety concerns. While these were of little concern to global capitalists and neo-liberal ideologues they are quite important to the social contracts of nations around the world. They are also of increasing importance to consumers.

Unfortunately, the currently prevailing US political beliefs about how markets should work have been baked by regulators into WTO rules. Many of these are deeply flawed and are being forced on an unwilling world. Even countries like Canada are being challenged to abandon efforts aimed at promoting "green" development because they are deemed an unacceptable meddling by government in the market. Labor protections are also skewed toward enabling companies unfettered power to drive down wages fueling the same inequality trends found in the US. Consumer demands to know whether child labor or GMOs are involved in production processes are often left to individual companies for compliance with little to no regulatory support or enforcement. However, the pressure to address these failings is mounting all over the world.

Paradoxically this evolution is slowly beginning to turn the original formulation on its head. These standards are no longer things that only emerging markets need to care about. This is no longer smug, self-satisfied, members of the "Washington establishment" telling the rest of the world what to do. What's now happening is the golden straitjacket is going truly global and is beginning to dictate to the west what western firms must do to be competitive. Tom Friedman referred to this stage as the "flattening" of the global basis of competition.

In a "flat" market firms must put together a *globally* optimized combination of production factors aimed at delivering unique value to a particular target market. Most operational efficiency strategies rely in one form or another on economies of scale. Any strategy based on production economies of scale that does not include globalized markets will be sub-optimal to strategies that do encompass those markets. Similarly, many customer intimacy strategies rely on economies of scope to bring diverse value to one's customers. Any such strategy that excluded global sources of goods would be disadvantaged to strategies that could readily draw from the full range of global offerings. The same truth applies to strategies based on innovations. No firm can assume that the only innovations that matter come from any single nation. All three of the fundamental pillars or value creation now depend on access to global markets to sustain their competitiveness.

These academic descriptions are always more complex in the real world. An entertaining example are the KitKat candy bars sold in Japan. The KitKat brand is owned by Nestle and is available in numerous countries around the world. In most regions, the flavors are limited to a small handful of basics like chocolate or caramel. In Japan, however, it's an entirely different story. For completely random reasons of history the brand name happens to be very close to the Japanese phrase "Kitto Kattsu" which can be loosely translated as "You will surely win" and is considered a sign of good luck. Recognizing this, Nestle developed a number of marketing and promotion campaigns designed to exploit this coincidence. The Japanese also have a penchant for both unique flavors as well as a distinct sweet tooth. Nestle realized they could use their optimized production processes to enable short production runs with unique colors and flavors. They combined these production capabilities with strong local market insights to bring well over 300 different versions of the KitKat to the Japanese market. These included things like green tea and soy sauce flavored candy bars. In 2014, they began opening specialty shops around Japan with even more unique recipes developed locally by a Japanese chef. They are now the number one selling candy in the country.

As this example illustrates, winning strategies blend global and local elements in a seamless fashion. That sort of seamless flexibility is precisely what is being enabled by the modern version of Friedman's original Golden Straitjacket. The straitjacket for nations has shown the potential to be a rocket powered flying suit for companies. Those who understand this reality are developing and executing strategies that cannot be matched by those who limit their thinking to local markets alone. These trends are true for large companies and small, for production processes and market targeting, and for industrial as well as service-oriented industries. This obviously varies by degree. Strategies for local producers at a weekend farmers market will be different from those adopted by global auto producers. However, one should not underestimate the hidden global dimensions of even those local farmers. Their customers may be demanding the production be locally certified as organic and the goods free from any GMOs. Their seeds may have been originally cultivated in Africa, refined in India, licensed to Europe, tested in America and planted by a trac-tor made in Japan. They may have had their taxes done by a local CPA, but the CPA may have used software developed in India and audited by back office operations in the Philippines. The global integration is increasingly seamless and quite often invisible. That is, unless its disrupted through ill-advised inter-ventions based on 19th century assumptions that ignore 21st century realities.

The regulations and standards that drive business decisions are also becom-ing both global and less visible to most consumers. A perfect example of this phenomena are the regulations around automotive fuel economy standards. Today's regulations around Corporate Average Fuel Economies (CAFÉ) in the US arose in response to the oil crisis of the 1970s. This crisis caused fuel econ-omy to shift from something almost no US customer cared about to become a top attribute for many customers and a relevant attribute for almost every-one. Standards quickly emerged for measuring and reporting what was now an important source of value in the market. Along with these came targets and mandates, not for individual vehicles, but for the average across all the vehi-cles produced by each manufacturer. Over time this mathematical algorithm evolved to give auto makers more flexibility to tune their compliance with the vagaries of actual consumer demands.

From the very beginning of this national process, California sought and was granted a unique waiver. The state had been dealing with serious pollution issues for decades before the rest of the country. They argued that the depth of their experience, their existing regulations and some of the unique aspects of the LA basin meant they were in a position to set their own standards. The federal government agreed, demanding only that any changes made to California law needed prior approval from federal agencies and needed to be at least as stringent as the national standards.

Several things happened as a result. The California standards were distinctly higher than those put in place by the federal agencies. Despite all their arguments against these higher standards, essentially all major auto producers chose to meet the standards to avoid losing access to the California market. Again, this didn't mean every vehicle met the standards. It meant the fleet averages did so. Making a model that could only be sold in California wasn't economically sensible. Having a sufficient range of models with high mileage that in aggregate met the California standards was essential. The California argument that they were simply ahead of the rest of the market has largely proven true. In 2017, 15 different states accounting for over 40% of the US population have chosen the higher California standard instead of the lower federal standard.

These days the decision for auto makers about whether to comply with the higher standards are pretty easy. Opting out would lose access to almost half the market. Most of the costs of compliance are in fixed cost areas like development and tooling. The key to managing fixed costs is to spread them over as large a volume as possible. Therefore, once you decide to comply you really want to spread that compliance as broadly as possible. Common vehicle "platforms" enable widely disparate vehicles to share costs. Having sub-assemblies and components that can be used widely across different models is now a standard practice. In recent years, Porsche has converted almost every engine they build to the use of turbochargers. These enable the high performance expected from the brand with much greater fuel efficiencies. A component that was once the exclusive defining feature for the top of the brand is now universal. This is directly due to the importance of meeting the highest standards in the market across as many vehicles as possible.

In practice, when large markets set high standards those standards create the invisible forces that shape the market as a whole. Niche markets will always exist but will not shape markets at scale. Large markets with low standards simply get subsumed by the economic forces driving the higher standards. Regulators who think they can reduce corporate costs by instituting lower local standards may find enthusiastic local supporters but little to no global impact.

Imagine now what happens as China embarks on the process of converting all new vehicles to electric power. This program is well under way. As we noted earlier, GM might have gone out of business entirely were it not for the Chinese market. That importance will only increase as China heads toward a super dominant scale on the world stage. There is literally no strategic question about GM adopting the Chinese standards that are emerging and making them their de facto global standards. In fact, essentially every auto manufacturer in the world is moving to electric vehicles in order to serve the Chinese market. Those who can't afford to sustain investments in both internal combustion engines and electric systems have been forced to choose and in every case have chosen the electric path. China is that important. Several years ago, the IBM senior executive responsible for our offerings and sales to the utility industry decided to locate his team in China specifically to be at the cutting edge of innovations in that industry. The overall market is flattening in all directions including having the future direction of major industries being set by policies in China.

The move to electric vehicles illustrates another invisible force that will drive strategies for the rest of the 21st century. Consumers all over the world are beginning to realize the threats and dangers to the planet arising from climate change. "Green" value propositions will become increasingly important in many, if not most, industries. In some cases, like the electric vehicle, the value will be embodied in the product itself. In other cases, like agricultural goods, the value will be embodied in the production processes. Farmers all over the world are well aware that some practices allow their soil to be effective in absorbing CO_2, while others strip the soil of this attribute. This difference is completely hidden from consumers today but could well become a substantial value attribute in the years to come.

"Green value" is another arena where China is moving strategically toward leadership. Solar panels, batteries, and high-speed rail are all important technologies for a "green" future and are all areas where China is setting the global pace. They have also realized there are certain raw materials, like the rare earth element, cobalt, that will be essential to these technologies and they have moved to secure long-term sourcing agreements with the suppliers of these materials. This is an enormous topic and beyond the scope of this particular book but is a category of value every strategist should be tracking.

China is not only a crucial market, it is poised to become a major source of global competition. Huawei is already one of the largest suppliers of telecommunications equipment and, with an extensive patent portfolio and well established clients, is the odds-on favorite to dominate the next generation of 5G deployments. Oppo Global is a provider of a wide range of home electronics offerings and is rapidly becoming one of the top competitors in mobile phones. There aren't many Chinese consumer brands who have yet made that sort of leap, but there is no doubt they're coming. My example of the Indian service companies' impact on IBM illustrates how profound these threats can be. This is another global dimension every strategist needs to track.

We began this section with a discussion on the sources of comparative advantages between nations. The vast majority of these potential sources of advantage have been harmonized in ways that allow businesses the ability to seamlessly construct strategies from anywhere. What then are the enduring sources of comparative advantage between nations? In some sectors access to raw materials still matters, but these days "ownership" can and often is scattered all over. Access to markets still matters, but mainly for localized insight and the kind of product tailoring exemplified by KitKat. Access to capital is no issue for those who have joined the flattened market. Weak, "friendly," local regulatory standards are being supplanted by more stringent global standards and are the antithesis of comparative advantage.

This flattening of the world makes the very boundaries between nations increasingly blurry. That's not a statement about the existence of physical borders, frontiers and fences. It's a statement about the things that actually impact our daily lives. From the candy bars in Japan to the vehicles driven in Texas the forces that shape the things we interact with are global. The invisible forces behind Coase's Theory are causing everything to become atomized and recombined in ways one would never predict solely by looking at their (presumed) place of origin. The small organic farmer selling to their local market could easily have dependencies on offerings from dozens of different nations. Even that tiny local business would find it quite difficult to unravel and discover all those global dependencies. For large global entities, it's no longer even an intelligible question.

In this environment, the one enduring source of national comparative advantage is human capital. People and their cultures define nations. Their energies, values and innovations are what fuel markets. Global capitalists can develop all kinds of strategies, but the execution of those strategies depends at the end of the day on the people who carry them out. In the 21st century the most important priority for the development of global comparative advantage are investments in people. This must include education, healthcare, and a full range of human services. Rather than hunting for the lowest common denominator leaders need to engage these empowered populations with a shared set of values and vision. The same is true for our business leadership.

CONCLUSIONS

Value endures, is built upon. . . . Power fades, is eventually conquered

WE LIVE IN a large, complex world that is constantly evolving. The wave of technology currently building is likely to bring as much if not more change than we have seen over the last 40 years. And, that change will unfold all over the world. Many of the most crucial innovations could well first arise in China or India. They will almost certainly entail collaborative efforts across many firms and many countries. These are those proverbial "interesting times."

This book has covered a great deal of ground on the topic of strategy, providing insights and tools to help businesses grapple with the challenges arising from this complex world. Everything from the basics of decision making, understanding markets and the concepts of strategic business design to the modern strategy frontiers around data, archetypes, AI, experiences and the arrival of China and India as primary markets. I have shown through the IBM examples the vital importance of preserving your core business at the same time as you generate new sources of value. I've also made the point repeatedly that when markets change, strategy must change; and, when strategies change, execution must change.

If there's a single golden thread through all of this, it's a focus on the creation of value. I am a firm believer that the purpose of business is precisely that—to create value for customers. As I have illustrated throughout, this is not a simple, naïve homily. It's a firm conviction from decades of experience dealing with issues and opportunities from across the spectrum and around the world.

There are five final points I believe are crucial to understand and embrace. The first of these is that Value is more important than Control. This is not to say that market power, entry barriers and the like have no place. They do. We just need to keep them in their place and not allow the pursuit of control or power to supplant the creation of value as our primary purpose.

The second key point is that value creation always builds on some sort of foundation. Whether that's adding services to existing products or leveraging open-source assets to create something new, we always build. This is not new. From the earliest days of raw material extraction and industrial production we have always created value by adding value. It has, however, become vastly more complex. Today's global network of physical and digital building blocks along with services encompassing every aspect of business is unlike anything that has ever existed. The old image of a factory with steel flowing in one side and cars flowing out the other is hopelessly archaic.

The third point is that all of this activity is now global. It's inescapable. There's no magic doorway leading to a world that isn't economically interconnected. The means of production, the potential markets to serve, the standards we must adhere to and the competitors we must confront are all global. This doesn't mean local values and craftsmanship have vanished. They simply operate within a context of an economy driven by invisible global forces. In fact, some of the greatest opportunities for the next generation of value will emerge when those with local insights, capabilities and values are able to leverage global resources and scale to maximize the value they create.

The fourth point is that at the end of the day all this value is created by people. Economists always want to add capital into the equation. They're not wrong, but the philosopher in me sees capital as a means of conveyance for a prior generation of value, and that value was also rooted in people. Yes, it's turtles all the way down.

Those people are fueled by their beliefs, knowledge, insights, skills and values. They create value through their collaboration with others, and those collaborations span the globe. Human capital is the root of the most powerful invisible forces shaping businesses and nations.

Which leads to my closing point. One of the most important themes found throughout this book is the importance of leadership. From the opening section describing the dramatic impact Lou Gerstner brought to IBM to the last chapter on nations and the forces that shape them, leadership has been central.

We've covered a number of critical factors business leaders must address. These include establishing a foundation of shared facts, vision and values along with the specific strategies, business design and execution elements. Those are necessary, but the greatest power is the creation of an environment and culture that enables people to flourish, both as individuals and in teams. In the modern world that power is limited only by the laws of nature. Until some properly motivated and enabled team of people decides to repeal those laws on behalf of their customers.

That's just what leaders enable people to do.

INDEX

W

Wang, Charles, 22

Washington Consensus, 225, 229–230, 238

Washington establishment, 238

Watson, x, 20, 112, 174–182, 184–185, 196, 211, 213, 215

Weather Company, The (TWC), 172, 200

Websphere, 19–21, 23, 51, 69, 71–73, 168–169

Wikipedia, 174, 180

Wild ducks, 20

Windows, 17–18, 36, 38–39, 43, 45–49, 51–52, 97

Wittenbraker, John, 217

World Trade Organization (WTO), 225–228, 231, 238

Y

Year 2000 (Y2K), 14, 29